Extracting
Development

The **ISEAS – Yusof Ishak Institute** (formerly Institute of Southeast Asian Studies) is an autonomous organization established in 1968. It is a regional centre dedicated to the study of socio-political, security, and economic trends and developments in Southeast Asia and its wider geostrategic and economic environment. The Institute's research programmes are grouped under Regional Economic Studies (RES), Regional Strategic and Political Studies (RSPS), and Regional Social and Cultural Studies (RSCS). The Institute is also home to the ASEAN Studies Centre (ASC), the Singapore APEC Study Centre and the Temasek History Research Centre (THRC).

ISEAS Publishing, an established academic press, has issued more than 2,000 books and journals. It is the largest scholarly publisher of research about Southeast Asia from within the region. ISEAS Publishing works with many other academic and trade publishers and distributors to disseminate important research and analyses from and about Southeast Asia to the rest of the world.

Extracting Development

Contested Resource Frontiers in Mainland Southeast Asia

EDITED BY

OLIVER TAPPE · SIMON ROWEDDER

YUSOF ISHAK INSTITUTE

First published in Singapore in 2022 by
ISEAS Publishing
30 Heng Mui Keng Terrace
Singapore 119614

E-mail: publish@iseas.edu.sg
Website: http://bookshop.iseas.edu.sg

All rights reserved. No part of this publication may be reproduced, stored in a retrieval system, or transmitted in any form or by any means, electronic, mechanical, photocopying, recording or otherwise, without the prior permission of the ISEAS – Yusof Ishak Institute.

© 2022 ISEAS – Yusof Ishak Institute, Singapore.

The responsibility for facts and opinions in this publication rests exclusively with the authors and their interpretations do not necessarily reflect the views or the policy of the publisher or its supporters.

ISEAS Library Cataloguing-in-Publication Data

Name(s): Tappe, Oliver, editor. | Rowedder, Simon, editor.
Title: Extracting development : contested resource frontiers in Mainland Southeast Asia / edited by Oliver Tappe and Simon Rowedder.
Description: Singapore : ISEAS-Yusof Ishak Institute, 2022. | Includes bibliographical references and index.
Identifiers: ISBN 9789815011197 (soft cover) | ISBN 9789815011463 (pdf) | ISBN 9789815011517 (epub)
Subjects: LCSH: Natural resources—Southeast Asia. | Natural resources—Political aspects—Southeast Asia.
Classification: LCC HC441 Z65E96

Cover photo: Mekong river bank, Vientiane, Lao PDR (photo by Oliver Tappe).

Cover designed by Lee Meng Hui
Index compiled by Raffaie Nahar
Typeset by International Typesetters Pte Ltd
Printed in Singapore by Markono Print Media Pte Ltd

Contents

Acknowledgements   vii

The Contributors   viii

1. Contested Resource Frontiers in Mainland Southeast Asia: An Introduction
   Simon Rowedder and Oliver Tappe   1

2. Ontological Politics of the Resource Frontier: A Hydrosocial Analysis of the Mekong River in Northern Thailand
   Thianchai Surimas and Carl Middleton   28

3. Reassembling Frontiers for Middle-Income Peasants: Rubber Expansion and Livelihood Ecosystem Transformation in a Northeast Thai Village
   Wataru Fujita   49

4. "Only the Best Fruits for China!": Local Productions of a 'Fruit Frontier' in the Borderlands of China, Laos and Thailand
   Simon Rowedder   79

5. Commodity Frontiers in Motion: Tracing the Maize Boom across the Lao-Vietnamese Borderlands
   Robert Cole   106

6. New Frontier Spaces: Complex Entanglements and Power Relations (Re)shaping Land Governance in Laos 129
Diana Suhardiman and Jonas Kramp

7. Moving Away from the Margins? How a Chinese Hydropower Project Made a Lao Community Modern and Comfortable 143
Floramante S.J. Ponce

8. Frontier Capitalism in Colonial and Contemporary Laos: The Case of Tin Mining 172
Oliver Tappe

9. Chinese Investments and Resource Frontiers in Cambodia: Systemic Transformation 198
Vannarith Chheang

10. The Open Issues: Cases between Chinese Investment Companies and Local People in Myanmar 221
Su Yin Htun

11. Internationalization of RMB and Tin Ore Trade in China-Myanmar Frontier Governance: Views from Yunnan Province 240
Dominik Mierzejewski

Index 261

Acknowledgements

The book is an outcome of the workshop "Contested Resource Frontiers in Mainland Southeast Asia" held in the ISEAS – Yusof Ishak Institute, Singapore on 6 March 2020 under its Regional Social and Cultural Studies (RSCS) Programme's "China in Southeast Asia" Project. The editors wish to express their gratitude to former RSCS director Benjamin Loh and his team for making this event possible just before the COVID-19 pandemic put an end to academic life as we knew it. Thanks go to those participants of the workshop who could not join this publication project but whose insightful presentations and contributions to the discussions greatly helped us to shape our ideas on contested resource frontiers in Southeast Asia. Special thanks are reserved for new RSCS Coordinator Norshahril bin Saat for the untiring support of our publication project, Rainer Einzenberger (University of Vienna) for his helpful critical reading of the introduction chapter, and Charlotte Wagner for editorial support.

Oliver Tappe wishes to thank ISEAS for the kind hospitality and inspiring working atmosphere during his visiting fellowship in (pre-pandemic) Singapore. He also would like to acknowledge the support of his and other contributors' research by the Competing Regional Integrations in Southeast Asia (CRISEA) interdisciplinary research programme, funded by the European Union's Horizon 2020 Framework Programme.

Simon Rowedder wishes to express special thanks to the students at the National University of Singapore (NUS) who have attended his classes on Sino-Southeast Asian frontiers in the past couple of years. Their engaged debates and creative comments greatly contributed to the ideas developed in this book.

the Contributors

Vannarith Chheang is President at the Asian Vision Institute and Visiting Fellow at the ISEAS – Yusof Ishak Institute, Singapore.

Robert Cole is a Research Associate of the Asia Research Institute, National University of Singapore; and an adviser on responsible agricultural investment at the Mekong Region Land Governance project in Vientiane, Laos.

Wataru Fujita is Associate Professor at the Graduate School of Sustainable System Sciences, Osaka Metropolitan University, Japan.

Su Yin Htun is Professor at the Department of Law, University of Mandalay, Myanmar.

Jonas Kramp works for the Land Governance Team of the German Agency of International Cooperation (GIZ).

Carl Middleton is Assistant Professor in the Graduate Studies in International Development Studies Program (MAIDS-GRID) and Director of the Center for Social Development Studies in the Faculty of Political Science of Chulalongkorn University, Thailand.

Dominik Mierzejewski is Associate Professor at the Department of Asian Studies, and Chair at the Centre of Asian Studies at the University of Lodz, Poland.

The Contributors

Floramante S.J. Ponce is a PhD candidate at the Max Planck Institute for Social Anthropology in Halle, Germany.

Simon Rowedder is Assistant Professor at the Chair of Development Politics, University of Passau, and affiliate member of the Max Weber Foundation Research Group on Borders, Mobility and New Infrastructures at the Faculty of Arts and Social Sciences, National University of Singapore.

Diana Suhardiman is Director of the KITLV/Royal Netherlands Institute of Southeast Asian and Caribbean Studies in Leiden/Netherlands.

Thianchai Surimas is Researcher at the Center for Social Development Studies, Faculty of Political Science, Chulalongkorn University, Thailand.

Oliver Tappe is Senior Researcher at the Institute of Anthropology, University of Heidelberg (Germany), and Associate Fellow at the ISEAS – Yusof Ishak Institute, Singapore.

1

CONTESTED RESOURCE FRONTIERS IN MAINLAND SOUTHEAST ASIA
An Introduction

Simon Rowedder and Oliver Tappe

INTRODUCTION

Mainland Southeast Asia, the upland regions in particular, has a long history as contested reserve of valuable minerals and forest products. Moving along transregional trade networks—at times bones of contention between competing regional powers—these resources continue to shape present-day economic and political dynamics. While mining and logging remain contested fields of resource extraction, new resource frontiers emerge: Transboundary investments in land or water reserves reveal new tendencies of resource struggles in the region.

This edited volume investigates recent trends and issues of resource extraction in Mainland Southeast Asia and their effect on local economies and social relations. Case studies from different countries analyse the socio-political dimensions of natural and agrarian resources such as minerals, water, land and cash crops. Some contributions focus on the significance of China's resource hunger for these commodities, and how local communities in the region perceive the opportunities and risks of the Belt and Road Initiative (BRI). However, this volume also aims to shift the focus on competing actors of resource extraction and governance within Southeast Asia and the contingent outcomes of (and local responses to) transregional economic dynamics, political entanglements and related socio-ecological transformations.

Contemporary Southeast Asia offers manifold test cases to discuss how local "frontier assemblages" (Cons and Eilenberg 2019a) relate to different (overlapping) resource regimes, corresponding discourses and changing patterns of (hybrid) resource governance (Barney 2009; Dzüvichü and Baruah 2019; Kelly and Peluso 2015; Li 2014; Miller et al. 2020). This volume brings together contributions that (re)examine different local frontier configurations and dynamics across up- and lowland Southeast Asia from various disciplinary vantage points. Providing an impressive breadth and depth of fresh empirical insights from the region, conceptually enriched by an intriguing combination of different disciplines and scales of analysis, this collection importantly highlights the complexity and diversity of actors involved. It foregrounds their intricately linked, often contesting and conflicting but sometimes surprisingly converging, interests in imagining, co-producing or challenging new frontiers of infrastructural development, resource extraction and land commoditization.

This multifaceted attention to complexity is much needed to address the ubiquitously cited rise of China's geopolitical and economic influence in Southeast Asia, most prominently expressed in the BRI (Chong and Pham 2020; Sidaway et al. 2020; Mierzejewski 2021). Going beyond rather one-sided and sensational depictions of Southeast Asia "under Beijing's Shadow" (Hiebert 2020), "in the Dragon's Shadow" (Strangio 2020) or as "China's Backyard" (Morris-Jung 2017), this volume aims to complicate narratives of Chinese economic and geopolitical expansion in Southeast Asia. Consequently, many contributors shift the focus on local agency, indigenous actors as well as marginal Chinese ones (for example, migrant workers, petty traders, or local cross-border entrepreneurs). This collection adds to the emerging scholarly body of more nuanced ethnographic, micro-scale accounts of local engagements and encounters with various forms and actors of a rapidly asserting

China (Saxer and Zhang 2017; Nyíri and Tan 2017; Woodworth and Joniak-Lüthi 2020).

Many chapters thus highlight the relevance of region-specific geographies and histories for understanding new frontier dynamics. While sharing Woodworth and Joniak-Lüthi's (2020, p. 4) overall leading question of "how ... local people navigate the complex institutional and cultural terrains of China's rapidly changing borderlands", this volume further examines how local actors also actively contribute to these moments of rapid change. Closely examining local perceptions of capitalist expansion and corresponding interactions on the ground, the contributions to this volume present different contexts in which local actors are sometimes passive recipients or victims, but sometimes also active agents of frontier development—or even both at the same time.

CONTESTED RESOURCE FRONTIERS: CONCEPTUAL APPROACHES

When in 2004 the Asian Development Bank (ADB) described Laos as a "new frontier" of economic opportunities, this reflected the establishment of a "neoliberal-inspired discourse of the Mekong as an untapped resource frontier" that served "as a legitimating ideology for a particular strategy of large-scale resource development and regional integration" (Barney 2009, p. 147). Since then, Laos in particular has undergone an unprecedented land rush (Dwyer and Vongvisouk 2017; Kenney-Lazar 2018; Suhardiman, Keovilignavong, and Kenney-Lazar 2019; for Cambodia, Loughlin and Milne 2020; Chheang, this volume). China has emerged as the dominant economic player in Southeast Asia, with specific ideas of the allegedly "empty", untapped and available frontiers of Laos, Myanmar and Cambodia that reveal a striking resemblance with colonial imaginaries.

Given its variety of frontier contexts (Brown 2018), Laos covers quite some space in this volume. Case studies include land and water (Ponce, Suhardiman and Kramp), cash crops (Cole, Rowedder) and mining (Tappe). Other Southeast Asian frontier contexts presented in this volume include land contestation in Cambodia (Chheang), Chinese investment in northern Myanmar (Htun, Mierzejewski), northern Thailand's rubber boom (Fujita) and hydropower dams in the Greater Mekong Subregion (Thianchai and Middleton). A transboundary dimension marks most case studies discussed in this volume. Sino-Southeast Asian exchanges are intersected here by multi-layered transnational and translocal dynamics within mainland Southeast Asia.

Before addressing different aspects of specific resource frontiers, we tackle the question of what constitutes a "resource frontier", or what is a "resource" in the first place (and how it is contested and by whom). The term "frontier" carries some ideological baggage since Frederick Jackson Turner (1921) described it as the expansion of civilization or a civilization-to-come. And yet, the concept remains useful as a heuristic tool to explore dynamic and ambiguous spaces of economic and social transformation—"sites of potential" (Li 2014, p. 13)—especially in the sense of an expanding capitalist frontier (Tsing 2003; Joseph 2019; Haug, Grossmann, and Kaartinen 2020). While the "frontier" often denotes remote borderlands such as the Southeast Asian upland margins bordering China (Anderson and Whitmore 2015; Giersch 2006; Scott 2009; Michaud and Forsyth 2011; Turner, Bonnin, and Michaud 2015), the concept does not necessarily imply marginality or remoteness (Saxer and Andersson 2019). New resource frontiers are also emerging in urban areas such as Sihanoukville as discussed in Vannarith Chheang's contribution to this volume.

Following Cons and Eilenberg (2019a), this volume focuses on processes of frontier (co-)production—or frontierization—in particular places and moments in time. Their model of "frontier assemblages" includes imaginations of the expansive capitalist frontier and the Turnerian clash between civilization and savagery—a model that highlights the "intertwined materialities, actors, cultural logics, spatial dynamics, ecologies, and political economic processes that produce particular places as resource frontiers" (Cons and Eilenberg 2019b, p. 2). As Rasmussen and Lund point out, the corresponding frontier dynamics "dissolve existing social orders—property systems, political jurisdictions, rights, and social contracts" (Rasmussen and Lund 2018, p. 388). Thus, frontiers imply a liminal or transitional dimension, allowing for disruptions of existing patterns of resource control to make way for new forms of appropriation.

The notion of frontier as expansion and appropriation is a key element of the capitalist *resource frontier* in the sense of enclosure through new institutions and infrastructures that transform landscapes and livelihoods. In contrast to James Scott's (2009, p. 278) idealistic "open common property frontier" of yore, the capitalist frontier is marked by processes of exclusion and dispossession. People inhabiting such frontier zones often find themselves confronted with extractive industries that negatively affect their social and natural environment. As in the example of ADB's labelling of Laos as "new frontier", imaginaries of resource-rich and allegedly underdeveloped regions fuel the fantasies of entrepreneurs and investors. And yet we must not overlook local agency and strategies within this emerging field of tension: searching for new opportunities, subverting institutional constraints and (re-)producing social networks.

Processes of frontierization go hand in hand with resourcification—the intertwined institutional, material and discursive processes that render a natural resource a valuable resource that invites extraction and accumulation. Timber and minerals are perhaps the most evident examples, even if contested, but also communal land and water, agrarian resources (see Rigg 2020; Ishikawa and Soda 2020) and perhaps even human resources (as labour). National and international laws settle questions of ownership and resource governance, restrict access, and shape frontier dynamics along new infrastructures, trade linkages (as yet another contested resource) and corresponding narratives of development.

Thus, discussing contested resource frontiers seeks to answer the following question: What is a resource? And, in extension, who defines what a resource is? Processes of resourcification "produce" resources (discursively as well as legally) that become open for extraction—but for whom? Such questions imply moral assessments of what is and shall remain an open-access resource, taking into account the economic and/or cultural values and the limits of resourcification or, rather, commoditization. Not surprisingly, those questions are heavily contested between a variety of actors on different scales and contexts, from international and state-level to the local domain.

Our idea of contested resource frontiers explores not only the dialectic between relentless exploitation and dispossession, but also "liminal spaces open for production and inventiveness" (Cons and Eilenberg 2019b, p. 7) that imply (contested) potentiality and creativity. Therefore, we pay attention to local perspectives and individual experiences in such spaces of capitalist expansion and appropriation of "nature". Disruptions may create (temporary) spaces of potentiality and change, with contingent outcomes. How do people perceive the opportunities and risks emerging from the transformative processes occurring on the frontier?

COMMODITIZATION AND FRONTIER CAPITALISM

Investigating Southeast Asian resource frontiers through the lens of capitalist expansion—from the colonial *mise en valeur* to the Chinese BRI—we need to pay particular attention to processes of commoditization (Taylor 2016). A specific resource or raw material becomes a commodity or, rather, is attached economic value to when successfully moved out of the natural environment. Commodities are further moved and circulated as traded goods (or electricity in the case of hydropower) across multiple scales (from local to transnational).

Arguably, the resource frontier "captures an important empirical 'reality' concerning the political economy of rapid and uneven development in the country" (Barney 2009, p. 150). As Edo Andriesse (2014) has pointed out for the example of Lao frontier capitalism (Laungaramsri 2012), the institutional frameworks and general conditions of underdevelopment privilege foreign (state-owned) companies that target different economic sectors in Laos (such as Chinese investors in the mining and plantation economy). This is certainly true as well for Myanmar (Einzenberger 2018; Htun, this volume) and Cambodia (Chheang 2021, this volume). However, institutional and legal ambiguities continue to complicate processes of appropriation and extraction, as Lu and Schönweger (2019) have vividly described with the example of Chinese investors on the Lao plantation frontier.

The emergence of capitalist frontiers does not only reveal institutional and infrastructural ramifications but also affects local economic and socio-cultural configurations. This is particularly true with regard to processes of exclusion and dispossession, questions of ownership and (customary) land use rights. Who declares and claims something a "resource" and how? The state, "the market" or local communities? As Thianchai Surimas and Carl Middleton (this volume) alert us for the case of water, ideas of what is a resource and who is entitled to exploit it might diverge fundamentally along ontological horizons (Götz and Middleton 2020). As the various contributions to this volume show, the question of what "nature" or "natural resources" are, is contested on the ground, based on contrasting ideas and moralities.

Accordingly, frontier capitalism entails a field of tension, marked by contested extractivism, the rapid and widespread removal of resources for exchange in global capitalist markets (Acosta 2013). As Jerry Jacka points out: "Extractivism is the 500-year history, associated with imperialism and colonialism, of a mode of accumulation whereby raw materials were removed from the Americas, Asia, and Africa to enrich the centers of the world economy" (Jacka 2018, p. 62). In our volume, this appears even more complicated as we highlight the south-south dimension of capitalist expansion in Southeast Asia—not only with regard to the BRI but also to the diversity of economic actors hailing from the emerging economies of Malaysia, Thailand and Vietnam, for example, and "gate-cities" such as Singapore (Breul and Revilla Diez 2021). Here, the expansion of corporations and non-governmental organizations into ever-growing resource frontiers (see Tsing 2005) is perhaps characteristic for expanding extractivism and corresponding frontierization processes in contemporary Southeast Asia.

The history of commoditization of natural resources, and related discourses of open mineral and gemstone frontiers, hark back to colonial ones (Ross 2014)—for example, the persistent cliché of resource-rich Laos as "oriental Klondike" (Deloncle 1930; Tappe this volume). And yet this is also true for the discursive legacy of Chinese frontier imperialism (Giersch 2006; Tagliacozzo and Chang 2011). The binary "resource-rich vs resource-hungry" arguably intersects the political economy of Southeast Asia (including the neighbouring Chinese provinces of Yunnan and Guangxi). Today as in the (colonial, imperial) past, capitalists aim to extract resources from allegedly "underdeveloped" regions, often negatively affecting local communities and their livelihoods.

Contributions to this volume reflect the ambiguities of livelihood transformation on shifting resource frontiers. As Robert Cole (this volume) demonstrates with his example of Vietnamese investment on the Lao maize frontier—as capitalist expansion beyond Vietnam's own upland frontier—contract farming offers both economic opportunity and precarity for local communities shifting from agricultural subsistence based on upland rice to maize and the corresponding dependency on Vietnamese investors and volatile market prices. Wataru Fujita (this volume) shows how a capitalist resource frontier unfolds in the context of Thailand's agribusiness, and how local communities manoeuvre in this emerging space of opportunity and risk.

Among the risks for the local population on capitalist resource frontiers are certainly the increasing land pressure through generous tax exemptions for agribusiness and extractive industries and related processes of accumulation and dispossession (Rigg 2020; Baird 2011; Harvey 2003). Hydropower dams are perhaps the most blatant examples where displaced communities seem to endure the closure of a frontier—displaced and excluded from any benefits. However, as Floramante Ponce (this volume) indicates, affected people are not necessarily unanimous and united in resistance, but diverse in their criticism and desires for new horizons, between hope and disillusionment.

We thus can identify not only differences between corporate actors but also contestations within groups. Even if a general agreement with political agendas of socio-economic development prevails, debates about the concrete goals of and ways to "improvement" (Li 2007) might differ between individuals. In the tin mines of Laos, while there is no disagreement about the legitimacy of large-scale extraction, we witness contestation about resource access and distribution. As Oliver Tappe shows in his contribution to this volume, local Lao villagers claim customary rights to extract minerals, not in opposition to international mining operations but in the sense of cohabitation (Luning and Pijpers 2017). Ambiguities in the Law on Minerals allow for such arrangements on the Lao frontier (Keovilignavong 2019; Tappe 2021).

However, investors usually eschew legal ambiguities (Lu and Schönweger 2019; Mierzejewski 2021, this issue). Conflicts about rights to access and extract resources are inevitable results. Patterns of compliance may break up and rearrange again in the course of the co-production of the capitalist frontier. Ideologies of extractivism (see below) complement or contradict the variegated patterns of resource use and governance on the ground (Kenney-Lazar and Mark 2021). Su Yin Htun's description (this volume) of resource frontiers in Myanmar illustrates the ambiguities and inherent tensions of emerging capitalist resource frontiers.

The complicity and/or contestation of nation-states and international investors in turning allegedly empty and underdeveloped "land into capital" (Dwyer 2007; Kenney-Lazar, Dwyer and Hett 2018), and how local communities navigate in and contribute to (re)emerging frontier assemblages, constitutes a key focus of this volume. Frontiers of capitalism combine resource frontiers with trade frontiers, as Simon

Rowedder posits (see below and Mierzejewski this volume). From informal local border crossings to the grand transnational routes of the BRI, spatial configurations shift and re-shuffle, thus constantly producing new forms of (im)mobility and territorialization where processes of frontierization unfold.

FRONTIER TERRITORIALITIES

Commodified resource frontiers are embedded in the, often conflictual, entanglement of spatial fixity and mobility. Processes of locating, cultivating and extracting natural resources are first and foremost tied to issues of land and territory. Depending on the respective commodity and environmental conditions—including geological, topographical and climatic factors—different technologies are required to physically move natural resources out of their ecological spatial embeddedness (e.g., on the ground, in the soil, underground, underwater), or to translate movement of natural resources into energy as in the case of hydropower. More importantly, at least for the purposes of this volume, the interplay of spatiality and movement of resource frontiers does not only impact the workings of natural ecosystems, but also often collides with pre-existing human ways of building livelihoods around different usages of land. Operating within complex, at times opaque, legal regimes of land classification and property rights (see Suhardiman and Kramp this volume), resource frontiers thus often lead to the enforced movement and resettlement—spatial dispossession—of local populations. Floramante Ponce's chapter demonstrates for the case of a large-scale hydropower plant in northern Laos how resource frontier-induced relocation programmes create in turn new specific frontier spaces of "resettlement communities" which need to navigate non-rural discourses and notions of development, modernity and convenience.

Causing, and caused by, physical movement, the production of resource frontiers unleashes dynamics of territorialization, deterritorialization and reterritorialization (unmaking and remaking of spatial orders, cf. Rasmussen and Lund 2018), thereby also triggering incisive socio-spatial transformations and related socio-economic hierarchies and inequalities. Relational frontier studies (Barney 2009; Li 2014) point to the wide range of actors on the ground differently involved in producing complex frontier assemblages, importantly not only including state or corporate agents but also directly affected local villagers and farmers who act out of various pragmatic motivations and aspirations. Aspirations to somehow partake in promises of frontier-based development might even be complicit in processes of state-driven relocation and resettlement, disclosing "the complex, situated and cumulative nature of local social and environmental transformations which reproduce frontier space, inequality and marginality, sometimes in unexpected ways" (Barney 2009, p. 148). Resource frontiers do not only mobilize local communities (across the spectrum of forced or voluntary movement and with local agency ranging from resistance to collaboration) but also induce migration flows from further afar. Examining the rubber boom in northeastern Thailand, Wataru Fujita's chapter demonstrates that rubber aspirations and experimentations of both local peasants and officials have been joined by already experienced rubber investors and cultivators from southern Thailand where rubber had been established much earlier.

Forced out-migration and aspirational in-migration are thus both essential parts of the discursive imagination, material production and actual workings of resource frontiers, fuelling the "frontier myth" of settling open, empty and resource-abundant lands. These two migration dynamics and directions are clearly observable in upland Southeast Asia, for instance. In Laos, upland populations (mostly ethnic minorities) have been resettled downhill to make room for state policies of large-scale resource extraction in the highlands and to become more "settled" within an intensified agriculture in rapidly modernized lowlands (Évrard and Goudineau 2004; Baird and Shoemaker 2007; High 2021; Ponce this volume). In Vietnam, people from highly populated lowlands have been moved uphill to settle and "tame"—to stabilize politically and develop economically—the highlands as part of the state's "New Economic Zone" scheme, established in North Vietnam and extended to the South after reunification in 1975 (Hardy 2003). More recently, different frontier materialities and imaginations across mainland Southeast Asia have lured a wide range of new migrant entrepreneurs, agriculturalists and workers from China. Most visibly in Chinese-backed Special Economic Zones (SEZs), emblematic of frontierized "enclave development" (Chettri and Eilenberg 2021; Laungaramsri 2019; Nyíri 2012, 2017), Chinese newcomers have been following the "call of the frontier" also in more "ordinary" urban and rural localities. Their small-scale entrepreneurial experimentations have not been paid much attention to in scholarship. Further fine-grained studies on everyday encounters and social relations between Chinese (small-scale) migrant entrepreneurs and local residents are needed to uncover newly emerging social infrastructures of conviviality, possibly forming specific social configurations of "frontier cultures" (Tsing 2005)—entailing "the intrinsic ambivalence of living together across local differences" (Marsden and Reeves 2019, p. 758), which Chinese-induced frontier development brings along on the ground. Looking at the rubber frontier, expanding from China across the border into northern Laos, Chris Lyttleton and Yunxia Li (2017) examine personal and intimate relations between Chinese rubber investors and Lao (mainly Akha) rubber plantation workers. Certainly not without its problems, they conclude that "the influx of Chinese people and goods into Laos has created a spectrum of opportunities based on proliferating personal connections" (Lyttleton and Li 2017, p. 323). Their case of "rubber's affective economies" across the China-Laos border points to yet another aspect of underlying mobility: resource frontiers do not only entail, or induce, various forms of movement; they are themselves moving within and across national borders and across time. Previous successful experiences with rubber are subsequently duplicated elsewhere: from Xishuangbanna Dai Autonomous Prefecture in the tropical south of China's southwestern Yunnan province to adjacent regions in northern Laos, or from southern Thailand to northeastern Thailand (see Wataru Fujita, this volume).

FRONTIER MOBILITIES

Similar to the entanglement of mobility and fixity, the multi-layered—top-down and bottom-up—political, economic and social production of spatially and temporally shifting resource frontiers is rooted in the tension of ideological projections of endless opportunities (flexibility) and complex realities of regulation and governance (rigidity). Importantly, both frontier imagination/ideology and frontier governance are not articulated and enacted merely by state and corporate actors but also by various local stakeholders. They disclose frontier micropolitics on the ground which contain dynamics of resistance and conflict, as well as of (possibly surprising) alliances and collaborations. Regarding the latter, Andrew Walker (1999, pp. 111–12) writes in his seminal work on the borderlands of Laos, Thailand, Myanmar and China of "collaborative borders" that reveal "complex and subtle collaborations between local initiative and state power". Key to these co-productions of border regimes is regulation as an underlying social practice historically shared by a multitude of borderland actors. While Walker's observations are primarily related to cross-border trade networks and regimes, the co-productive aspect across the state-society divide also applies to resource frontiers.

After all, trade is essential for the proper working of commodified resource frontiers, guaranteeing access to the market, whose generated (anticipated or at times simply imagined) demand justifies the making of resource frontiers in the first place. As Robert Cole's chapter exemplarily demonstrates, Vietnamese traders are the key drivers of the maize frontier expanding across the borderlands of Vietnam and Laos, fuelling a maize boom within the general intensive development of various crop booms in Southeast Asia (Hall 2011; Hurni and Fox 2018). Generally, crop booms, as particular temporal moments and patterns of resource frontier dynamics, constitute venues where the interplay of trade-oriented and agrarian frontier livelihoods becomes visible. Simon Rowedder's contribution to this volume illustrates how fruit cultivators in Thailand and mobile small-scale traders in adjacent Laos both fully align their livelihoods to, and consequently facilitate and sustain, the China-driven fresh fruit boom. Their flexibility and creativity are rooted in local arrangements of regulating and coordinating—*governing*—their frontier resources of village-level fruit orchards and cross-border mobility (production of local trade regimes combining formal and informal channels).

Often imagined top-down as empty and ungoverned spaces suitable for capitalist extraction and exploitation, resource frontiers are on the ground often highly governed assemblages of various local actors and interests. Thus, territorial (re)configuration and governance is not only the tool of high-level state-corporate frontier projects, but also key to local translations of and reactions to (newly emerging) frontier dynamics, possibly resulting in land grabs and accumulation "from below" (Chettri 2020; Woods 2020). Regarding the rubber boom in northeastern Thailand, Wataru Fujita demonstrates fascinatingly how different actors, with otherwise conflicting interests, all act in some form or another towards further enabling, and not necessarily resisting, large-scale rubber planting despite possible negative ecological and socio-economic consequences—at times acting against legal norms and, more importantly, modifying customary rights and establishing new legal-territorial regimes at the village-level.

The local aspirational embracing of the monetarily promising rubber frontier does not fully exclude alternative, subsistence-oriented livelihood strategies such as paddy fields or communal forests that still might exist along and within (albeit in different scope) the shifting frontier patterns. Thus, the local translation, and in turn (re)production, of state-driven neoliberal discourse and policies of frontier development is a contingent, multi-directional, self-governing, and oftentimes seemingly self-contradictory process. These locally produced, smallholder-driven crop booms (Junquera and Gret-Regamey 2019; Hall 2011) illustrate the temporality and volatility of resource frontiers. Embedded in dynamic, often unpredictable, boom-bust cycles, they provide instant cash income and prosperity for some, but often with devastating long-term environmental and socio-economic consequences, especially in regard to indebtedness. Thus, cash crop frontiers exemplify, and potentially exacerbate, political, social and economic vulnerabilities and precariousness on the ground (Zuo et al. 2021). Local precariousness is even more pronounced in frontier configurations where there is no room for smallholders' active participation in and co-production of frontier capitalism, namely when facing large-scale plantations and infrastructural megaprojects.

Simon Rowedder's chapter illustrates the uncertainties among small-scale fruit cultivators and traders in the face of China's rapidly expanding large-scale plantation frontier encroaching upon northern Laos as well as northern Thailand, which might override the previous small-scale agrarian-cum-trade frontier constellation of skilfully satisfying China's demand for tropical fruits. China might be able to appease its growing fruit appetite by itself, by experimenting with tropical fruit cultivation in southern China and in extraterritorial plantations in northern Laos and beyond. This concomitant large-scale frontier exploitation or "closure" is furthermore observable in processes of fully "infrastructuring" the frontier through megaprojects such as dams (Htun, Ponce, Thianchai and Middleton), mines (Htun, Tappe), oil and gas pipelines (Htun), maritime and river ports (Chheang), and roads or railways (Rowedder), or in dynamics of exclusionary zoning of frontiers in form of Special Economic Zones or cross-border trade zones (Mierzejewski).

FRONTIER TEMPORALITIES

Large-scale plantations, infrastructures and development zones can be all understood as tools or manifestations of different levels of state governance—in terms of territoriality, sovereignty, security and finance. Mierzejewski's chapter shows how China's southwestern border province of Yunnan has been aggressively pushing for establishing a comprehensive system of cross-border governance, including cross-border infrastructures of transport connectivity, energy supply (oil and gas), political exchanges and security dialogue, trade zones, nodes and corridors, and financial integration and interdependence (internationalization of the Chinese RMB). China's (and Yunnan's) underlying ultimate motive, or claim, to secure an economically, politically and ethnically stable border is based on the overall discursive representation of the Yunnan-Myanmar frontier as backward and less civilized. Although Chinese central and local officials complain about uncertainties and fragmented sovereignty across the border, the latter might in some contexts even further enable, and not hinder, Chinese efforts to "pacify" or "tame" this "unruly" frontier. Thus, Chinese stakeholders might skilfully utilize competing and conflicting central and local entanglements of political elites and corporate interests within Myanmar.

Frictions and ruptures—as "'open moments' when opportunities and risks multiply, when the scope of outcomes widens, and when new structural scaffolding is erected" (Lund 2016, p. 1202)—are essential ingredients of long-term frontierization processes. The latter are in their emergence and workings never linear, teleological, absolute, finite or finished, although they are often officially represented and praised as such (Haug, Grossmann, and Kaartinen 2020). As with cash crops outlined before, frontier capitalism in general often develops in volatile boom-bust cycles. The lifespan of frontiers is longer than its single projects. Failure, discontinuation or suspension of frontier projects can lay the ground for new imaginaries and materializations of frontier-making, giving way to new actors and trajectories. This is especially manifest in infrastructure projects and development zones.

Akhil Gupta (2018, p. 62) calls for a dynamic conceptualization of infrastructure "as a process, not a thing: a thing-in-motion, ephemeral, shifting, elusive, decaying, degrading, becoming a ruin but for the routines of repair, replacement, and restoration (or in spite of them)." Once an infrastructure project officially starts construction, its trajectory is, despite meticulous future-oriented planning, open-ended, with different possible temporalities at play. For Gupta (2018, pp. 68–72), "suspension" constitutes a central modality of infrastructural time. More than merely the in-between time within the teleological timeline of working towards finishing a project, Gupta (2018, p. 70) sees suspension "as a condition in its own right", as a central and open progress of (non) construction through which one can better grasp the actual material and social life of infrastructure.

Similarly, Alessandro Rippa (2021) sees suspension as an essential part of the overall trajectory of the Boten Special Economic Zone at the China-Laos border. There, longer periods of decay, abandonment and incipient ruination, following the enforced shutdown of its booming, but increasingly scandalous and criminal, casino landscape in 2011, laid the foundation for its subsequent sanitized re-branding as "Boten Beautiful Land Specific Zone" by new Chinese state-backed investors in 2015, then officially endorsed as a central transportation and logistics hub of China's BRI (see also Rowedder 2020). Thus, ruins of the past are at the same time productive sites of future development. Frontiers "emerge at particular conjunctures and disappear at others. They have lifecycles, deaths, and occasionally, particular rebirths" (Cons and Eilenberg 2019b, p. 11). In the case of temporarily abandoned Boten, development re-emerges through practices of "waiting" with patience and boredom as key elements (Rippa 2021, p. 235).

The cyclical, open-ended, contingent, multi-layered modality of "frontier time" (Cons and Eilenberg 2019b, p. 12) is also evident in Oliver Tappe's chapter on tin mining in Laos. Abandoned large-scale mines—ruins of previous extractive booms—become venues for future-oriented local livelihoods of artisanal and small-scale miners. Following economic aspirations or simply trying to survive amidst an increasingly marketized local economy and mining-induced environmental degradation, local miners eventually reproduce the inherent inequality of frontier development, accepting and thus sustaining precarious and hazardous working conditions. Tappe's historically informed focus on the continuity, or persistence, of precarious labour relations throughout different configurations of Laos's mining frontier reminds of C. Patterson Giersch's (2006, p. 9) notion of "persistent frontiers" in his Qing history of the Yunnan-Southeast Asian borderlands where "it is impossible to identify first contacts, and it is equally difficult to settle on an era for the decisive closure of the frontier." Giersch eventually sees the frontier largely closed from the middle of the twentieth century onwards, amidst rapid processes of nation-building and -consolidation. However, the underlying frontier topos of economically and politically utilizing, or imagining, non-occupied, open, empty yet resource-rich spaces slated for "development" (see also section below) has been, and will be, living on. As James Anderson and John Whitmore (2015, p. 46) put it in their long-term history of the Sino-Southeast Asian land frontier, "[a]t any particular moment, the frontier continues in the internal/external overlapping conceptions of its territory, as the variety of actors work to enact their particular views of the territory." In this connection, in mainland Southeast Asia, the focus of this book, long-term "frontier continuities" can be seen for the Mekong River as both a geo-strategic routeway and energy supplier, extraction of minerals, and railway aspirations, which all now have again found their way into China's recent BRI formulations.

FRONTIER IMAGINARIES

Apart from their spatial, material and temporal aspects, resource frontiers are marked by multi-layered discursive and affective dimensions. The idea of the "empty" and "undeveloped" frontier, open for appropriation and extraction, is perhaps the most obvious and influential frontier imaginary. Different frontier imaginaries may be contested between a variety of actors (nation-states, public/private companies, international investors, NGOs, and different local actors), thus contributing to the formation of dynamic frontier assemblages. Investigating frontier discourses and imaginaries that overlap, complement, or contrast with each other, helps to understand relational conceptualizations of frontier contexts.

As Tania Murray Li (2014, p. 13) puts it, frontiers constitute "coveted places, envisaged by various actors as sites of potential". They are future-oriented, constituting a nexus of (contesting) hopes and aspirations, "a space of desire" (Tsing 2005, p. 32). This affective dimension highlights the limitations of a mere focus on technical framings of capitalist "development" frontiers (Ferguson 1994). "Scientific" discourses of "underdevelopment" underpinned by economic data are certainly important for understanding frontier processes (see e.g. the contributions by Mierzejewksi, and Suhardiman and Kramp). However, the way local communities perceive such discourses and link them with their own specific frontier imaginaries and corresponding aspirations provides a crucial lens to explore the contingent co-production of shifting frontier assemblages.

In his contribution to this volume, Wataru Fujita offers a longitudinal perspective on rubber aspirations in the context of agrarian change in northern Thailand, including its counter-movements. He points at the hopes and contestations of different agents that contribute to the evolution of frontier regimes and corresponding discourses of rights to access and control agrarian resources. Simon Rowedder (this volume) stresses the imaginative aspects of the fruit frontier in discussing the search for opportunities of local actors that share an experimental ethic (High 2013) and co-produce the resource frontier along with states and public enterprises. Exploring the (fruit) frontier of opportunity from the ground, Rowedder illustrates the everyday practices and tactics of transnational small-scale traders who manoeuvre the physical and discursive spaces shaped by frontierization processes in the Lao-Sino-Thai borderlands (see as well Cole's contribution on the Lao-Vietnamese maize frontier).

As noted before, the concept of resource frontier is linked to the phenomenon of extractivism as a form of (colonial) accumulation through the commoditization of any natural resources aiming at enriching world economic centres (Jacka 2018). Part and parcel of extractivism is an ideological mindset of removing resources under the guise of "development" (benefitting mainly wealthy countries). Investors in Southeast Asia justify extractive practices with claims on allegedly "underdeveloped" regions and thus create the discursive precondition of extractivism. Official Chinese views of the Southeast Asian frontier as an extension of the "deficient" margins of China (discussed by Dominik Mierzejewski in his contribution to this volume) are a case in point.

This is only one side of the imaginary dimension of frontierization, though. A variety of local actors engage in the multi-scalar and co-productive processes of frontier making. They bring in their specific ontologies of nature and environment that either foster or limit natural resource extraction. As Thianchai Surimas and Carl Middleton show in their contribution to this volume, naturalist/"scientific" notions of natural resources co-exist with indigenous ways of conceptualizing resources and questions of access and control. Their example of the Mekong River highlights the contested nature—and corresponding imaginaries—of resources such as water. Adding a socio-cosmological dimension to the question of river water use, Thianchai and Middleton complicate the frontier assemblages by including non-human beings such as fish and ghosts (see also Johnson 2020) that are often overlooked in studies of contested resource frontiers.

Southeast Asian frontier assemblages are marked by power asymmetries and corresponding discursive formations as many chapters of this book reveal. Developmentalist imaginaries such as "Cambodia-China Community of Shared Future" (discussed by Vannarith Chheang in his contribution to this volume) on the national level pave the way to dispossession and exploitation on the ground, benefiting mainly investors and corrupt elites to the detriment of local communities and creating social tension and disillusionment. The same is true for Laos where local communities generally accept the developmentalist agenda of the government but sense an increasing discrepancy between the promise of prosperity and modernity and the everyday experiences of socioeconomic marginalization (see Ponce's discussion of hydropower-induced displacement in this volume). Hegemonial discourses of extractivism that privilege capitalist accumulation in Southeast Asia are confronted with individual aspirations and alternative future-making, resulting in the typical contradictions and ambiguities of frontier spaces.

People's imaginations and aspirations are certainly drivers of frontierization processes. Frontier-making from below complements top-down processes of capitalist expansion and accumulation. Linking these two perspectives offers a more detailed picture of resource capitalism in Southeast Asia. The question of how locals perceive—and agree or disagree with—the "will to improve" (Li 2007) of external developers, calls for meticulous empirical inquiry on the ground. The ethnographic examples in this volume illustrate this co-productive dimension of frontierization.

CONCLUSION

This volume investigates the multi-layered co-production and contestations of resource frontiers in mainland Southeast Asia and the various actors and factors at stake. It considers not only the perspective of investors and venturers but also the stakeholders on the ground such as local communities and NGOs. The transdisciplinary contributions to this volume address the question of how capitalist frontier visions correspond with the hopes and aspirations, as well as anxieties, of communities living in and with capitalist resource frontiers.

Despite the huge diversity of actors that practically and discursively co-produce and shape Southeast Asian resource frontiers, China certainly remains the big elephant in the room. Frontier politics envisaged in Beijing or Kunming, and the corresponding large-scale infrastructure projects (such as BRI), have a profound impact on frontierization processes in mainland Southeast Asia—including both economic and geopolitical dimensions. And yet we should not underestimate the complicity and contestations by domestic actors that result in the contingent outcomes of frontier capitalism and its contradictions as analysed in many contributions to this volume.

That said, our aim to shift the focus away from "China in Southeast Asia" was perhaps only a vain attempt to add more nuances to the *longue durée* of frontierization processes in China-Southeast Asian borderlands. From the Qing era to the present, social and political dynamics in China certainly triggered transformations and disruptions on its southern fringes. However, only focusing on Chinese "encroachment" would not do justice to the manifold complicity and contestations on the ground—the agency of frontier populations in manoeuvring the opportunities and risks of shifting frontier assemblages.

Thus, this volume is perhaps only a selected taking stock of a specific frontier moment in the long history of contested resource frontiers in mainland Southeast Asia. It is arguably marked by livelihood transformation and dispossession, by new (transboundary) regimes of resource governance, increasing investment and debt traps, and environmental risks. New economic opportunities contrast with precariousness and uncertainties. It remains to be seen how the current COVID-19 pandemic disrupts or exacerbates these frontier processes in one way or the other.

At the present moment, the COVID-19 pandemic provokes questions about the future of the frontierization processes discussed in this volume. Limited mobility, new border regimes and economic downturns have certainly affected the transboundary frontier dynamics and livelihoods in Southeast Asia. On the other hand, after initial setbacks, interruptions and down-scaling of several BRI projects due to the emerging pandemic, analysts still see a bright future for the BRI in the long run, already gathering pace along China's post-pandemic economic recovery, especially in Southeast Asia amidst economic pressure and infrastructural demand exacerbated by the pandemic (Liu, Tan, and Lim 2021, pp. 13–16; Ye 2021; Yu 2021). The flagship project of the China-Laos railway opened on 2 December 2021, just in time for the Lao National Day. China was quick to package the BRI as a remedy for the pandemic recession in Southeast Asia and beyond. It has also served as a channel of its COVID-19 health diplomacy, thereby reactivating and intensifying the "Health Silk Road" scheme already formulated in 2015 (Jiahan 2020). Consequently, in the case of geopolitically significant Chinese energy investment in Myanmar, the pressing concern is not so much the pandemic, but recent political unrest and uncertainty following the military coup in February 2021. However, the expectation that "Myanmar will likely remain a long-term destination for Chinese investment, particularly in the energy, mining and infrastructure sectors" (Yu 2021, p. 6), only attests again to the long-term character of continual frontierization, interspersed with specific periods or moments of rupture, remodelling and intensification. Regarding the latter, the COVID-19 pandemic has boosted another inherent feature of frontier constellations: illicit economies, especially cross-border drug trade (Ghosh 2021).

While the still unfolding pandemic with all its uncertainty and volatility confounds any serious attempt at a prognosis of future resource frontier developments in the region, a historically informed, longitudinal—and not episodic—understanding of many-faceted frontier continuities and ruptures might be a good start to make sense of, and to anticipate, processes of both production and disruption of resource frontiers in mainland Southeast Asia.

References

Acosta, Alberto. 2013. "Extractivism and Neo-extractivism: Two Sides of the Same Curse". In *Beyond Development: Alternative Visions from Latin America*, edited by Miriam Lang and Dunia Mokrani, pp. 61–86. Quito: Rosa Luxemburg Foundation.

Anderson, James A., and John K. Whitmore. 2015. "Introduction. The Fiery Frontier and the *Dong* World". In *China's Encounters on the South and Southwest: Reforging the Fiery Frontier Over Two Millennia*, edited by James A. Anderson and John K. Whitmore, pp. 1–55. Leiden: Brill.

Andriesse, Edo. 2014. "Laos: Frontier Capitalism". In *The Oxford Handbook of Asian Business Systems*, edited by Michael A. Witt and Gordon Redding. Oxford: Oxford University Press. 10.1093/oxfordhb/9780199654925.013.002 (accessed 9 October 2021).

Baird, Ian G. 2011. "Turning Land into Capital, Turning People into Labour: Primitive Accumulation and the Arrival of Large-Scale Economic Land Concessions in Laos". *New Proposals: Journal of Marxism and Interdisciplinary Inquiry* 5, no. 1: 10–26.

──────, and Bruce Shoemaker. 2007. "Unsettling Experiences: Internal Resettlement an International Aid Agencies in the Lao PDR". *Development and Change* 38, no. 5: 865–88. https://doi.org/10.1111/j.1467-7660.2007.00437.x (accessed 9 October 2021).

Barney, Keith. 2009. "Laos and the Making of a 'Relational' Resource Frontier". *Geographical Journal* 175, no. 2: 146–59. http://dx.doi.org/10.1111/j.1475-4959.2009.00323.x (accessed 9 October 2021).

Breul, Moritz, and Javier Revilla Diez. 2021. "One Thing Leads to Another', But Where? Gateway Cities and the Geography of Production Linkages". *Growth and Change* 52, no. 1: 29–47. http://dx.doi.org/10.1111/grow.12347 (accessed 9 October 2021).

Brown, Alan. 2018. "Laos's Peripheral Centrality in Southeast Asia: Mobility, Labour, and Regional Integration". *European Journal of East Asian Studies* 17, no. 2: 228–62. https://doi.org/10.1163/15700615-01702005 (accessed 9 October 2021).

Chettri, Mona. 2020. "From Shangri-La to de-facto SEZ: Land Grabs from 'Below' in Sikkim, India". *Geoforum* 109: 57–66. https://doi.org/10.1016/j.geoforum.2019.12.016 (accessed 9 October 2021).

──────, and Michael Eilenberg, eds. 2021. *Development Zones in Asian Borderlands*. Amsterdam: Amsterdam University Press. https://doi.org/10.1515/9789048551811 (accessed 9 October 2021).

Chheang, Vannarith. 2021. "Cambodia's Embrace of China's Belt and Road Initiative: Managing Asymmetries, Maximizing Authority". *Asian Perspective* 45, no. 2: 375–96. https://doi.org/10.1353/apr.2021.0005 (accessed 9 October 2021).

Chong, Alan, and Quang Minh Pham, eds. 2020. *Critical Reflections on China's Belt & Road Initiative*. Singapore: Palgrave Macmillan.

Cons, Jason, and Michael Eilenberg, eds. 2019a. *Frontier Assemblages: The Emergent Politics of Resource Frontiers in Asia*. Oxford: Wiley. 10.1002/9781119412090 (accessed 9 October 2021).

Cons, Jason, and Michael Eilenberg. 2019b. "Introduction: On the New Politics of Margins in Asia: Mapping Frontier Assemblages". In *Frontier Assemblages: The Emergent Politics of Resource Frontiers in Asia*, edited by Jason Cons and Michael Eilenberg, pp. 1–18. Oxford: Wiley. https://doi.org/10.1002/9781119412090.ch0 (accessed 9 October 2021).

Deloncle, P. 2011. "The Development of Laos". In *Laos in the 1920s: The Gods, Monks and Mountains of Laos*, edited by Jean Renaud, pp. 103–21. Bangkok: White Lotus. First published 1930.

Dwyer, Michael. 2007. *Turning Land into Capital. A Review of Recent Research on Land Concessions for Investment in the Lao PDR*. Vientiane: Land Information Working Group (LIWG)

_____, and Thoumthone Vongvisouk. 2017. "The Long Land Grab: Market-assisted Enclosure on the China-Lao Rubber Frontier". *Territory, Politics, Governance* 7, no. 1: 96–114. https://doi.org/10.1080/21622671.2017.1371635 (accessed 9 October 2021).

Dzüvichü, Lipokmar, and Manjeet Baruah, eds. 2019. *Objects and Frontiers in Modern Asia: Between the Mekong and the Indus*. New York: Routledge.

Einzenberger, Rainer. 2018. "Frontier Capitalism and Politics of Dispossession in Myanmar: The Case of the Mwetaung (Gullu Mual) Nickel Mine in Chin State". *Austrian Journal of South-East Asian Studies* 11, no. 1: 13–34. https://doi.org/10.14764/10.ASEAS-2018.1-2 (accessed 9 October 2021).

Évrard, Olivier, and Yves Goudineau. 2004. "Planned Resettlement, Unexpected Migrations and Cultural Trauma in Laos". *Development and Change* 35, no 5: 937–62. https://doi.org/10.1111/j.1467-7660.2004.00387.x (accessed 9 October 2021).

Ferguson, James. 1994. *The Anti-Politics Machine. 'Development', Depoliticization, and Bureaucratic Power in Lesotho*. Minneapolis: University of Minnesota Press.

Giersch, C. Patterson. 2006. *Asian Borderlands: The Transformation of Qing China's Yunnan Frontier*. Cambridge: Harvard University Press.

Ghosh, Nirmal. 2021. "Asia's Illegal Drug Trade Thriving Even as COVID–19 Pandemic Batters Economies". *Straits Times*, 10 June 2021. https://www.straitstimes.com/asia/se-asia/asias-illegal-drug-trade-is-thriving-even-as-pandemic-batters-economies (accessed 1 July 2021).

Götz, Johanna M., and Carl Middleton.2020. "Ontological politics of hydrosocial territories in the Salween River basin, Myanmar/Burma". *Political Geography*

78: 102–15. https://doi.org/10.1016/j.polgeo.2019.102115 (accessed 9 October 2021).

Gupta, Akhil. 2018. "The Future in Ruins: Thoughts on the Temporality of Infrastructure". In *The Promise of Infrastructure*, edited by Nikhil Anand, Akhil Gupta and Hannah Appel, pp. 62–79. Durham: Duke University Press. https://doi.org/10.1215/9781478002031-003 (accessed 9 October 2021).

Hall, Derek. 2011. "Land Grabs, Land Control, and Southeast Asian Crop Booms". *Journal of Peasant Studies* 38, no. 4: 837–57. https://doi.org/10.1080/03066150.2011.607706 (accessed 9 October 2021).

Hardy, Andrew. 2003. *Red Hills: Migrants and the State in the Highlands of Vietnam*. Singapore: Institute of Southeast Asian Studies.

Harvey, David. 2003. *The New Imperialism*. Oxford: Oxford University Press.

Haug, Michaela, Kristina Grossmann, and Timo Kaartinen. 2020. "Introduction: Frontier Temporalities: Exploring Processes of Frontierization, Defrontierization and Refrontierization in Indonesia and Africa". *Paideuma: Mitteilungen zur Kulturkunde* 66: 171–82.

Hiebert, Murray. 2020. *Under Beijing's Shadow: Southeast Asia's China Challenge*. Lanham: Rowman & Littlefield.

High, Holly. 2013. "Experimental Consensus: Negotiating with the Irrigating State in the South of Laos". *Asian Studies Review* 37, no. 4: 491–508. https://doi.org/10.1080/10357823.2013.794188 (accessed 9 October 2021).

———. 2021. *Projectland: Life in a Lao Socialist Model Village*. Honolulu: University of Hawai'i Press.

Hurni, Kaspar, and Jefferson Fox. 2018. "The Expansion of Tree-based Boom Crops in Mainland Southeast Asia: 2001 to 2014". *Journal of Land Use Science* 13, no. 1–2: 198–219. https://doi.org/10.1080/1747423X.2018.1499830 (accessed 9 October 2021).

Ishikawa, Noboru, and Ryoji Soda, eds. 2020. *Anthropogenic Tropical Forests: Human-Nature Interfaces on the Plantation Frontier*. Singapore: Springer.

Jacka, Jerry K. 2018. "The Anthropology of Mining: The Social and Environmental Impacts of Resource Extraction in the Mineral Age". *Annual Review of Anthropology* 47, no. 1: 61–77.

Jiahan, Cao. 2020. "Toward a Health Silk Road: China's Proposal for Global Health Cooperation". *China Quarterly of International Strategic Studies* 6, no. 1: 19–35. https://doi.org/10.1142/S2377740020500013 (accessed 9 October 2021).

Johnson, Andrew Alan. 2020. *Mekong Dreaming: Life and Death along a Changing River*. Durham: Duke University Press. https://doi.org/10.2307/j.ctv14t48xn (accessed 9 October 2021).

Joseph, Sabrina, ed. 2019. *Commodity Frontiers and Global Capitalist Expansion: Social, Ecological and Political Implications from the Nineteenth Century to the Present Day*. London: Palgrave.

Junquera, Victoria, and Adrienne Gret-Regamey. 2019. "Crop Booms at the Forest Frontier: Triggers, Reinforcing Dynamics, and the Diffusion of Knowledge and Norms". *Global Environmental Change* 57: 101929. https://doi.org/10.1016/j.gloenvcha.2019.101929 (accessed 9 October 2021).

Kelly, Alice B., and Nancy Lee Peluso. 2015. "Frontiers of Commodification: State Lands and Their Formalization". *Society and Natural Resources* 28, no. 5: 473–95. https://doi.org/10.1080/08941920.2015.1014602 (accessed 9 October 2021).

Kenney-Lazar, Miles. 2018. "Governing Dispossession: Relational Land Grabbing in Laos". *Annals of the American Association of Geographers* 108, no 3: 679–94. https://doi.org/10.1080/24694452.2017.1373627 (accessed 9 October 2021).

_____, Michael Dwyer, and Cornelia Hett. 2018. *Turning Land into Capital: Assessing A Decade of Policy in Practice*. Vientiane: Land Information Working Group (LIWG).

_____, and SiuSue Mark. 2021. "Variegated Transitions: Emerging Forms of Land and Resource Capitalism in Laos and Myanmar". *Environment and Planning A: Economy and Space* 53, no. 2: 296–314. https://doi.org/10.1177%2F0308518X20948524 (accessed 9 October 2021).

Keovilignavong, Oulavanh. 2019. "Mining Governance Dilemma and Impacts: A Case of Gold Mining in Phu-Hae, Lao PDR". *Resources Policy* 61: 141–50. https://doi.org/10.1016/j.resourpol.2019.02.002 (accessed 9 October 2021).

Laungaramsri, Pinkaew. 2012. "Frontier Capitalism and the Expansion of Rubber Plantations in Southern Laos". *Journal of Southeast Asian Studies* 43, no. 3: 463–77. https://doi.org/10.1017/S0022463412000343 (accessed 9 October 2021).

_____. 2019. "China in Laos: Enclave Spaces and the Transformation of Borders in the Mekong Region". *Australian Journal of Anthropology* 30, no. 2: 195–211. https://doi.org/10.1111/taja.12319 (accessed 9 October 2021).

Li, Tania. 2007. *The Will to Improve: Governmentality, Development, and the Practice of Politics*. Durham: Duke University Press.

_____. 2014. *Land's End: Capitalist Relations on an Indigenous Frontier*. Durham: Duke University Press.

Liu, Hong, Kong Yam Tan, and Guanie Lim. 2021. "Introduction: Southeast Asia and the Belt and Road Initiative: The Political Economy of Regionalism, Trade, and Infrastructure". *Singapore Economic Review* 66, no 1: 1–20. https://doi.org/10.1142/S021759082102001X (accessed 9 October 2021).

Loughlin, Neil, and Sarah Milne. 2020. "After the Grab? Land Control and Regime Survival in Cambodia since 2012". *Journal of Contemporary Asia*. 5, no. 3: 375–97. https://doi.org/10.1080/00472336.2020.1740295 (accessed 9 October 2021).

Lu, Juliet, and Oliver Schönweger. 2019. "Great Expectations: Chinese Investment in Laos and the Myth of Empty Land". *Territory, Politics, Governance* 7, no. 1: 61–78. https://doi.org/10.1080/21622671.2017.1360195 (accessed 9 October 2021).

Lund, Christian. 2016: "Rule and Rupture: State Formation Through the Production of Property and Citizenship". *Development and Change* 47, no. 6: 1199–228. https://doi.org/10.1111/dech.12274 (accessed 9 October 2021).

Luning, Sabine, and Robert J. Pijpers. 2017. "Governing Access to Gold in Ghana: In-Depth Geopolitics on Mining Concessions". *Africa: The Journal of the International African Institute* 87, no 4: 758–79. https://doi.org/10.1017/S0001972017000353 (accessed 9 October 2021).

Lyttleton, Chris, and Yunxia Li. 2017. "Rubber's Affective Economies: Seeding a Social Landscape in Northwest Laos". In *Changing Lives in Laos: Society, Politics, and Culture in a Post-Socialist State*, edited by Vanina Bouté and Vatthana Pholsena, pp. 301–24. Singapore: NUS Press.

Marsden, Magnus, and Madeleine Reeves. 2019. "Marginal Hubs: On Conviviality beyond the Urban in Asia: Introduction". *Modern Asian Studies* 53, no. 3: 755–75. https://doi.org/10.1017/S0026749X18000495 (accessed 9 October 2021).

Michaud, Jean, and Tim Forsyth, eds. 2011. *Moving Mountains: Ethnicity and Livelihoods in Highland China, Vietnam, and Laos*. Vancouver: UBC Press.

Mierzejewski, Dominik. 2021. *China's Provinces and the Belt and Road Initiative*. London: Routledge.

Miller, Michelle Ann, Carl Middleton, Jonathan Rigg, and David Taylor. 2020. "Hybrid Governance of Transboundary Commons: Insights from Southeast Asia". *Annals of the American Association of Geographers* 110, no. 1: 297–313. https://doi.org/10.1080/24694452.2019.1624148 (accessed 9 October 2021).

Morris-Jung, Jason, eds. 2017. *In China's Backyard: Policies and Politics of Chinese Resource Investments in Southeast Asia*. Singapore: ISEAS – Yusof Ishak Institute.

Nyíri, Pál. 2012. "Enclaves of Improvement: Sovereignty and Developmentalism in the Special Zones of the China-Lao Borderlands". *Comparative Studies in Society and History* 54, no. 3: 533–62. https://doi.org/10.1017/S0010417512000229 (accessed 9 October 2021).

——. 2017. "Realms of Free Trade, Enclaves of Order: Chinese-Built 'Instant Cities' in Northern Laos." In *The Art of Neighbouring: Making Relations Across China's Borders*, edited by Martin Saxer and Juan Zhang, pp. 57–71. Amsterdam: Amsterdam University Press. http://library.oapen.org/handle/20.500.12657/31928 (accessed 9 October 2021).

——, and Danielle Tan, eds. 2017. *Chinese Encounters in Southeast Asia: How People, Money, Ideas from China are Changing a Region*. Seattle and London: University of Washington Press.

Rasmussen, Mattias, and Christian Lund. 2018. "Reconfiguring Frontier Spaces: The Territorialisation of Resource Control". *World Development* 101: 388–99. https://doi.org/10.1016/j.worlddev.2017.01.018 (accessed 9 October 2021).

Rigg, Jonathan. 2020. *Rural Development in Southeast Asia: Dispossession, Accumulation and Persistence*. Cambridge: Cambridge University Press.

Rippa, Alessandro. 2021. "From Boom to Bust – to Boom Again? Infrastructural Suspension and the Making of a Development Zone at the China-Laos Borderlands". In *Development Zones in Asian Borderlands*, edited by Mona Chettri and Michael Eilenberg, pp. 231–51. Amsterdam: Amsterdam University Press. https://doi.org/10.1515/9789048551811-012 (accessed 9 October 2021).

Ross, Corey. 2014. "The Tin Frontier: Mining, Empire, and Environment in Southeast Asia, 1870s–1930s". *Environmental History* 19, no. 3: 454–79. https://doi.org/10.1093/envhis/emu032 (accessed 9 October 2021).

Rowedder, Simon. 2020. "Railroading Land-Linked Laos: China's Regional Profits, Laos' Domestic Costs?". *Eurasian Geography and Economics* 61, no. 2: 152–61. https://doi.org/10.1080/15387216.2019.1704813 (accessed 9 October 2021).

Saxer, Martin, and Ruben Andersson. 2019. "The Return of Remoteness: Insecurity, Isolation and Connectivity in the New World Order". *Social Anthropology* 27, no. 2: 140–55. https://doi.org/10.1111/1469-8676.12652 (accessed 9 October 2021).

―――, and Juan Zhang, eds. 2017. *The Art of Neighbouring: Making Relations Across China's Borders*. Amsterdam: Amsterdam University Press. http://library.oapen.org/handle/20.500.12657/31928 (accessed 9 October 2021).

Scott, James. 2009. *The Art of Not Being Governed: An Anarchist History of Upland Southeast Asia*. New Haven, CT: Yale University Press.

Sidaway, James D., Simon Rowedder, Chih Yuan Woon, Weiqiang Lin, and Vatthana Pholsena. 2020. "Politics and Spaces of China's Belt and Road Initiative". *Environment and Planning C: Politics and Space* 38, no. 5: 795–847. https://doi.org/10.1177%2F2399654420911410 (accessed 9 October 2021).

Strangio, Sebastian. 2020. *In the Dragon's Shadow: Southeast Asia in the Chinese Century*. New Haven: Yale University Press.

Suhardiman, Diana, Oulavanh Keovilignavong, and Miles Kenney-Lazar. 2019. "The Territorial Politics of Land Use Planning in Laos". *Land Use Policy* 83: 346–56. https://doi.org/10.1016/j.landusepol.2019.02.017 (accessed 9 October 2021).

Tagliacozzo, Eric, and Chang, Wen-chin, eds. 2011. *Chinese Circulations: Capital, Commodities, and Networks in Southeast Asia*. Durham: Duke University Press.

Tappe, Oliver. 2021. "Artisanal, Small-Scale and Large-Scale Mining in Lao PDR". *ISEAS Perspective*, no. 2021/44, 14 April 2021. https://www.iseas.edu.sg/articles-commentaries/iseas-perspective/2021-44-artisanal-small-scale-and-large-scale-mining-in-lao-pdr-by-oliver-tappe/ (accessed 17 August 2021).

Taylor, Philip. 2016. "Frontier Commoditisation in Post-Socialist Southeast Asia". *Asia Pacific Viewpoint* 57, no 2: 145–53. https://doi.org/10.1111/apv.12125 (accessed 9 October 2021).

Tsing, Anna L. 2003. "Natural Resource and Capitalist Frontiers". *Economic and Political Weekly* 38, no. 48: 5100–106. https://www.jstor.org/stable/4414348 (accessed 9 October 2021).

———. 2005. *Friction: An Ethnography of Global Connection*. Princeton: Princeton University Press.

Turner, Sarah, Christine Bonnin, and Jean Michaud, eds. 2015. *Frontier Livelihoods: Hmong in the Sino-Vietnamese Borderlands*. Seattle: University of Washington Press.

Walker, Andrew. 1999. *The Legend of the Golden Boat: Regulation, Trade and Traders in the Borderlands of Laos, Thailand, China and Burma*. Honolulu: University of Hawai'i Press.

Woods, Kevin M. 2020. "Smaller-Scale Land Grabs and Accumulation from Below: Violence, Coercion and Consent in Spatially Uneven Agrarian Change in Shan State, Myanmar". *World Development* 127: 104780. https://doi.org/10.1016/j.worlddev.2019.104780 (accessed 9 October 2021).

Woodworth, Max D., and Agnieszka Joniak-Lüthi. 2020. "Exploring China's Borderlands in an Era of BRI-Induced change". *Eurasian Geography and Economics* 61, no. 1: 1–12. https://doi.org/10.1080/15387216.2020.1727758 (accessed 9 October 2021).

Ye, Min. 2021. "Adopting or Atrophying? China's Belt and Road after the COVID-19 Pandemic". *Asia Policy* 16, no. 1: 65–95.

Yu, Kaho. 2020. "The Belt and Road Initative in Southeast Asia after Covid-19: China's Energy and Infrastructure Investments in Myanmar". *ISEAS Perspective*, no. 2021/39, 6 April 2021. https://www.iseas.edu.sg/articles-commentaries/iseas-perspective/2021-39-the-belt-and-road-initiative-in-southeast-asia-after-covid-19-chinas-energy-and-infrastructure-investments-in-myanmar-by-kaho-yu/ (accessed 18 August 2021).

Zuo, Zhenting, Jennifer C. Langill, Sarah Turner, and Jean-François Rousseau. 2021. "Spices as the Saviour? The Complex Vulnerabilities of three Commodity Crop Booms and Ethnic Minority Livelihoods in Yunnan's Agrarian Frontier". *Asia-Pacific Viewpoint* 62, no. 1: 100–15. https://doi.org/10.1111/apv.12291 (accessed 9 October 2021).

2

ONTOLOGICAL POLITICS OF THE RESOURCE FRONTIER
A Hydrosocial Analysis of the Mekong River in Northern Thailand

Thianchai Surimas and Carl Middleton

INTRODUCTION

In Chiang Khong District, northern Thailand, the current governance and plans of the Mekong River are contested, as are the future imaginaries for the river. Here, over the past two decades, the hydrological and ecological characteristics of the Mekong River have changed due to the construction and operation of hydropower projects upstream in China, with consequences for the lives of those who depended on river resources (Santasombat 2011; Räsänen et al. 2017). The changing river conditions have also held consequences for local social and cultural practices and beliefs connected to the river (Johnson 2019;

Yong 2020). In 2019 and 2020, a serious regional drought and low and unpredictable river flows left sand bars and rocky outcrops exposed along many stretches of the river and placed at risk ecosystems, fishing and farming livelihoods, and wider food security, creating severe hardship (Middleton et al. 2021). These conditions intersected with the operation of China's large hydropower dams upstream, as well as a period of intensifying geopolitics between the US and China, further escalating the already present resource politics in northern Thailand and across the wider region (Keovilignavong, Nguyen, and Hirsch 2021). In this liminal context, the Mekong River as a resource frontier remains unsettled.

In this chapter, in the context of the severe low flows, we examine the resource politics of the Mekong River in northern Thailand as revealed through the practices, narratives and knowledge productions of several competing networks that shape the Mekong River as a resource frontier. These include the community and civil society movement-led Ing People's Council (IPC), the intergovernmental Mekong River Commission (MRC) and the Lancang-Mekong Cooperation (LMC). Our conceptual approach reflects the growing recognition of the heterogeneity of water cultures and histories (or "water worlds") in recent academic literature (Barnes and Alatout 2012), and the multiple ontologies of water that underpin them (Vogt and Walsh 2021). We draw in particular on hydrosocial literature that emphasizes how rivers are entwined within social processes that produce multiple forms of water-society assemblage (Wesselink, Kooy, and Warner 2017). Linton and Budds (2014, p. 175), for example, observe that "different kinds of waters are realized in different hydrosocial assemblages; in one such assemblage, water is constituted as a public good, while in another, it is constituted as a commodity". This leads to our interest in how resource politics at the resource frontier reveal an enactment of multiple ontologies (Mol 1999) and their ontological politics, whereby human actors compete to further their own interests by naturalizing their ontology while marginalizing others (Yates, Harris, and Wilson 2017; Götz and Middleton 2020).

Our chapter is based on ethnographic fieldwork mainly conducted between September and December 2019, as well as a longer-term engagement until the present as part of the first author's doctoral research. The study was primarily conducted in five villages in Chiang Khong District and one village in Vieng Kean District, both in Chiang Rai Province. Participant observation was the main method for data collection through observing economic, social and cultural practices, as well as networking activities among the groups engaged in the Mekong River issues. We observed the everyday lives of people around water, such as agricultural activities and fishing, participated in meetings of civil society groups, and observed several cultural and ritual ceremonies, namely an "illuminated boat procession" (*Lai Rua Fai*) (October 2019) and a "prolong river and forest ordination" ceremony (December 2019). We also conducted seven in-depth interviews with civil society members, two with village leaders, and sixteen with community members. We also organized six group interviews, with nineteen participants in total.

In the next section, we briefly detail the 2019–20 low flows, and the knowledge politics that emerged towards explaining it. We then introduce the riverside communities and their perceptions of the impacts of China's upstream dams, to suggest that the ceremonies and everyday practices that we observed reveal an ontology whereby local cultures, lives and meanings are intimately woven together with the Mekong River that includes its material human and non-human dimensions inclusive of supernatural things. This maintains an ontology of the river as simultaneously a resource sustaining local livelihoods and economies, and that also embodies local cultural and sacred values. We also show how this relationship, which has been patterned by the river's natural seasonal flow, is increasingly disrupted due to the changing river conditions. We further expand on this theme by outlining the formation, purpose and activities of the IPC. In the last section, before the conclusion, we show how the state-led MRC and LMC pursue variants of ecological modernization, holding the meaning of the Mekong River to be an economic resource for sustainable management. Overall, we argue that politics at the resource frontier are ontological politics contesting the very meaning of the Mekong River and its future form, be it as embedded in and patterning the socio-cultural relations of riverside communities in northern Thailand, or as part of an ecological modernization and economic integration and growth agenda as envisioned by the region's governments.

MEKONG RIVER DROUGHT AND LOW FLOWS

The low flows in the Mekong River during 2019 and 2020 have been some of the driest river conditions in living memory. While the region faced a drought over these two years, compounded by the El Niño weather pattern, it has been vigorously debated whether large dams in the basin have either exacerbated the impact of the drought or could have been operated differently to better mitigate its impacts. A significant focus has been on the role of China's cascade of eleven dams in the upper Mekong (Lancang), given that a significant proportion of the river's dry-season flow originates from China, from the glacial melt of the river's headwaters in the Tibetan Plateau, and more recently due to the significant reservoir storage now in place. Moreover, China's operation of the Jinghong Dam—the lowest in China's Lancang (upper Mekong) cascade—which China reports in advance to the MRC for major fluctuations has led to reductions in river water flow and abnormal fluctuations downstream including during the 2019–20 drought (MRC 2020). The extent to which climate change is nowadays shaping river conditions in the basin is also an important question (Evers and Pathirana 2018). The debates have also intensified scrutiny of transboundary water governance institutions, including the MRC and LMC.

Public debate on the Mekong River's low flows also intensified with the publication of a report in April 2020 by the research consultancy "Eyes on the Earth" that presented a model of the pre-dam flow of the Lancang River to then predict the impact of the dams onto northern Thailand downstream, drawing on satellite data (Basist and Williams 2020). Overall, the study showed how since dams in the Lancang cascade began to be commissioned in the early 1990s there had been a decrease in wet season river levels and an increase in dry season levels, and more irregular and rapid fluctuations in water levels in both seasons. The Eyes on Earth report drew significant media attention (e.g., *New York Times*, 13 April 2020), as it was drawn upon by several civil society groups as well as representatives of the US Government to claim that it provided evidence that China was responsible for the severity of the 2019–20 low flows (Johnson and Wongcha-um 2020). This led to responses from China's diplomats (e.g., Hu and Lin 2020) and researchers (e.g., Tian, Liu, and Lu 2020), the MRC (2020) and significant debate among researchers on the report's findings (e.g., Ketelsen, Räsänen, and Sawdon 2020). The 2019 and 2020 low flows occurred at a time of intensified geopolitics between the United State and China in Southeast Asia and globally, leading to a hydropoliticization of the drought and the research related to it (Keovilignavong, Nguyen, and Hirsch 2021; Middleton et al. 2021). As this at times very heated debate unfolded at the national, regional and even global level, the impacts of the changing river conditions were experienced most directly by those whose lives depend directly upon the river, and it is to this experience that we now turn.

LIVING WITH THE MEKONG RIVER

For the members of the communities we visited nearby the Mekong River, the operation of China's dams has challenged their way of relating to the river. Many of those whom we spoke with, who tied their life and livelihood to the river, stated that the Mekong River needed to flow naturally and to reflect the previous seasonal conditions. Having related to the Mekong River for their whole life, the seasonal flow—low in the dry season and high in the rainy season—has been important for patterning their economic, social and cultural activities, as well as situational knowledge produced by observing and learning from seasonal changes. In the rainy season, when the water level is high, fishing was the main income because fish migrate at this time and are more abundant. In the winter season, the river level starts to lower and the deposited sediment yields a good quality of soil for riverbank gardening. In the dry season, river weeds (*kai*) can be collected, while riverbank gardening also continues. The seasonal calendar of the community that relies on the natural flow of the river is nowadays disrupted. Many of those we spoke with said that they could not rely on the river, with its unusual and fluctuating flows that had defined their previous way of life around the river.

The seasonal conditions also connect to the traditional cultural, ritual and ceremonial practices. During the high flow season, several festivals are hosted. In the twelfth month of the Thai lunar calendar,[1] the *Loy Krathong* festival is hosted, during which community members and villagers float *krathong*[2] in the river. Among the Lao ethnic communities, another festival called *Lai Rua Fai* (the illuminated boat procession) (Figure 2.1) is organized during the eleventh month of the Thai lunar

FIGURE 2.1
The launch of the illuminated boat procession (October 2019)

Source: Photo by Thianchai Surimas.

calendar for which Buddhist monks, the master of ceremony,[3] community leaders and members help prepare by decorating an illuminated boat. Both the *Loy Krathong* and *Lai Rua Fai* festivals are organized to pay respect to and worship the *Kongka* Goddess, which is the goddess of rivers and is a common belief in the region (Johnson 2019). People organize both festivals to ask for forgiveness for consuming from the river the whole year, which may damage the river intentionally or unintentionally, and to thank the goddess for providing the river and its resources for them. They also believe that when the illuminated boat and *krathong* float away, bad luck, sickness, misfortune and suffering also flow away from them. On the last day of Buddhist Lent, *Boon Suang Rua* (longboat racing) is hosted by the Huay Xai district in Laos and joined by people from both sides of the river. From September to October, young men gather to practise before competing. Those we interviewed mentioned that this competition helped bring together communities along both sides of the river, and to prepare the young men who participate to be brave. This festival also helps them learn about the river system and local beliefs.

In the dry season, when the water level drops and the flow becomes slower, it signals the time when traditionally the Mekong giant catfish (*pla buek*) would migrate to the Chiang Khong area to the upper areas of the Mekong for breeding. It is believed that *pla buek* is owned and protected by ghosts called *Chao Pong* and *Chao Luang*, and if these ghosts do not allow fishermen to catch fish, then they will neither see nor be able to catch them. In Had Krai village, on 18 April, an annual ceremony and ritual is held, joined by fishermen, folk doctors and other community members, to worship these ghosts and ask for permission before setting out to catch the *pla buek*. During this ceremony, they also worship *Mae Ya Nang* who is the guardian of boats, and they also worship ghosts and spirits that surround the area to protect fishermen from anything dangerous that could happen while they are out on the river (Meebun 1998; Tanakit 2013). After the ceremony, fishermen will spend multiple days and nights on islands (*don*) in the middle of the Mekong River seeking to catch *pla buek*. These *don* are only exposed during the low-flow periods when the *pla buek* will come to eat *kai* that only grows in the clean and clear water characteristic of the low-flow period. Even though *pla buek* are nowadays rarely found in the area, the fishermen still practice this ceremony, which has become a part of the identity of Chiang Khong and which has been recently used by the local government to promote tourism (Vieng Chiang Khong Municipality 2021), while the whole process of preparing and then seeking to catch *pla buek* remains important to the fishermen who engage in it.

These festivals and ceremonies are not only cultural activities but also important social gatherings within the village and with other communities both in Thailand and from Laos across the river. The relationship between people and the river is complex, and the Mekong River is related to their life in multiple ways. These ceremonies, however, reveal how local people tie their relationship economically, socially, culturally and religiously with the Mekong River and its seasonal cycles. Through our hydrosocial lens, it reveals the social and cultural embeddedness of the Mekong River, which holds a value different from that of a commodified economic resource. This way of living with the Mekong River is not defined by property rights to control or own the river, but rather that the local people whom we spoke with only wish to draw from the river alongside respect for its nature. Ontologically, the everyday practices and ceremonies suggest that the Mekong River assembles human and non-human things together, making it a powerful source of life.

IMPACTS OF CHINA'S DAM OPERATION: PERSPECTIVE OF DOWNSTREAM FISHERS AND FARMERS

For those who we spoke with, it was ubiquitously commented that since the construction of upstream dams in China unusual flow conditions had occurred with impacts on fishing and riverbank farming practices, and on the ecosystems of the river itself. For the riverbank gardening, the rapid fluctuation of water levels and flows during the winter and dry season—released from the dam to facilitate boat navigation—swept away vegetables and tobacco crops as well as tools. One farmer who grows vegetables along the river said:

> When water level increases overnight without warning it causes me to lose my beansprouts and vegetables, which cannot survive being in the water. I lose all my products and sometimes I lose my tools. The money that I spent on seeds and beans flows away too (Interview, 18 October 2019).

Another farmer, whose family has been farming the riverbank for two generations, spends most of his working time alongside the river growing beansprouts. He said:

> I have worked on the riverbank for the past 20 years, and there have been dramatic changes in the flow of the river. It flows unnaturally. At first, when the flow started to change, I didn't know why the water level was high in the dry season, but now I know that there are dams above. I observe the water every day. The Mekong does not depend on the season anymore.... This year, the water level is extremely low. Normally, from the end of July, we have to move everything—our buckets and sandbags—to the concrete road, but this year we haven't had to because the water level is low (Interview, 17 October 2019).

The unpredictable flow also caused losses for fishermen. Many in Chiang Khong have lost their expensive fishing gear when leaving it out overnight during the low flow season, as "water comes without rain (from the upstream dams)". For fishermen in Chiang Khong District, it was difficult to predict the flow and difficult to access information about the dam operation upstream (also Middleton et al. 2021). These unusual flow conditions challenge the situational knowledge and life of people along the river who rely on fisheries for food and income (Yong 2020). The quantity and number of species of Mekong's fish have been dramatically decreased, with some species no longer in the area and many species hard to find. The decline is widely viewed by fishers to relate to the operation of dams and the unusual flow conditions, as well as other local development projects such as the construction of the Fourth Thai-Lao Friendship Bridge.

On the one hand, there have been important local initiatives to protect fisheries through establishing village-led conservation zones and coordinating fishing practices (Yong 2020). But the difficulties of the fishery decline are still a challenge. In Had Krai village, fishermen still gather every day to fish. However, unlike in the past when everyone was allowed to fish, nowadays they have to queue because only one or two fishing boats are permitted to catch fish at a time due to the decrease in fish. We spoke with one ex-fisher, for example, who had spent two decades on the river but quit five years ago due to the fisheries decline (Interview, 10 October 2019). He observed that the number of active boats had over halved from seventy-two boats five years ago to less than thirty nowadays who only fish part-time. Some ex-fishers have migrated to urban areas seeking work, while others have become daily labourers working locally.

The fisheries of the Ing River, a major Mekong River tributary in northern Thailand, have also been affected by the changes. Earlier community-led (*Thai Baan*) research found that fishes from the Mekong River migrate to this tributary to breed and lay their eggs, with fish migrations shaped by both the flow and temperature differences between the tributary and the mainstream (Wises, Yodmuang, and Jaikla 2006). One local fisherman explained:

> During the rainy season, the Mekong River is supposed to be flooded and water from the mainstream should overflow into the Ing River, while the Ing River flow also increased so that the lower part of the Ing River Basin was always flooded. This is an important ecosystem because fish can migrate to breed and lay their eggs in the wetland areas. Then they migrate back to the Mekong when they become adults.

> In recent years, we found fishes [in the Mekong] with their stomach full of eggs, ready to lay their eggs, but they were unable to migrate to the wetland because the river levels are extremely low (Interview, 13 October 2019).

This statement both demonstrates the situational knowledge of the ecosystems held by local fishers, and locally experienced impacts due to China's upstream dams as well as changes caused by development projects and trends that are also occurring in the Ing watershed (e.g., Wajjwalku 2019).

FORMATION AND ACTIVITIES OF THE ING PEOPLES COUNCIL

The Ing People's Council (IPC) was established in 2013 as a network of community and civil society organizations in the Ing watershed that spans Phayao and Chiang Rai provinces. Before its institutionalization in 2013, the IPC existed as an informal network of local people and civil society who shared the network's values. The network first emerged in response to a concern towards a large-scale state-led plan for a water diversion from the Kok-Ing-Nan River Basins to the Chao Phraya River Basin, together with a more general concern for the Ing River's environmental degradation that at first was from deforestation and water pollution in the upper part of the river basin, which was impacting livelihoods. Those in the network are also concerned about the rapids blasting for a navigation project on the Mekong River, as well as the construction of large dams on the mainstream both in China and downstream in Laos, as these changes also affected the Ing River. Therefore, the network collaborated in campaigns, such as those organized by the NGO Rak Chiang Khong, towards these issues (Interview and informal group interview, 3 December 2019). It was formalized as a "People's Council" to allow for a more systematic strategy and effective communication of the network's concerns for natural resource management emphasizing a community-led approach (Living Rivers Siam Association 2013; Wajjwalku 2019; Wises 2019).

The IPC's purpose, as stated on its website, is to: support local community participation in natural resources management; conserve and recover the natural resources in Ing River Basin (animals, wetland, watershed forest area and others); build a systematic and empirical mechanism for resources management in the Ing River Basin; and support local community economies from local resources (IPC 2021). Its activities include organizing network meetings and local events to share ideas about how to protect and use natural resources based on the cultural ecology of the river basin, increase the participation of local people, and support local projects and initiatives to the extent that its limited funding allows.

Knowledge production is a key strategy of the IPC, including conducting community-led *Thai Baan* research (also known as *Tai Baan* and *Jao Baan*). Many studies have covered a range of topics including fisheries, animal species, vegetables and herbs, food security, seasonal food calendar, fishing gear and equipment, and riverbank gardening. It has also documented the participation of women in environmental management, the significance of cultural activities, and changes due to development projects including the fluctuating flows of the Mekong River (Ing Peoples Council 2021, Living Rivers Siam Association 2021, Mekong Community Institute 2021). In *Thai Baan* research, local community members are the researchers who design, collect information, analyse, write, publish and utilize the study drawing on their local (situational) knowledge. It is the knowledge that draws from the lives of those who interact every day with the research topic. Sometimes it is used to influence policy and political processes related to the river, including to challenge state and project developers' studies, but it is also an empowerment process for the community members (who are the researchers) to organize their knowledge systematically, to trust the knowledge that they have and to share this knowledge between generations. Regarding *Thai Baan* as a research method, one interviewee commented: "Local knowledge is important and when local people have it, and they can deliver it, they feel empowered" (Interview, 3 December 2019). The IPC also collaborates with civil society, international and local NGOs, and academic researchers to produce studies based on conventional social and physical science methods, which they view as complementing *Thai Baan* generated knowledge. These studies also evidence the impact of some development projects on society and the environment in the Ing River Basin.

Overall, the IPC leadership view knowledge production that demonstrates the inseparability of water from local social and ecological context as vital to challenging the studies of powerful state and private actors whose (scientific) studies emphasize the material value of water. Reflecting on the significance of the *Thai Baan* knowledge production, and demonstrating the embeddedness of water in social relations, one community leader of the IPC interviewed said: "People have sets of knowledge from what they see in everyday life. But the Mekong River Commission and Lancang Mekong Cooperation construct the knowledge from scientific and engineering data. So, it leads to a different way of looking at the river." (Interview, 9 October 2019).

The IPC also plays an important role in supporting the community management of local resources. For example, in December 2019, an annual forest ordination ceremony at Muang Chum village was organized that emphasized the importance of protecting the community's wetland and fishery conservation zone. Given the severe drought over the past years, and the resulting degradation of the wetland ecosystem, including insect infestation affecting the trees, the ceremony was named the "Prolong Forest and River" ceremony. The ceremony entails preparing various materials and structures over three days that are commonly used in northern Thailand when people are facing bad luck or feeling sick; this ceremony is now also used with nature, such as rivers and forests, as a recognition that nature is alive in the same way that people are and can be treated through ceremonies in a similar way. It is a synthesis of Buddhist rituals, Brahmanism, animism, local beliefs in spirits, and local knowledge, and has been accepted because the ceremony is considered to be a successful practice in the preservation of forests and rivers (Sriviraj, Kaosesand, and Thidpad 2019). The ceremony is led by monks and involved a master of the ceremony, the elders, leaders from the community, local government, civil society and the IPC, and some invited government agencies, such as the Office of Forest Department and the Department of Water Resource at the regional level. The monk's opening speech emphasized the importance of the forest for food security, livelihood, and nature as a foundation of life, and after the speech the ceremony participants tied saffron fabric around trees as a symbol of ordination, and a wish for the trees to be healthy (Figure 2.2). The practices and values of this ceremony—and others like it—reveal how rivers and forests are embedded in the social and cultural context, which are deeper and more complex than merely being natural resources for human consumption and economic activity.

FIGURE 2.2
Monks speak at the "Prolong Forest and River" ceremony (December 2019)

Source: Photo by Thianchai Surimas.

INTERGOVERNMENTAL INSTITUTIONS FOR TRANSBOUNDARY WATER GOVERNANCE

In this section, we focus on how the Mekong River Commission (MRC) and Lancang-Mekong Cooperation (LMC) have approached the 2019–20 drought, to enquire into each institution's underpinning practices, knowledge production, planning and values towards the Mekong River. As mentioned above, much of the public debate about the drought and low flows has taken place in the context of intensified geopolitics between China and the US, which has been analysed in other recent research (Keovilignavong, Nguyen, and Hirsch 2021; Middleton et al. 2021).

In 1995, the governments of Cambodia, Laos, Vietnam and Thailand jointly established the MRC in order to strengthen transboundary water governance. Guided by the 1995 Mekong Agreement and its various procedures (MRC 1995), on paper, it is intended to facilitate rules-based decision making amongst its members. The MRC's secretariat has built an extensive knowledge base that largely is based on expert scientific knowledge. Recent key studies have included a strategic environmental assessment of Mekong mainstream dams, a State of the Basin report series (most recently for 2018), a broader comprehensive "Council Study" that examines the implications of various development pathways across the basin, and a basin development plan currently for 2021 to 2030.

Regarding drought, the MRC has launched a drought management strategy published in November 2019 in the context of its climate change strategy (MRC 2019a). This strategy mostly recommends technical measures, including dry season flow monitoring, drought forecasting and early warning, capacity building in drought assessment and planning, and information sharing systems (including with China). While the strategy and its related studies and plans contain important technical analysis, various long-standing challenges for the MRC remain. These include its ability to influence national governments' plans, its ability to ensure meaningful participation of communities and civil society, and its cooperation with China, including the LMC (e.g., Boer et al. 2016). Fundamentally, the plan reflects the MRC's overall technical approach towards the river, which is founded on Integrated Water Resource Management (IWRM) principles (Cooper 2012). There is much hydrosocial literature that emphasizes how an IWRM approach enables technical water management based on claims of "neutral" scientific principles rather than as always embedded within assemblages of social and human-nature relationships (Linton 2010; Linton and Budds 2014). In short, it can be summarized that the MRC's approach to water management and sustainable development, including in relation to the drought, aligns with an ecological modernization ontology.

The intergovernmental institutions for transboundary water management of the Mekong River are, however, in flux. The Lancang Mekong Cooperation (LMC) was launched at a summit in Hainan Province, China, in March 2016. At this first summit, leaders from China, Myanmar, Thailand, Cambodia, Laos and Vietnam committed to cooperation in five priority areas, including economic integration and water resource management. Two years later, in Phnom Penh, Cambodia, at a second summit a Five-Year Plan of Action on Lancang-Mekong Cooperation (2018–22) was announced. Within the Phnom Penh plan, it is detailed that the LMC will deepen Lancang-Mekong River flood and drought disaster emergency management, carry out a joint assessment of flood control and drought relief in the Mekong basin, and carry out a joint study on the early setting up of communication lines/channels for sharing information in emergency cases of flood and drought on the Lancang-Mekong river (LMWRC 2018). New LMC organizations related to water have been launched, namely the Lancang-Mekong Water Resources Cooperation Center (LMWRC) launched in March 2017, and the Lancang-Mekong Environmental Cooperation Center (LMECC) in November 2017. Under the LMC, a "Green Mekong" strategy has been promoted through the LMECC that emphasizes sustainable infrastructure, green industrial investment, and environmental governance. Meanwhile, cooperation around water is set to be achieved by policy dialogue, improved water quality monitoring and information and data sharing, technical cooperation and exchanges, joint research, and capacity building, to be implemented through the LMWRC. These plans have been accompanied by significant financial resources for projects, as well as China's capacity to now regulate to a significant degree the river's flow via the Lancang dams. There is a growing body of academic research comparing the role and strategies of the LMC and MRC towards water governance, including their seemingly competing mandates (Middleton and Allouche 2016; Biba 2018; Williams 2020). However, the LMC's core approach is comparable to that of the MRC in its emphasis on scientific management principles and connecting water management to economic growth, which is also reflective of an ecological modernization agenda. This includes China's viewpoint that the operation of the Lancang dams allows for the improved management of the Mekong River flows, including flood and drought mitigation. As discussed above, from the perspective of downstream communities in northern Thailand, this is certainly a heavily contested claim.

Since the LMC's launch, the MRC and LMWRC have explored areas for collaboration. In December 2019, a first MoU was signed between the two organizations that propose collaboration on data and information exchange, basin-wide monitoring, and joint assessment of Mekong water and related resources (MRC 2019b). This agreement suggests that these organizations, at their core, are compatible in terms of their ecological modernization ontology of the Mekong River. As an initial step, both sides agreed to conduct joint research on the 2019 drought and low flow situation in the Mekong River basin, aiming to identify the causes and impacts of drought and low flow conditions in 2019.

The collaboration between the MRC and LMC on the causes and impacts of the 2019 low flows, and potentially in the longer term on the cascade management of dams in the upper and lower basin has the potential to more optimally manage the Mekong River judged from an ecological modernization perspective. Yet in the context of the past impacts of China's dam operation on farmers and fishers in northern Thailand, it is also likely to be a contentious one. The leader of a civil society group in Chiang Khong told us that:

> When we talk about the impact of the dams, they [governments, dam developers, and investors] will talk about compensation. From my perspective, the loss cannot be counted, and some losses are uncountable [in economic terms]. How can we calculate the compensation for losing fish and animal species? .... When they talk about compensation, it reflects that the Mekong River is only for humans. They want to compensate humans but never think about the river and other species (Interview, 9 October 2019).

This insightful comment strongly suggests how divergent ontologies fundamentally underpin politics over the Mekong River in northern Thailand. It also demonstrates that there are deep differences in the vision for the future of the Mekong River. Large dams have over the past three decades been progressively constructed that are—nowadays—claimed to be aspiring towards the goals of ecological modernization. Yet, the activities of community and civil society networks continue to articulate other visions for the Mekong River defined by human-nature relations that existed before the dams were constructed—even as communities increasingly must adapt to the hydrological and ecological changes that the dams create.

CONCLUSION

This chapter has examined the impact of the 2019–20 drought on the Mekong River in northern Thailand, understood as a resource frontier where over the past two decades the Mekong River's ecological and hydrological characteristics have changed to a significant degree due to the hydropower projects operated upstream in China. Viewed through a hydrosocial lens, we have examined the practices, narratives, and knowledge productions of riverside communities, the community and civil society-led Ing Peoples Council, and the intergovernmental Mekong River Commission (MRC) and the Lancang-Mekong Cooperation (LMC).

The community- and civil society-led IPC maintains a value of water that is simultaneously a resource that sustains local livelihoods and local economies, but also recognizes cultural values as well. Knowledge for governing and imagining the future of the basin is produced through community networks, community-led *Thai Baan* research, as well as by seeking partnerships with civil society and academic researchers. The response to the drought has been a combination of drawing on cultural practices, and advocacy towards the state including the MRC and LMC. In contrast, the state-led MRC and LMC pursue variants of ecological modernization that ultimately hold the value of water to be an economic resource that should be managed to maximize efficiency and utility. For the MRC and LMC, the response to the drought is to be viewed as primarily a technical challenge that at least in part can be addressed through large dam operations. Knowledge is produced by state officials and sanctioned scientist experts in the form of scientific studies and technical planning exercises. Between these two networks, politics at the resource frontier on the Mekong River in northern Thailand are ontological politics contesting the very meaning of the Mekong River and what constitutes a "resource", with significance for the river's use, value, governance and future.

ACKNOWLEDGEMENT

The authors would like to sincerely thank all of those who took the time to speak with us and share their knowledge. This research was kindly supported by the Competing Regional Integrations in Southeast Asia (CRISEA) interdisciplinary research program funded by the European Union's Horizon 2020 Framework Program.

Notes

1. Coincides approximately with November in the Roman calendar.
2. A *krathong* is a decorated small float placed in the river, often with a candle, incense and flowers on it.

3. In Thai language, the Master of Ceremony is referred to as "doctor" (*mor*), who is locally considered as a folk doctor. They play a key role in the ceremony, including calling the ghosts.

References

Barnes, Jessica, and Samer Alatout. 2012. "Water Worlds: Introduction to the Special Issue of Social Studies of Science". *Social Studies of Science* 42, no. 4: 483–88. https://doi.org/10.1177/0306312712448524

Basist, Alan, and Claude Williams. 2020. *Monitoring the Quantity of Water Flowing through the Upper Mekong Basin Under Natural (Unimpeded) Conditions*. Bangkok: Sustainable Infrastructure Partnership.

Biba, Sebastian. 2018. "China's 'Old' and 'New' Mekong River Politics: The Lancang-Mekong Cooperation from a Comparative Benefit-Sharing Perspective". *Water International* 43, no. 5: 1–20. https://doi.org/10.1080/02508060.2018.1474610

Boer, Ben, Philip Hirsch, Fleur Johns, Ben Saul, and Natalia Scurrah. 2016. *The Mekong: A Socio-legal Approach to River Basin Development*. Abingdon and New York: Earthscan.

Cooper, Rachel. 2012. "The Potential of MRC to Pursue IWRM in the Mekong: Trade-offs and Public Participation". In *Politics and Development in a Transboundary Watershed: The Case of the Lower Mekong Basin*, edited by Joakim Öjendal, Stina Hansson, and Sofie Hellberg, pp. 61–82. Dordrecht, Heidelberg, London, New York: Springer.

Evers, Jaap, and Assela Pathirana. 2018. "Adaptation to Climate Change in the Mekong River Basin: Introduction to the Special Issue". *Climatic Change* 149, no. 1: 1–11. https://doi.org/10.1007/s10584-018-2242-y

Götz, Johanna M., and Carl Middleton. 2020. "Ontological Politics of Hydrosocial Territories in the Salween River Basin, Myanmar/Burma". *Political Geography* 78: 102–15. https://doi.org/10.1016/j.polgeo.2019.102115

Hu, Yuwei, and Xiaoyi Lin. 2020. "US-backed Institutions Hyping China's 'Dams Threat' in Mekong River Riddled with Loopholes: Expert". *Global Times*, 11 September 2020. https://www.globaltimes.cn/content/1200571.shtml (accessed 30 September 2021).

IPC (blog). 2021a. "Khor Moon Sang Kom Lae Wat Ta Na Tham Ing". http://www.ingcouncil.org/index.php/soc-cultures (accessed 22 September 2021).

———. 2021b. "Ing People Council Frontpage". http://www.ingcouncil.org/index.php (accessed 22 September 2021).

Johnson, Andrew A. 2019. "The River Grew Tired of Us: Spectral Flows along the Mekong River". *HAU: Journal of Ethnographic Theory* 9, no. 2: 390–404. https://doi.org/10.1086/706045

Johnson, Kay, and Panu Wongcha-um. 2020. "Water Wars: Mekong River Another Front in U.S.-China Rivalry". *Reuters*, 24 July 2020. https://www.reuters.com/article/us-mekong-river-diplomacy-insight-idUSKCN24P0K7 (accessed 27 September 2021).

Keovilignavong, Oulavanh, Tuong Huy Nguyen, and Philip Hirsch. 2021. "Reviewing the Causes of Mekong Drought Before and During 2019–20". *International Journal of Water Resources Development*. https://doi.org/10.1080/07900627.2021.1967112 (accessed 21 September 2021).

Ketelsen, Tarek, Timo Räsänen and John Sawdon. 2020. "Did China Turn Off the Lower Mekong? Why Data Matters for Cooperation". *Southeast Asia Globe.com* (blog), 13 May 2020. https://southeastasiaglobe.com/china-mekong-river-flow/ (accessed 5 October 2021).

Linton, Jamie. 2010. *What Is Water? The History of a Modern Abstraction*. Vancouver: University of British Columbia (UBC) Press.

———, and Jessica Budds. 2014. "The Hydrosocial Cycle: Defining and Mobilizing a Relational-Dialectical Approach to Water". *Geoforum* 57: 170–80. https://doi.org/10.1016/j.geoforum.2013.10.008

Living Rivers Siam Association. 2013. *Sa Rup Phon Kan Pra Chum Sa Pha Lum Nam Ing*. Phayao: Living River Siam Association.

———. 2021. "Ngan Vi Jai Tai Baan Nai Tae La Puen Tee". http://www.livingriversiam.org/2work/tb_research.html (accessed 20 September 2021).

LMWRC. 2018. "Five-year Action Plan on Lancang-Mekong Water Resources Cooperation (2018–2022)". http://www.lmcwater.org.cn/cooperative_achievements/important_documents/files/202008/t20200825_162726.html (accessed 9 October 2021).

Meebun, Vichian. 1998. "Pi Thi Jub Pla-Buek Nai Lum Nam Khong: Ban Had Krai, Tumbon Vieng, Chiang Khong, Chiang Rai". MA thesis, Mahasarakham University.

Mekong Community Institute. 2021. "Print Publications". Mekong Community Institute. http://www.mekongci.org/index.php/publication/print (accessed 22 September 2021).

Middleton, Carl, and Jeremy Allouche. 2016. "Watershed or Powershed? A Critical Hydropolitics of the 'Lancang-Mekong Cooperation Framework'". *International Spectator* 51, no. 3: 100–17. https://doi.org/10.1080/03932729.2016.1209385

Middleton, Carl, Anisa Widyasari, Kanokwan Manorom, Davis J. Devlaeminck, and Apisom Intralawan. 2021. *Strengthening Water Diplomacy Through Water Data Sharing and Inclusive Evidence-Based Transboundary Governance*. Bangkok: Center for Social Development Studies, Chulalongkorn University.

Mol, Annemarie. 1999. "Ontological Politics. A Word and Some Questions". *Sociological Review* 47: 74–89.

MRC. 1995. *Agreement on the Cooperation for the Sustainable Development of the Mekong River Basin, 5 April 1995*. Vientiane: Mekong River Commission.

———. 2019a. *Drought Management Strategy for the Lower Mekong Basin 2020–2025*. Vientiane: Mekong River Commission.

———. 2019b. *MRC Secretariat, LMC Water Center Ink First MOU for Better Upper-Lower Mekong Management*. 18 December 2019. Vientiane: Mekong River Commission Secretariat. http://www.mrcmekong.org/news-and-events/news/mrc-secretariat-lmc-water-center-ink-first-mou-for-better-upper-lower-mekong-management/ (accessed 29 September 2021).

———. 2020a. *Understanding the Mekong River's hydrological conditions: A brief commentary note on the "Monitoring the Quantity of Water Flowing Through the Upper Mekong Basin Under Natural (Unimpeded) Conditions" study by Alan Basist and Claude Williams (2020)*. Vientiane: Mekong River Commission Secretariat.

———. 2020b. *Weekly Dry Season Situation Report for the Mekong River Basin Prepared on: 07/01/2020, Covering the Week from 31 Dec 2019 to 5 Jan 2020*. Vientiane: Mekong River Commission. https://reliefweb.int/sites/reliefweb.int/files/resources/2020-01-06%20Weekly%20Dry%20Season%20Situation.pdf (accessed 29 September 2021).

New York Times. 2020. "China Limited the Mekong's Flow. Other Countries Suffered a Drought". 13 April 2020. https://www.nytimes.com/2020/04/13/world/asia/china-mekong-drought.html (accessed 7 October 2021).

Räsänen, Timo A., Paradis Someth, Hannu Lauri, Jorma Koponen, Juha Sarkkula, and Matti Kummu. 2017. "Observed River Discharge Changes Due to Hydropower Operations in the Upper Mekong Basin". *Journal of Hydrology* 545: 28–41. https://doi.org/https://doi.org/10.1016/j.jhydrol.2016.12.023

Santasombat, Yos. 2011. *The River of Life: Changing Ecosystems of the Mekong Region*. Chiang Mai: Mekong Press.

Sriviraj, Suteepong, Prarop Kaosesand, and Pairat Thidpad. 2019. "Tree Ordainment: Indigenous Knowledge for Forest Conservation in Northern Thailand Community through Buat-Pah Ritual". *Humanity and Social Science Journal, Ubon Ratchathani University* 10, no. 1: 121–44.

Tanakit Pipat. 2013. "Writing Knowledge, Making Memory: Pla-Buek and Local Communities in Chiang Khong, Chiang Rai, Thailand". *Journal of Sociology and Anthropology* 32, no. 1: 146–73.

Tian, Fuqiang, Hui Liu, and Hu Lu. 2020. "Trust Key to Lancang-Mekong Cooperation". *China Daily*, 25 August 2020. https://www.chinadailyasia.com/article/141177 (accessed 20 September 2021).

Tian, Fuqiang, Hui Liu, Shiyu Hou, Kunbiao Li, Hui Lu, Guangheng Ni, and Xiangpeng Mu. July 2020. *Drought Characteristics of Lancang-Mekong River Basin and the Impacts of Reservoir Regulation on Streamflow*. Beijing: Centre for International Transboundary Water and Eco-Security, Tsinghua

University, Department of Hydraulics, China Institute of Water Resources and Hydropower Research.

Vieng Chiang Khong Municipality. 2021. "Pra Chum Ha Rue Kan Jad Phi Thi Buang Suang Chao Phor Pla-Buek". 29 March 2021. https://www.wckmunic.org/ (accessed 30 August 2021).

Vogt, Lindsay, and Casey Walsh. 2021. "Parsing the Politics of Singular and Multiple Waters". *Water Alternatives* 14, no 1: 1–11.

Wajjwalku, Siriporn. 2019. "Civil Society and Water Governance in Northern Thailand: Local NGOs and Management of Mekong's Tributaries in Chiang Rai". In *Interactive Approaches to Water Governance in Asia*, edited by Kenji Otsuka, pp. 123–54. Singapore: Springer Singapore.

Wesselink, Anna, Michelle Kooy, and Jeroen Warner. 2017. "Socio-hydrology and Hydrosocial Analysis: Toward Dialogues across Disciplines". *WIREs Water* 4, no. 2: e1196. https://doi.org/https://doi.org/10.1002/wat2.1196

Williams, Jessica M. 2020. "Is Three a Crowd? River Basin Institutions and the Governance of the Mekong River". *International Journal of Water Resources Development* 37, no. 4: 720–40. https://doi.org/10.1080/07900627.2019.1700779

Wises, Sahathaya. 2019. "People Council of Ing River Basin: Civil Society Dynamic in Natural Resource Management in Ing River Basin". *Journal of Buddhist Studies* 10, no. 2: 331–45.

———, Nutthakarn Yodmuang, and Sangdoun Jaikla. 2006. *Ha Yoo Ha Gin: Vi Thi Chi Vit Lum Nam Ing Ton Play*. Phayao: Phayao Development Foundation.

Yates, Julian S, Leila M. Harris, and Nicole J. Wilson. 2017. "Multiple Ontologies of Water: Politics, Conflict and Implications for Governance". *Environment and Planning D: Society and Space* 35, no. 5: 797–15. https://doi.org/10.1177/0263775817700395

Yong, Ming Li. 2020. "Reclaiming Community Spaces in the Mekong River Transboundary Commons: Shifting Territorialities in Chiang Khong, Thailand". *Asia Pacific Viewpoint* 61, no. 2: 203–18. https://doi.org/https://doi.org/10.1111/apv.12257

3

REASSEMBLING FRONTIERS FOR MIDDLE-INCOME PEASANTS

Rubber Expansion and Livelihood Ecosystem Transformation in a Northeast Thai Village

Wataru Fujita

INTRODUCTION

A bus from Ubon Ratchathani city to N village, located near the Mekong River on the border between Thailand and Laos, goes through rolling hills. In the lower lands spread paddy fields, while in the higher lands bush and forests. This scenery seen from the bus window, reflecting a typical rural landscape in northeast Thailand, rapidly changed. During trips to N village in 2008 and 2010, I was astonished that many forests were replaced by rubber gardens. Several years later, I also noticed that the villagers' lifestyle became somehow "urbanized". Indeed, in the village, still calm and peaceful at a glance, various things were reassembled.

This chapter analyses the rapid expansion of rubber cultivation in N village, exemplifying a resource frontier. Unlike traditional understandings of frontiers as geographically peripheral places where state power and control are weak (Korf and Raeymaekers 2013), resource frontiers are venues where configurations of institutional relationships over natural resources take place, mainly due to the development of capitalism, and where existing social, cultural, political and ecological orders are reassembled into new territorial orders. Assembling or reassembling exploitation and production in resource frontiers is directed by the negotiation of multiple meanings of resources (Rasmussen and Lund 2018; Cons and Eilenberg 2019; see as well the introduction to this volume by Rowedder and Tappe). Social orders and human-nature relationships in particular locales are transformed by the development of neoliberal capitalism in relation to various actors and processes in multiple geographical scales (Barney 2009). In this chapter, I demonstrate for the case of rubber expansion in N village how resource frontier assemblages are formed that transform the people's lives and environments in Thailand's context of a contemporary rural agrarian society.

In the study site of N and neighbouring villages, community-based sustainable natural resource management had been established since the 1990s, before it turned into a frontier of rubber cultivation in the 2000s. In examining the formations of assemblages in this study site, I focus on the differences in characteristics of resource frontiers in northeast Thailand, a middle-income region, from surrounding countries. The northeast was for long the poorest region in Thailand. However, recently, the people's income and living standards have been significantly upgraded by a variety of migrant labour to urban areas and abroad, small-scale businesses and commercial agriculture. The resource frontier of rubber will be analysed in the context of such agrarian changes (as commonly observed in Southeast Asia; see, e.g., Rigg 2020). In addition, since the 1990s, the local community's rights over surrounding natural resources have become increasingly, though not perfectly, respected. Therefore, as far as rubber is concerned, large-scale land grabbing or resource exploitation by large-scale projects, often reported in Laos or Cambodia (Barney 2009; Baird and Barney 2017), are unlikely to be the important elements in resource frontier assemblages in Thailand. Instead, the expansion of rubber cultivation has been driven mainly by smallholders' spontaneous efforts.

In the following, I will first provide an overview of rubber expansion and agrarian change in northeast Thailand. I will then examine various actors' responses to ecological degradation due to rubber expansion on a broader scale while focusing on the resulting changes in the living environments in N village caused by the transformative dynamics of emerging rubber frontier assemblages. Finally, I will put the characteristics of these frontier assemblages in the study site in the larger socio-political context of a middle-income country with established democratic institutions.

The arguments in this chapter draw on field research in N Village in Si Muang Mai District, Ubon Ratchathani Province and in surrounding villages. I have made regular visits to N and neighbouring villages since 1997 and carried out ethnographic research on relationships between villagers' livelihoods and natural resource use. The description and arguments are based mainly on ethnographic data from participant observation prior to 2015, as well as on questionnaire surveys held in 2012 and 2015, interviews with key informants both in Bangkok and the area around N village, and analysis of documents such as newspapers and websites.

RUBBER BOOM AND AGRARIAN CHANGE IN NORTHEAST THAILAND

Farmers in Thailand have been committed to a market economy longer and more deeply than in many other countries and areas. In northeast Thailand in particular, upland cash crops such as kenaf, cassava and maize have been widespread since the 1960s (Phongpaichit and Baker 1995, pp. 48–90). Before the 1990s, the high volatility of crop prices, accompanied by a poor or lacking social safety net, kept farmers socially marginalized and economically vulnerable (Hirsch 1990). Instead, as many previous studies (Rigg, Promphaking, and Le Mare 2014; Rigg et al. 2018; Rigg and Salamanca 2011, 2015) have argued, migrant work in Bangkok and other urban areas, as well as various non-farm activities, were long the main source of cash income while engaging in farming decreased.

Since the 2000s, however, the growth of global market needs kept high prices of industrial crops such as rubber and cassava. I observed in this study that rubber cultivators have become rich; they are able to purchase cars, tractors and electrical appliances, as well as daily food materials. Their children can attend college. They have never experienced such an economic boom before. The statistics also show that the average income in Ubon Ratchathani Province, where this study is located, almost reached the national average in 2011, but the gap subsequently widened following a decline in the price of rubber (Figures 3.1 and 3.2).

Many previous studies that argued for an agrarian change in northeast Thailand dismissed the impact of this rise in crop prices, probably because those studies were conducted in Khon Kaen and Maha Sarakham Provinces, where no more frontier land for upland crop expansion remained in the 1980s (Rigg and Salamanca 2011, 2015). However, in other case studies in Khon Kaen Province, a significant contribution of rubber cultivation to villagers' income was reported, both for owners of rubber gardens and hired labourers (Kroeksakul, Naipinit, and Promsaka Na Sakolnakorn 2011; Tongkaemkaew and

FIGURE 3.1
Average Income: National and Ubon Ratchathani Province

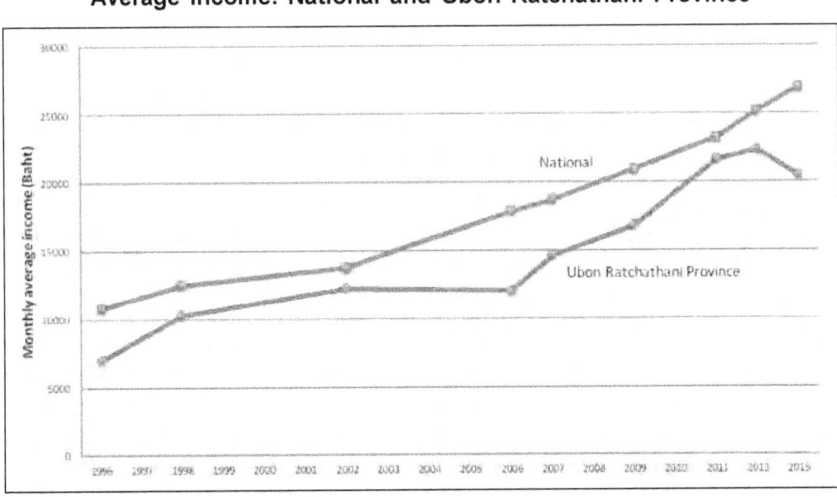

Sources: Thailand, National Statistics Office (1996; 1998; 2006; 2007; 2009; 2011; 2015); Ubon Ratchathani Provincial Statistical Office (2002).

FIGURE 3.2
Price of Rubber, 1997–2015

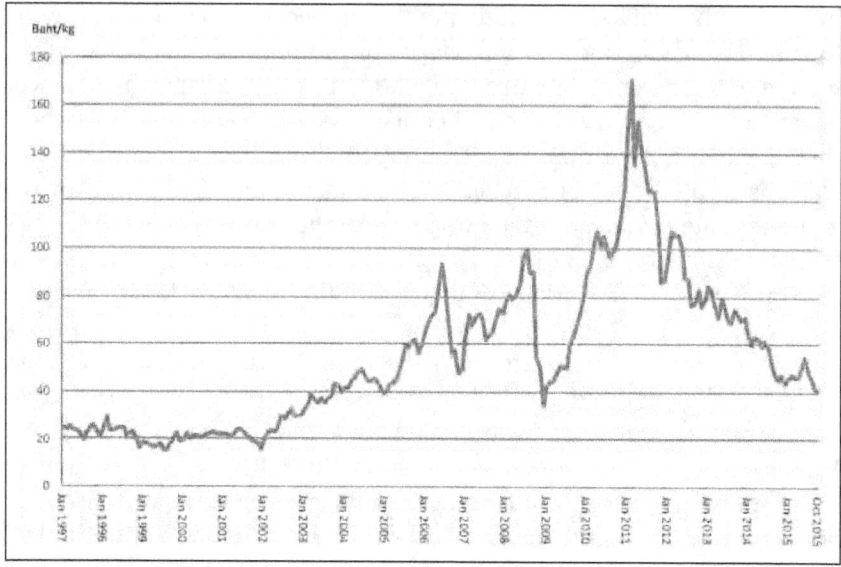

Source: Thailand, Office of Agricultural Economics (2015b).

Patanothai 2013). Thus, the spread of cash-crop cultivation and its economic impact are not uniform. In the areas suitable for rubber cultivation, rubber played a crucial role in the agrarian change.

In the past, rubber cultivation was limited to southern and eastern parts of Thailand. Except for a negligible number of people who had experience in working as rubber tappers in the South and began to cultivate rubber earlier, major rubber cultivation in the northeast began only in 1989, when the government initiated a promotion policy after seeing successful results from previous rubber experimentation. The first phase until 1996 resulted in approximately 280,000 *rai*[1] of cultivation area in the northeast. The promotion of rubber in this phase is aimed at reforestation as well. The following phase, from 1997 to 2001 (and then extended), targeted additional growth of 200,000 *rai*, and a total cultivation area of 800,000 *rai* (Phu chat kan rai wan 1997; Matichon 2001). Two further phases, 2003 to 2006 and 2011 to 2013, set more ambitious targets of an additional 1,000,000 *rai* (700,000 *rai* in the northeast and 300,000 *rai* in the north) and 800,000 *rai* (500,000 *rai* in the northeast, 150,000 *rai* in the north, and 150,000 *rai* in the central region), respectively (*Khao sot*, 9 May 2003; Deli niu 2009; Krungthep thurakit 2011; Phongthong 2013). In each phase, the promotion project provided participating farmers with rubber seedlings at no cost and low-interest loans to support expenditures until rubber began to be harvested. However, the farmers were not convinced that rubber could grow in the northeast in the initial period.

Farmers in the northeast began to plant rubber enthusiastically around 2002–3 (Figure 3.3), the period when the Thaksin government considered the accelerated promotion policy, often called the "1 million *rai* project". It is true that the government made a significant policy shift to boost the target to an additional 1,000,000 *rai* of cultivated area and that the Thaksin government needed to revoke a previous cabinet resolution that limited the rubber cultivation area in the whole country to not more than 1,200,000 *rai* (*Khao sot*, 14 June 2003). Expecting the project to be the basis of improving living standards, many people formed a long queue to join the project (*Phu chat kan rai wan*, 12 July 2007; *Krungthep thurakit*, 15 January 2011). However, the government's

FIGURE 3.3
Expansion of Rubber Cultivation Area by Region

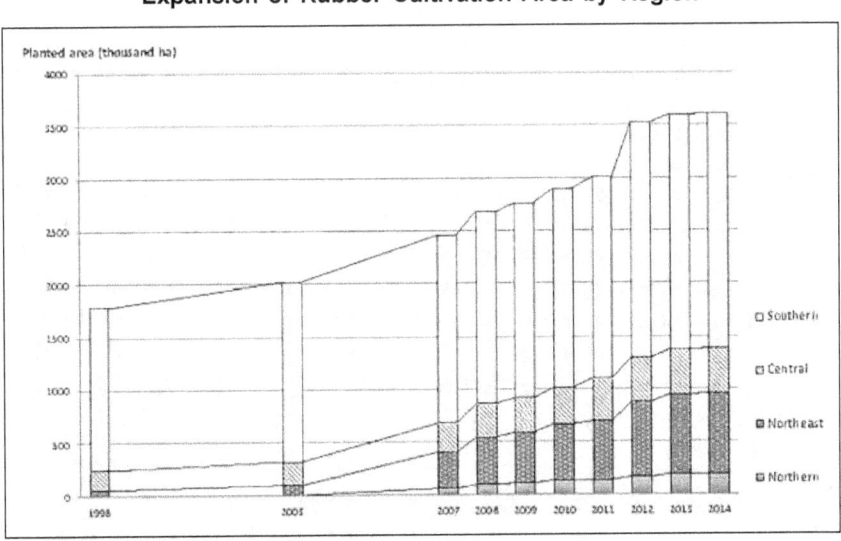

Sources: Khana Kamakan Nayobai Yang Thamachat (2010); Thailand, Office of Agricultural Economics (2010; 2012; 2015a).

project was not the main driving force behind farmers' interest in planting rubber. The government's project was so problematic that it did not fully benefit farmers. Production of seedlings could not keep up with demand. Seedlings arrived too late in the season for planting, in insufficient numbers, and were of poor quality. Additionally, corrupt politicians were involved in this process (Thitikak 2011). Farmers planted many more rubber trees without any support from the project. Of the 4 million *rai* increase in rubber cultivation area between 2003 and 2009, 3.2 million *rai* were planted spontaneously through farmers' own investments. Some obtained informal loans at high-interest rates to pay the initial costs of rubber cultivation (*Phu chat kan rai wan*, 12 July 2007). The continued high price of rubber caused a rubber boom in which people were affected by directly witnessing rich consumption lifestyles enjoyed by others, thanks to rubber cultivation.

ECOLOGICAL DEGRADATION AND ACTORS IN THE RUBBER BOOM

Ecological Degradation

The rapid expansion of rubber cultivation was inevitably accompanied by ecological changes. As discussed above, the promotion of rubber cultivation was aimed initially at rehabilitating degraded forestlands. Northeast Thailand in general had experienced severe deforestation up until the 1980s due to agricultural expansion. In fact, in some places, rubber did come to replace existing crop fields in the way that the project originally assumed.

However, it was revealed that rubber cultivation caused much more deforestation than it contributed to forest rehabilitation in some areas. National forestlands, including protected forests, such as national parks and wildlife sanctuaries, were illegally encroached on and cleared for rubber cultivation. In the northeast, probably the biggest deforestation case was that of 1,250 *rai* in Thap Lan National Park in Nakhon Ratchasima Province, while in Ubon Ratchathani Province, a case was exposed in the Buntharik–Yot Mon Wildlife Sanctuary (Sarnsamak 2011). Not only locals were engaged in the illegal cultivation of supposedly protected forests. Businessmen, mostly from the South, bought land that the locals had cleared. A case in Loei Province involved businessmen buying local peoples' land with "So Po Ko 4–01" deeds,[2] which could not be legally sold, by formally claiming them to be "rentals". Other businessmen who could not buy "So Po Ko 4–01" land employed local inhabitants to clear the forests illegally. The fee for the land clearing would be paid about two years after planting rubber seedlings. In the event of subsequent official exposure, the businessmen insisted that they bought land already cleared by the local population. In this way, businessmen invaded protected areas step by step (Chindahem 2006).

Countrywide, about 90 per cent of newly planted rubber gardens from 2003 to 2014 were converted from low vegetation areas, probably crop fields, while only about 10 per cent were converted from natural forests (Hurni and Fox 2018). Praweenwongwuthi et al. (2017) reported higher percentages for Nakhon Phanom Province: 827 ha out of a total of 1,353 ha of rubber gardens planted in Mueang District between 2006 and 2010 were converted from natural forests, as were 1312 ha out of a total of 5498 ha in That Phom District. These data show that in some areas, conversion to rubber gardens caused much more severe deforestation compared with the general trend. Only 10 per cent was enough to damage the last remaining natural forests, including rich natural ecosystems, in some protected areas.

A case of ecological degradation of the villagers' living environments like N village was reported in Dong Khum Kham and the Dong Phu Kham Forest area, in the same district as N: rubber cultivation destabilized the villagers' subsistence basis, leading to conflicts among villagers over natural resources (Samakhom Pa Chumchon Isan n.d.). In the Dong Saramoen Forest area, also adjacent to N, rubber cultivators even attacked the community forest.[3] In both areas, village groups had been making efforts to encourage sustainable resource use. However, they did not prevent the cultivation of rubber.

Government Policies and Implementations

As an almost inevitable side effect of this rubber boom, forest destruction and other related environmental changes occurred. Many actors, government authorities, non-government organizations (NGOs) and local entities were involved in this process. However, all of them tended to show adaptive attitudes, except for occasional strong measures taken by the conservation section. With respect to government authorities, the development and extension of rubber cultivation is the responsibility of the Rubber Research Institute, the Office of Rubber Replanting Aid

Fund (ORRAF) and, partially, the Provincial/District Agricultural Office. The Office of Agricultural Economics is also involved in policy-making, especially as the National Natural Rubber Policy Committee is headed by the vice prime minister.

Those authorities, directly committed to rubber policy in terms of agricultural development, seemed little concerned about environmental issues. Basically, the government's scheme of support for rubber cultivation in the northeast, planned and funded by the Ministry of Agriculture and Cooperatives and implemented mainly by ORRAF, officially required that only lands with legal titles were eligible for support. The Innovative Farmers Association, the first organization to carry out a rubber promotion project around the study site in 1989, also had the same regulation. However, according to an ORRAF officer in the Ubon Ratchathani branch, the district/provincial agricultural office implemented part of the promotion project, in which they, despite the official guidelines, granted support to lands without legal title, which might also have included recent illegal, encroached lands. The ORRAF officer further reported that ORRAF had also endorsed lands without titles to be supported by the project, pressured by a parliament member petitioned by the farmers. Once planted, supported by the project or not, having a land title or not, rubber gardens can all be registered with ORRAF, so that replanting can be funded by ORRAF.

There remains the view, although it is not widely held, that rubber contributed to environmental improvement. Mr Montri, secretary-general of the Progressive Farmers Association, stressed that rubber gardens provided fuelwood that could substitute timber from the forests.[4] Mr Sukhum Wong-ek, Director of the Rubber Research Institute at the end of 2007, also stated that planting rubber could substitute green forests because rubber could generate moist environments and enrich the land much more than many other crops (Susewi 2007). Officers in charge of rubber at the Office of Agricultural Economics were astonished when I told them that many natural forests had been converted to rubber gardens because they thought that rubber had replaced other annual crops, not natural forests, while a ranking officer of the Rubber Research Institute presented his personal opinion that rubber should be planted on suitable land, which did not include previous paddy fields, steep slopes or national forest reserves. He did not want villagers to burn the forests and believed the degradation of forests by rubber cultivation was not beneficial to villagers.

Foresters' Dilemmas

The responsibility for the conservation of natural resources is shared by two governmental departments: the Royal Forest Department for land outside protected areas, and the National Park, Wildlife, and Plant Conservation Department for protected areas. These departments did not effectively prevent the conversion of the forests to rubber gardens. As shown above, even protected areas were invaded. As organizations, they were caught between their legally required task of conservation and favouring a social climate geared towards rubber. In 2007, it was revealed that the National Park, Wildlife, and Plant Conservation Department was ready to submit a report on the illegal occupation of national forest reserves to the Minister; the Director-General of the Department pointed out that the government's rubber promotion policy had caused illegal occupation and cultivation of national forest reserves, and that officers felt pressured in that the initiation of legally correct measurements would have gone against the government's policy, and that, therefore, they could not strictly control and protect the forests. Because of these conditions, many officers resigned. The Director-General questioned whether society would accept the disappearance of protected forests. He stressed that society should make that decision; otherwise, the Department alone could not conserve the forests (Matichon, 13 July 2007).

There has been no clear evidence showing that the government prioritized the expansion of rubber cultivation over nature conservation. However, as the Director-General pointed out, the officers perceived such a sentiment spreading through society and that the government would favour it. As I will show below, turning a blind eye to forest clearing was also observed in N and neighbouring villages, mainly due to the local-level officers' sympathy with the villagers. It was also reported that some corrupt officers took part in illegal encroachments. In a case in Kanchanaburi Province, brought to light in 2011, it turned out that officers, including some from the Royal Forest Department, the Department of Land, and the Department of Local Administration, had illegally "sold" national forest lands to investors from the South for rubber cultivation. After an investigation, the Royal Forest Department decided to transfer twelve officers and established a hearing committee (Phongrai 2011). Apart from this scandal, a forestry officer working in Ubon Ratchathani, a close friend of mine, told me that officers in the Forest Protection Unit accepted bribes from farmers to allow illegal clearing of the forests to cultivate rubber. Not simply bowing to social sentiment, some forest officers took positive advantage of the rubber boom.

However, there were eventually several campaigns against illegal encroachments of national forest land and in protected areas in particular. The most well-known took place during 2011 and 2012, when Damrong Phidet was the Director-General of the National Park, Wildlife, and Plant Conservation Department. As with physically destroying resort hotels illegally constructed and operated by powerful businessmen in Khao Yai National Park, Damrong ordered the taking of strong measures against illegal rubber gardens in a way that had rarely materialized under previous directorships. In Buntarik District, Ubon Ratchathani Province, villagers cultivated rubber in a wildlife sanctuary. They resisted officers by blockading roads. Then, the Director of Protected Area Management Office 9 (Ubon Ratchathani), under the National Park, Wildlife, and Plant Conservation Department, sent all officers under his control out at dawn to destroy all rubber gardens as quickly as possible and to return before the road was blockaded.[5] In 2015, the current military government also ordered that all rubber trees in the protected areas must be removed by the end of July. Otherwise, the officers in each protected area, national park or wildlife sanctuary, would destroy them. As I observed in a village in Pha Taem National Park, this order was implemented. However, these strong measures were not taken on a regular and systematic basis and so did not change the social sentiment generally supporting the rubber boom.

Local Administration and NGOs

Considering ecological changes due to rubber, the lack of commitment by either national or local environmental NGOs is remarkable, especially in comparison with previous local environmental movements, such as those concerning anti-logging efforts and community forests. In previous times, NGOs had supported local movements seeking sustainable natural resource usage. However, in facing such apparent threats to local environments, as shown above, almost all the NGOs kept quiet. However, at the study site, some local initiatives emerged to advocate more balanced resource use, although none of them negated rubber. Officially, local municipalities and sub-district level Tambon Administrative Organizations (TAOs) adopted policies that called attention to the environment and supported conservation actions by villagers. Both TAOs of the NT subdistrict, to which N village belongs, and the adjacent NP subdistrict, had presidents with a background of working in local community forests. Both supported villagers' activities regarding the maintenance of community forests in terms of budget allocation. However, this was a small part of the total budget, and they naturally had to respond to the various needs of the people. The NT TAO also organized a training course on rubber cultivation for the villagers.

A more evident and concrete initiative was the "family forest" project (*pa khropkhruea*), substantially carried out by Mr Lom, ex-President of NT TAO. He had undertaken this project before he was elected as the TAO President. Lom had grown up in a different province. After graduating from university, he joined a local NGO, Nature Care, as a volunteer and later became a staff member. His task was to give advice to local people on the establishment of community forests and to organize an inter-village network. Even after leaving Nature Care, Lom stayed in the area and worked as an adviser for the villagers' community forest network. Although the network organization became inactive for several reasons, Lom obtained funds from UNDP and implemented the project with his staff in 2008 and 2009. This project assisted villagers in turning parts of privately owned secondary forests adjacent to farmlands (*pa hua rai plai na,* literally meaning "forests fringing paddy fields") into "family forests" with clearly demarcated boundaries and written regulations established at participants' meetings in each village. Although the project targeted 100 participants in NT and NP subdistricts, it attracted more than 150, whose family forests totalled 1,076 *rai*. Throughout the project, participants seemed well aware of the importance of family forests, even though the number of such participants was limited. Except for one household with nine participants in N, eight households who preserved family forests in 2010 still do so. This project, as shown later, reflected a change in the villagers' mindset regarding natural resources.

As shown above, the attitudes varied by the organization due to administratively or socially assumed roles. However, they commonly declined to take negative actions against rubber. The social climate that required prioritization of the economic benefits of rubber was so strong that the Director-General and other officers of the Department of National Parks and Wildlife Conservation assumed that it was an unspoken government policy and hesitated to follow legal provisions strictly. At the local level, the officers could not regulate rubber cultivation out of sympathy for the poor villagers trying to improve their economic status through rubber. This nationwide social climate resonated with the farmers' hopes at a grassroots level. Local actors were agents of such a social climate while they simultaneously held on to the contradictory position of sustainable forest management, which was suppressed or represented only in an indirect way, as in the "family forest" project. In this way, conflicts (and contradictions) between the elements within the rubber boom assemblage were internalized in each actor.

TRANSFORMATION OF ASSEMBLAGES IN N VILLAGE

N Village is located adjacent to the Pha Taem National Park, established in 1991. Around the village, the land is gently sloped. The lower lands are occupied by paddy fields, while the hilly area was once cultivated for upland rice by a form of shifting cultivation that had been abandoned for decades because of reinforced forest patrols against swidden practices after the establishment of the National Park. The main form of subsistence has long been paddy cultivation, while various resources for daily living have been extracted from the surrounding natural environment, such as bamboo shoots and mushrooms from the forests, fish from the streams and paddy fields, and wild animals hunted in the forests. Unlike many other villages in the northeast, cash crops such as cassava, maize and kenaf had seldom been cultivated until cassava cultivation prevailed in N village and the surrounding area in the 2000s.

Before rubber and cassava cultivation prevailed in the 2000s, villagers' cash income derived mostly from migrant work in urban areas or miscellaneous wage labour around the village. Therefore, relatively rich natural forest resources were preserved, which allowed for a self-sufficient mode of life. Rubber, with its significant economic impact, not only replaced existing crop fields but also destroyed the scarce remaining natural forests.

Community Forest

In 1997, to secure sustainable use of natural forest resources, N villagers designated the hilly forest area in the village as a community forest. In the area surrounding N, all villages established their own community forest in the 1990s. In the past, villagers had extracted necessary forest resources without clear regulations. By establishing community forests, boundaries were clearly demarcated, management committees were organized, and written regulations were instituted.

The establishment of community forest in this area began with K village. In 1991, the Forest Industry Organization planned to establish industrial afforestation replacing natural forests from which K villagers extracted resources for daily life. K villagers resisted the plan. The District Office then revoked the plan. As a result of consultation between the villagers and the branch office of the Royal Forest Department (RFD), it was decided that the natural forest was to be K village's community forest. With the supervision of the staff of local NGOs and forest officers who had technical knowledge about community forest management, the villagers collectively made decisions on management organization and regulations. Boundary markers and firebreaks were also installed.

Afterwards, community forest promotion projects were carried out in this area by RFD. Project staff from RFD together with representatives of the villages that had already established community forests encouraged and assisted other villages to establish their own community forests. In the case of N village, the community forest was thus established, first, de facto, with approximately 80 per cent of the villagers in agreement, while its formal establishment, with complete agreement, was in 2002. After commercial logging had been stopped in 1989, RFD changed its main mission from timber production to nature conservation, designating core natural forests to be protected areas whereas promoting community-based management for other less valued forests. The villagers also recognized that forest resources were getting scarce so they had to use them in a sustainable way for future generations. Protecting the resources from outsiders who, for example, extracted a lot of mushrooms for commercial purposes, was also an important issue.

For a few years after the establishment of community forests, each village experienced breaches of regulations by the villagers and outsiders' invasion to extract resources from community forests. After that, these problems disappeared because information and understanding of community forests were widely shared. Since then, it has not been necessary to patrol community forests regularly. In N village, the villagers still extract from community forest timber necessary for house construction, mushrooms and bamboo shoots for daily consumption or for sale.

Rubber Expansion

Rubber cultivation began a rapid expansion in N village in the early 2000s, in line with the general trend in northeast Thailand, although some had practised it before. Large parts of the private forests were cleared and converted to rubber gardens as well as cassava fields.

Rubber was first cultivated in this area in 1989, when a few retired teachers migrated to P village, next to N village. In 1990, about ten more P villagers began cultivation, with the support of the project by an NGO, the Progressive Farmers Association. The villagers in N began to cultivate rubber around 2000. Since 2003, following the rubber price increase, rubber cultivation increasingly expanded. N villagers made their decision to plant rubber not only by watching the price in the market; they were more affected by realizing that those who had planted in advance were doing well. They learned that rubber grew well in the area and could reward them with enough income to support a livelihood without working in Bangkok, to buy a pick-up truck and a tractor and build a new house. Such first-hand learning about the success of their neighbours effectively pushed the villagers into rubber cultivation.

Not only farmers rushed into rubber. Mr Noi, a policeman at the nearest police station, bought land from a local farmer in 1995 and planted rubber in 2005 and 2009. He managed his rubber garden by hiring labour from neighbouring villagers. In fact, most of the staff at the police station also had rubber gardens. This was true for other public authorities, such as schools, forestry, and district office personnel. Moreover, many from the south purchased land for rubber gardens. The community forest of C village, next to N, was cleared illegally by a man from another district to plant rubber. A young girl in N, whom one of my friends knew, was married to a rich man from the South, who managed rubber gardens.

According to a questionnaire survey in N village in 2012, 59 of 109 households had rubber gardens occupying 664 *rai* within the village, while in 2015, 131 of 144 households had 973.3 *rai*. In 2012, only 17 out of 109 households still maintained secondary forests adjacent to farmlands (*pa hua rai plai na*, see above) of their own, totalling 88 *rai*. Figure 3.4 shows the years of cultivation and planting of rubber seedlings, covering 417 *rai* out of 664 *rai* in 2012. Forest clearing preceded the planting of rubber seedlings because the villagers tend to cultivate cassava for several years before planting rubber. Both clearing of secondary forests and planting of rubber seedlings markedly increased after 2003.

The community forest was well conserved, partly because the villagers respected their own regulations and partly because a large part of the community forest was located on rocky land that was unsuitable for cultivation. Expansion of rubber gardens accompanied various changes in their environment; on the one hand, it pushed the people into a more convenient lifestyle based on consumption by providing cash incomes and, on the other hand, it discouraged them from natural

FIGURE 3.4
Clearing and Planting of Rubber Trees

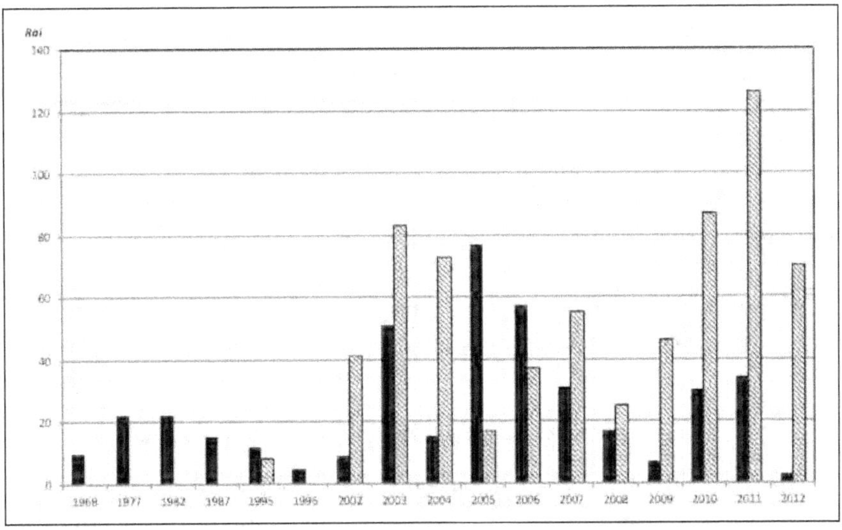

Note: Unshaded bars show the area of clearing that is current rubber gardens; shaded bars show the area of rubber planting.

Source: Questionnaire survey, 2012.

resource extraction, such as fishing and wild mushroom gathering, due to chemical pollution and decreases in natural resources. There were also changes in their daily lives. Some villagers may have once considered preventing resource degradation by regulating herbicide use; in the new reality, however, they tried to adjust their social and customary order of open access to natural resources regardless of land ownership to the new conditions brought about by rubber cultivation in which landowners could prohibit access to natural resources.

Indeed, a large proportion of the rubber gardens and cassava fields did not have any land title, except for those enduring farmlands that had "So Po Ko 4–01" titles or those recently investigated by forest officers and qualified to be given "So Tho Ko" titles.[6] In fact, the recent clearing of forests was mostly illegal. The land was all located outside the National Park. Thus, the park guards did not patrol the villagers' agricultural activities. The "forest protection unit" (*nuai pongkan raksa pa*) located near the village, and other forestry authorities in charge of managing national forest lands outside the park, turned a blind eye to the villagers' clearing of the forests, as the officers understood their need to generate a livelihood. NGOs, including one that had committed to promoting the establishment of community forests in this area and assisting the villagers, also did not publicly alert the authorities or rubber cultivation smallholders to the resulting environmental damage.

The rubber price dropped after 2012, as shown in Figure 3.2, to around THB40 per kilogram. However, in 2013, I still observed N villagers planting rubber. As reflected in questionnaire surveys, there was a higher percentage of rubber-growing households in 2015 than in 2012, as shown above. In 2014 and 2015, villagers no longer planted, and seedling suppliers near the village almost disappeared or ceased to do business. The villagers who had already begun to harvest the latex reported that they could tolerate the low price. The rubber boom has passed, but rubber remains at the centre of farmers' livelihoods.

ECOLOGICAL CHANGES DUE TO RUBBER

N villagers did not have conflicts with the national park, as they were not adjacent to it, although the boundary and inner villages allegedly practised illegal cultivation of rubber and other cash crops within the protected area. However, even outside the national park, degradation of the living environment of the villagers was a serious problem.

Most of the current rubber gardens, 973.3 *rai* according to the questionnaire survey in 2015, were either converted directly from secondary forests or following some years of cassava cultivation. In other words, the total area of forest disappeared, mostly in the last fifteen years. Thus, many villagers naturally pointed out that, due to the conversion of secondary forests to rubber gardens, the source of natural food materials had declined, and they had to rely more on the community forest that was still conserved by the villagers.

Some villagers attributed the floods of the Huai Se, a small river running through the village, that affected the village almost every year after 2010, to the loss of forests due to rubber cultivation. There was an argument against this, however; according to some of the elders, there had been more severe floods in the past when rubber was not yet planted and before the riverbed was dredged to prevent floods. Hence, the floods were not necessarily caused by deforestation.

What was more shocking, and more talked about by the villagers, was contamination by herbicides. In rubber gardens, weeds grow strongly, especially in the five years after planting seedlings until the closure of the crown. Weeding in this period is thought of as critical for growing the rubber seedlings and will be reflected in the harvest. Villagers, therefore, sprayed herbicides once or twice during the initial five years. Spraying herbicides once could keep a garden free of weeds for a few years. At the same time, however, the herbicides broadly contaminated the villagers' living environment. Sprayed in the rubber gardens, herbicides flowed into neighbouring land with rainwater. In the early 2000s, the villagers were shocked by an accident in which an old woman was killed by herbicide poisoning after eating wild mushrooms that she collected from villagers' own secondary forests adjacent to the rubber garden. Previously, the villagers had not been familiar with chemical contamination. However, after this accident, they became nervous about herbicides. Now, the middlemen who buy wild mushrooms that the villagers collect accept only mushrooms from the community forest, located on higher land and thus thought to be free from contamination. Some villagers reported that they had seen much dead fish in the stream. Others said that they could no longer collect edible plants alongside the street and eat them as they had before the expansion of rubber gardens. Even though the villagers felt threatened by herbicides, they could not regulate them. Thus, a general sense of anxiety prevailed regarding their living environment as a whole.

Additionally, several resources are disappearing due to the chain of changes in livelihood ecology. For example, *phak kadon*, shoots of *Careya sphaerica*, which were among the most popular wild vegetables in northeast Thailand, are now difficult to find. *Kadon* is a tree that typically grew on the dykes of paddy fields. The villagers were likely to conserve *kadon* trees naturally growing from seeds. However, recently, using large tractors in paddy fields has become common. Large tractors plough too deeply for the seedlings of *kadon* to shoot. Cow manure is also hard to find in the village now. The villagers once raised many cows and buffaloes. However, the expansion of rubber gardens has made it difficult to herd cows and water buffaloes that might eat or fall young rubber trees. Now, most villagers have abandoned cattle grazing, so they must buy manure to make organic fertilizer. Such a causal chain of events related to rubber has been gradually transforming the living world of the villagers. It is also changing their lifestyle, as shown in the next section.

Income from rubber cultivation in N village was estimated at THB10,195 per *rai* in 2014, after the sharp drop in rubber prices. Although initial investments and costs until the beginning of harvesting must be considered, this income would be enough to support basic consumption in everyday life. In fact, over the past years, the price was as high as THB100 to 180 per kg, which is more than two to four times the current price. Thus, some villagers could buy new cars and tractors, and build new houses. Their children were able to receive at least a high school education and, if they wanted, college was possible. In parallel with the degradation of their living environments, the high price of rubber caused the villagers' lifestyles to change. The increasing penetration of a cash economy is apparent in both daily consumption and livelihood work. They hire more labour and use machines for farm work, buy more food materials, and use fewer resources from the surrounding natural environments. The continued high price of rubber has partly facilitated their change of lifestyle to one oriented to a market economy.

Regarding labour, some villagers reported that, currently, they hired much more labour for paddy cultivation, such as transplanting and harvesting, to finish it in the shortest time and to minimize the loss of rubber harvesting time. However, the results of the questionnaire survey in 2015, containing questions on expenditures for paddy cultivation, were not consistent with this. The average expenditure for hired labour per one *rai* for paddy cultivation in 2014 was THB540.7 for the thirty-eight households who answered that they had rubber gardens to harvest, whereas it was THB636.8 in the seventy-two households who did not (the other thirty-four households did not answer). This contradicts the villagers' explanation that those who had rubber to harvest put more effort into finishing other farm work.

Regarding sources of food materials, many villagers reported that they bought more daily food materials than in the past because, as they explained, those who had rubber gardens to harvest did not have the time or energy to go hunting, fishing, or gathering after finishing the tapping and harvesting of rubber at night. In the past, few foods were purchased; most were extracted from the natural environment or planted/raised. The questionnaire survey in 2015 contained questions about sources of daily food materials other than rice, asking about the ratio extracted from nature versus planted/raised and purchased, both in 2015 and in 2000.

In 2015, those who had started to harvest rubber depended more on the market economy than did those who had not yet begun to harvest rubber. Additionally, not only the former but also the latter showed a higher percentage of purchases in 2015 than in 2000. That is, dependence on the market economy increased as a general trend regardless of their engagement in rubber cultivation. Rubber provided income opportunities not only for cultivators but also for those who did not have their own harvest because more labour was required either for paddy cultivation or work in rubber gardens.

VILLAGERS' ADAPTATION

Facing the ecological changes described above, N villagers at least recognized the problems and considered ways to solve them. Indeed, the regulation of a community forest for the village, established through village meetings, contained a provision that prohibited clearing without the permission of those with private forests. This provision could be a tool to prevent the extreme expansion of rubber cultivation. However, the villagers' understanding seems to have been vague. For example, the head of the community forest of the village almost forgot the rule, stating that, according to the regulations of the community forest, felling trees in private forests, unlike the community forest, did not need permission. However, the subdistrict headman (*kamnan*), recognizing the provisions of the community forest regulations, reported that villagers in the subdistrict, including N, would inform him before clearing private forests. He would check on-site to see whether there were large trees and send a report to the Forest Protection Unit so that clearing would be still allowed because the officers understood the villagers' need to do so for their livelihood. He explained that if he found a rich forest with large trees, he would refuse to report it to the Forest Protection Unit and persuade the holder not to clear it.

Since he took the position in January 2011, until I interviewed him in 2012, more than fifty cases in the subdistrict had been reported to him. Some of them were rejected, although he did not remember the exact number. However, not all villagers did inform the *kamnan* in advance. In the questionnaire survey in 2015, of thirty-six households that had cleared forests after 2000, lands that are currently rubber gardens, sixteen households answered that they had informed the *kamnan*, one answered that they directly informed the Forest Protection Unit, while thirteen households said they had not, and the other six did not answer. Furthermore, of those who answered that they informed the *kamnan*, four households answered that they cleared secondary forests with large trees or primary forests. This shows that even the *kamnan*'s guidelines could not be implemented completely. The *kamnan* himself had to loosen the standard because villagers had the idea that they could cultivate their own land in any way allowed in the local customary context. The *kamnan* cannot enforce action beyond the villagers' consensus as to the customary rule of the village. He could refuse to talk to the Forest Protection Unit and overlook uninformed cases but could not punish the villagers.

In this regard, any modification or addition to village custom needs majority approval, although there is no institutionalized process for this. The establishment of the community forest was a typical example. The community forest organization and regulations were established through a series of village meetings, to which all villagers were invited. The process of establishing the community forest was formally organized with forest officers' assistance. Consensus could be promoted in informal ways. Regulating rubber cultivation and related activities has not reached a consensus. For example, some villagers would like to regulate the use of herbicides. However, one explained it was impossible to regulate herbicide use through the villagers' own initiatives because those from outside bought land in the village and would not comply with group directives. However, this explanation is not reasonable. After all, there has never been any explicit attempt to regulate herbicide use, even among the villagers, although some villagers individually made decisions not to spray herbicides because their lands were near residential areas. The villagers have overlooked the issue of contamination because of convenience pertaining to their rubber cultivation.

Facing rapid ecological changes, the villagers' concerns about rights over resources, particularly private forests, have increased. Some have attempted to enclose their own resources and exclude others. Their custom was that everyone could take wild resources on anyone's land. For many years, extracting timber from private forests without the permission of the owner has been prohibited. However, collecting mushrooms and bamboo shoots, for example, has been considered open to anyone. This situation is now ambiguous.

The "family forest" project, described above, reflected the villagers' conflicting attitudes. Each participant was given signboards to be stuck at the entrance of the family forest, showing the regulations for family forests. At first glance, this project merely encouraged the owner to consider sustainable resource use, and thus, as some villagers suggested, its target seemed to be vague. However, this project contained important modifications to village customs, because the regulations, collectively established through village meetings and commonly applied to all participants within the village, included provisions that persons other than family members were not allowed to enter or extract resources from a family forest without permission. Moreover, penalties were provided. These were significant changes in custom. However, unlike the regulation of community forests, which most villagers respected because of passage through village meetings, participants in the "family forest" project seemed hesitant to respect family forest regulations. The discourse and actions of the villagers in relation to family forests remain ambiguous.

When I interviewed Mr Khon, the *kamnan*, in 2010, he stated that, despite the regulation of family forests, collecting mushrooms and bamboo shoots in others' forests was not prohibited because all villagers were living in cooperation with each other. Mr Sommai, a participant in the project, stressed that he had the right to conserve his own forest by himself. He stated that he still could allow his relatives to freely collect resources. However, I found that he did not put up a sign setting out the regulations. He explained that he had previously put it up at his family forest, but he kept it in his house now because he wondered whether the sign would be damaged by exposure to wind and rain. He further insisted that he would put it up again when officers came to inspect it so that he could show he was conserving the forest in the way the regulations stated. Mr Rin, another participant, told me that he put up the sign at his family forest. However, this was not true. In fact, no participant in N put up the sign.

Each village operated under different conditions. For example, in Na Thoi, adjacent to N, some participants did put up signs showing almost the same regulations as those for N, although all villagers apparently understood that, contrary to the regulations, collecting mushrooms and bamboo shoots were open to anyone. One participant in Na Thoi reported that, although other villagers had extracted timber from his forest before, they came to ask permission to do so in advance after the project was launched. Thus, the project substantially strengthened the control of family forests by the owners.

Regardless of the family forest project, among N villagers, the idea has been spreading gradually that natural resources should be extracted from one's own forests. When I interviewed an assistant of the *kamnan* at that time (and the current *kamnan*), Mr Sit, in 2010, he observed that they went to their own forest to collect bamboo shoots and fuelwood, or they needed to get permission from the owners if they entered another's forest. Mushrooms, however, were still open to all because mushrooms went bad quickly. According to him, this change in custom had been established since around 2002 when the community forest was formally established. Sit's explanation is contradicted by Mr Khon. Unlike Mr Khon's rather formal understanding, Mr Sit suggested what was actually happening on the ground. That is, the change in custom was still too uncertain at that time to formally enforce it against all villagers. As proof, a villager, who had converted all his forests to rubber gardens, did not hesitate to gather mushrooms and bamboo shoots in others' forests. However, nobody formally complained.

In 2013, I was astonished by the accounts of several different witnesses. One villager told me that some villagers had prohibited others from collecting mushrooms and bamboo shoots in their forests for two or three years because they were afraid that they collected too much for sale. When I asked Mr Khon about that, he revealed that most villagers had done so for the last five years, triggered by an incident in which a villager had guided an outside collector to extract large amounts of mushrooms and bamboo shoots in others' forests for the purpose of selling them. However, he added, it was supposed that villagers of N could collect in others' forests with permission from the owners. Mr Thip, a villager, present at that time, stressed that permission must be given upon request. However, there were cases in which the owner had refused to give permission. This is completely contradictory to what Mr Khon told me in 2010.

If the incident that caused changes in the villagers' behaviour occurred around 2010, the custom might have changed between 2010 and 2013 in that those villagers who refused others permission to collect mushrooms and bamboo shoots in their own forests gradually became the majority. There has never been any institutionalized mechanism for the modification or reinterpretation of customs in the village. The customs at each moment simply reflect the collective thoughts and actions of the villagers. The villagers, on the one hand, accepted ecological changes in exchange for the wealth they could acquire through rubber cultivation. At the same time, they came to consider the need to enclose their own forest resources, which had become increasingly scarce, due to rubber cultivation. The collective attitudes of the villagers resulted in changes in their customs.

As shown above, the responses of local communities to the ecological changes caused by rubber were complex. The *kamnan* tried to conserve private forests by requiring applications for clearing forests, but this failed. Some villagers believed that herbicide use should be prohibited, but this was not realized. Village customs changed to admit the enclosure of non-timber forest products in private forests. Village customs can be formed and modified by informal consensus, as well as through formal village meetings. Informal consensus is shaped as a collective response on the part of the villagers to an action inconsistent with existing customs. Individual interpretations are shared in daily chats among the villagers. When consensus is made in this way, the custom may change. Based on various events related to rubber, good and bad, individual opinions were established that might change village customs, as above. All these elements were features of a rubber boom assemblage in the village.

CONCLUSION

This chapter has examined how the expansion of rubber cultivation transformed the villagers' life and ecological conditions in N village and surrounding areas. Though geographically distant, concerned governmental agencies and NGOs are also committed to this transformation in various ways. In the 1990s, the area surrounding N village was the resource frontier of nature conservation and community-based sustainable natural resource management. For the villagers, an assemblage of community forests was formed with the following heterogeneous elements: the importance of sustainable use and management of natural resources for daily life; villagers' recognition of the decrease of local natural resources and attack from outsiders; and RFD's policy change and community forest promotion projects.

Since around 2003, however, the situation changed. The resource frontier of rubber reached N village fuelled by increasing demand in the global market. Seeing pioneer cultivators becoming remarkably rich due to high rubber prices, not only farmers but also civil servants rushed to plant rubber. The government partly assisted them through its promotion policy. Income from rubber enabled the villagers to avoid work migration, purchase cars and tractors as well as daily foods, and their children to attend college. On the other hand, their daily life was reorganized adapting to effective rubber production. Ecological conditions in their living environments were degraded by forest clearing, herbicides contamination and other indirect effects.

The villagers did not neglect the ecological degradation. However, it was impossible to regulate privately owned forest clearing or the use of herbicides due to lacking consensus, even though some villagers demanded a solution. On the other hand, the custom that everyone could extract non-timber forest resources regardless of ownership changed to the effect that others had to get permission from the owner.

When the owners started to prohibit others from resource extraction, most villagers accepted it. This reflected their collective recognition of increasing resource scarcity.

This transformation in N village due to rubber expansion was linked to the countrywide rubber boom. In addition to the high rubber price and promotion policy, important elements were governmental agencies' reluctance to take necessary measures even though there were legal provisions to do so. Few local NGOs that have been engaged in promoting sustainable natural resource management also dare to make an announcement against rubber expansion. These elements, affected and accelerated by the general social climate of the rubber boom, were interwoven with micro-level elements observed in N village to an assemblage of rubber frontier. Constituting central agents of this rubber frontier assemblage, the villagers of N have found remarkable ways to balance the emerging friction of economically promising rubber cultivation and threatening ecological degradation. Unlike the case of Anna Tsing's (2005) described friction between networks of conflicting values, N villagers internalized parts of seemingly contradictory frontier assemblages of both sustainable natural resource management and the commodification of rubber.

Some elements of the former were included in the latter. The fact that the community forest has never been invaded and is continuously maintained as precious is a good example. Change of custom to allow the owners to enclose their private forest resources also reflects the community's respect for natural resources. Moreover, the villagers' engagement with paddy cultivation, without abandonment or conversion to other more economically productive crops, demonstrates their strategy to avoid complete reliance on the market economy by securing basic staples. Transformations of resource frontiers, especially if mainly carried out by local smallholders, may not completely replace existing systems, but create an assemblage that balances contradicting elements of both old and new orders.

Notes

1. 1 *rai* equals to 0.16 ha.
2. "So Po Ko 4–01" is a limited land title granting cultivation rights, but not rights for sale and mortgage. It is issued by the Agricultural Land Reform Office.

3. Personal communication with members of the Dong Saramoen Forest Network.
4. Interview with Montri Kosalawat, 29 July 2014.
5. Personal communication with an officer of the Protected Area Management Office 9.
6. "So Tho Ko" is also a limited land title like "So Po Ko 4–01" granting cultivation rights, but not rights for sale and mortgage. It is, however, issued by the Royal Forest Department.

References

Baird, Ian G., and Keith Barney. 2017. "The Political Ecology of Cross-sectoral Cumulative Impacts: Modern Landscapes, Large Hydropower Dams and Industrial Tree Plantations in Laos and Cambodia". *Journal of Peasant Studies* 44, no. 4: 769–95.

Barney, Keith. 2009. "Laos and the Making of a 'Relational' Resource Frontier". *Geographical Journal* 175, no. 2: 146–59.

Chindahem, Wichai. 2006. "Nayobai pluk 'yang phara'—nayobai nun chao ban bukruk pa" [Rubber cultivation policy: Policy supporting villagers encroaching forests]. *Khao sot*, 9 March 2006.

Cons, Jason, and Michael Eilenberg. 2019. "Introduction: On the New Politics of Margins in Asia: Mapping Frontier Assemblages". In *Frontier Assemblages: The Emergent Politics of Resource Frontiers in Asia*, edited by Jason Cons and Michael Eilenberg, pp. 1–18. Oxford: Wiley.

Deli niu. 2009. "Dai thi dan kla yang phoem ik 1 lan rai" [Pressure for rubber seedlings for additional 1 million rai]. 8 October 2009.

Hirsch, Philip. 1990. *Development Dilemmas in Rural Thailand*. Singapore: Oxford University Press.

Hurni, Kaspar, and Jefferson Fox. 2018. "The Expansion of Tree-Based Crops in Mainland Southeast Asia: 2001 to 2014". *Journal of Land Use Science* 13, no. 1–2: 198–219.

Khao sot. 2003. "Nayok sang phoem phuenthi pluk yang nen phak nuea-isan" [Premier ordered to increase rubber cultivation area, putting emphasis on the North]. 9 May 2003.

———. 2003. "Kho cho ko. ploi ku phoem thuenthi pluk yang phara 1 lan rai" [Subcommittee for farmer support policy and measures provides more funds for 1 million rai rubber cultivation]. 14 June 2003.

Korf, Benedict, and Timothy Raeymaekers. 2013. "Border, Frontier and the Geography of Rule at the Margin of the State". In *Violence on the Margins: States, Conflict, and Borderlands*, edited by Benedict Korf and Timothy Raeymaekers, pp. 3–28. New York: Palgrave Macmillan.

Kroeksakul, Patarapong, Aree Naipinit, and Thongphon Promsaka Na Sakolnakorn. 2011. "The Economic and Social Effects of Farmers Growing Para Rubber in Northeast Thailand: A Case Study of Sapsomboon Village, Dun Sad Sub-District, Kranoun District, Khon Kaen Province". *Journal of Business Case Studies* 7, no 1: 113–18.

Krungthep thurakit. 2011. "Rat 'khik oof'-pluk yang 8 saen rai duean na" [Government "kicked off": Planting 800,000 rai rubber in the next month]. 15 January 2011.

Matichon. 2001. "Phaen ut Isan sot sai—ruk pluk yang 180,000 rai" [Plan to assist for a bright Isan: Push planting rubber on 180,000 rai]. 4 April 2001.

———. 2007. "Athibodi uthayan ngong nayobai pa sanguan nun pluk yang phara tham ngan lambak" [Director general of National Parks Department is confused over rubber policy that made his work difficult]. 13 July 2007.

Phongpaichit, Pasuk, and Chris Baker. 1995. *Thailand: Economy and Politics*. New York: Oxford University Press.

Phongrai, Chanchira. 2011. "Khabuankan 'kho ro ko. hua nai thun' plian pa pen suan yang" [Process by which corruption between officers and businessmen transformed forests into rubber gardens]. *Krungthep thurakit*, 8 May 2011.

Phongthong, Yuphin. 2013. "Kaset cho lom 'yang' 8 saen rai: Suan thang nayobai dan rakha" [Agricultural Ministry fells rubber trees on 800,000 rai as a measure to increase rubber price]. *Krungthep thurakit*, 14 January 2013.

Phu chat kan rai wan. 1997. "Dan tang khana ko ko. pongkan yang wikrit sam man" [Push to establish a committee to prevent a crisis in rubber like cassava]. 10 March 1997.

———. 2007. "Huan 'nayobai pluk yang isan 1 lan rai' lew kasetrakon siang khat thun het rat phaen rong rap" [Worried about "one million rai rubber cultivation policy" failing, farmers make a loss if the government supports the plan]. 12 July 2007.

Praweenwongwuthi, Sorat, Tewin Kaewmuangmoon, Sukanlaya Choenkwan, and A. Terry Rambo. 2017. "Recent Changes in Agricultural Land Use in the Riverine Area of Nakhon Phanom Province, Northeast Thailand". *Southeast Asian Studies* 6, no. 2: 357–65.

Rasmussen, Mattias Borg, and Christian Lund. 2018. "Reconfiguring Frontier Spaces: The Territorialization of Resource Control". *World Development* 101: 388–99.

Rigg, Jonathan. 2020. *Rural Development in Southeast Asia: Dispossession, Accumulation and Persistence*. Cambridge: Cambridge University Press.

_____, Buapun Promphaking, and Ann Le Mare. 2014. "Personalizing the Middle-Income Trap: An Inter-Generational Migrant View from Rural Thailand". *World Development* 59: 184–98.

_____, and Albert Salamanca. 2015. "The Devil in the Detail: Interpreting Livelihood Turbulence from a 25-Year Panel Study from Thailand". *Area* 47, no. 3: 296–304.

_____, and Albert Salamanca. 2011. "Connecting Lives, Living, and Location: Mobility and Spatial Signatures in Northeast Thailand, 1982–2009". *Critical Asian Studies* 43, no. 4: 551–75.

_____, Albert Salamanca, Monchai Phongsiri, and Mattara Sripun. 2018. "More Farmers, Less Farming? Understanding the Truncated Agrarian Transition in Thailand". *World Development* 107: 327–37.

Samakhom Pa Chumchon Isan [Isan Community Forest Association]. n.d. "Kan pluk yang phara kap phon krathop to pa hua rai plai na" [Rubber cultivation and its impact on forests adjacent to farmlands]. *Biothai Foundation*. http://www.biothai.net/sites/default/files/Annex3.pdf (accessed 25 February 2012).

Sarnsamak, Phongphon. 2011. "Forests Cleared for Illegal Plantations". *The Nation*, 9 June 2011.

Susewi, Phanphichaya. 2007. "Pluk yang chak phuenthi rap phoem phuenthi si khiao su phu khao" [Planting rubber increases green lands from flat areas to mountains]. *Deli niu*, 25 December 2007.

Thailand, National Statistical Office (NSO). 1996. *Report of the 1996 Household Socioeconomic Survey*. http://www.nso.go.th/sites/2014/Pages/Statistics%20from%20major%20Survey.aspx (accessed 6 September 2018).

_____. 1998. *Report of the 1998 Household Socioeconomic Survey*. http://www.nso.go.th/sites/2014/Pages/Statistics%20from%20major%20Survey.aspx (accessed 6 September 2018).

_____. 2006. *The 2006 Household Socioeconomic Survey*. http://www.nso.go.th/sites/2014/Pages/Statistics%20from%20major%20Survey.aspx (accessed 6 September 2018).

_____. 2007. *The 2007 Household Socioeconomic Survey*. http://www.nso.go.th/sites/2014/Pages/Statistics%20from%20major%20Survey.aspx, accessed 6 September 2018).

_____. 2009. *The 2009 Household Socioeconomic Survey*. http://www.nso.go.th/sites/2014/Pages/Statistics%20from%20major%20Survey.aspx (accessed 6 September 2018).

_____. 2011. *The 2011 Household Socioeconomic Survey, Ubon Ratchathani Province*. http://www.nso.go.th/sites/2014/Pages/Statistics%20from%20major%20Survey.aspx (accessed 6 September 2018).

_____. 2015. *Raidai lae kan krachai raidai khong khrua ruean pho. so. 2558 radap changwat* [Household income and distribution, 2015, provincial level]. http://

www.nso.go.th/sites/2014/Pages/Statistics%20from%20major%20Survey.aspx (accessed 6 September 2018).

Thailand, Office of Agricultural Economics. 2010. *Agricultural Statistics of Thailand 2009*.

———. 2012. *Agricultural Statistics of Thailand 2011*.

———. 2015a. *Agricultural Statistics of Thailand 2014*.

———. 2015b. *Yang phara: rakha yang phaen dip chan 3 rai duean thi kasetkon khai dai thi suan thang prathetpi2540–2558* [Phara rubber: monthly price of grade 3 unsmoked rubber sheet at farmyards, 1997–2015]. http://www.oae.go.th/download/price/monthlyprice/Horticulture/rubber3.pdf (accessed 7 November 2015).

Thitikak, Saran. 2011. "Nayobai kan mueang kap kan thucharit" [Policy, politics, and justice]. *Krungthep thurakit*, 13 May 2011.

Tongkaemkaew, Uraiwan, and Aran Patanothai. 2013. "Expansion of Rubber Plantations in Northeast Thailand: Income and Living Status of Full-time Hired Labors". *Khon Kaen Agriculture Journal* 41, no. 4: 497–506.

Ubon Ratchathani Provincial Statistical Office. 2002. *Report of the Socioeconomic Survey, 2002*.

4

"ONLY THE BEST FRUITS FOR CHINA!"
Local Productions of a "Fruit Frontier" in the Borderlands of China, Laos and Thailand

Simon Rowedder

INTRODUCTION

China has been recording an ever-rising demand for tropical fruits (above all, durian) over the last two decades, particularly from Thailand. Besides China's growing affluent and consumption-oriented middle class, increasingly concerned about health and food safety, and travelling to tropical destinations in Southeast Asia and beyond, the elimination of tariffs for fruits and vegetables in 2003 within the scope of the ASEAN-China Free Trade Area (ACFTA) contributed to this development. In 2017, China's import of fresh tropical fruits reached US$2.468 billion, up from US$1.378 billion in 2011 (Kubo and Sakata 2018, p. 1). Since 2002,

ASEAN countries contributed more than 90 per cent of all tropical fruit imports to China (Lei 2018, p. 7), with Thailand increasingly competing with Vietnam and the Philippines. China's surging demand for Thai durian in particular is even undaunted by the COVID-19 pandemic. In the first four months of 2020, it imported from Thailand US$567.29 million worth of durians, 78 per cent more than in the same period of 2019 (Theparat 2020).

While most of the fruits are shipped by sea, with Shenzhen, Shanghai and Tianjin as the most important ports, overland transport through China's border provinces of Guangxi Zhuang Autonomous Region and Yunnan has grown significantly, particularly since the establishment of ACFTA. While most fresh fruit overland imports are shipped through Guangxi's Pingxiang Port on the border with Vietnam, "making it one of China's most significant entry ports for ASEAN member fresh fruit shipments" (GIZ 2020, p. 30), Yunnan's Mohan port on the China-Laos border, and, by extension, Laos have gained in importance. Since the opening of the Kunming-Bangkok Highway in 2008, which links the markets of China and Thailand through a 228-km section traversing Laos' northwestern provinces of Luang Namtha and Bokeo, Yunnan province has been developing into an essential hub for imported Thai fruits. The opening of the 4th Thai-Lao Friendship Bridge in December 2013, linking Chiang Khong (Chiang Rai province, Thailand) and Huay Xai (Bokeo province, Laos) across the Mekong River, further boosted this development. Only by then, trucks did not need to take the time-consuming and inconvenient ferry trips anymore.

Constituting an integral part of the North-South Economic Corridor of the Greater Mekong Subregion (GMS) backed by the Asian Development Bank (ADB), it is not surprising that each province along the Kunming-Bangkok Highway embraces the same developmentalist entanglement of infrastructure projects, logistical hubs or ports and Special Economic Zones (SEZ). The unquestioned ideology of corridorized development has been further taken up by China's proposed China-Indochina Peninsula Economic Corridor as part of its Belt and Road Initiative (BRI), with the China-Laos Railway (opening in late 2021) as its flagship project (see Figure 4.1). As with previous, largely externally driven development initiatives, the Laotian government regards China's BRI as complementary to its national vision of turning from a land-locked into a land-linked country (Rowedder 2019, 2020b). However, it has been questioned whether Laos would indeed become more than a "pass-through country" (Sun 2017), merely acting as a thoroughfare serving larger gateway geographies of stronger Chinese and Thai economies. If again looking at the Kunming-Bangkok Highway, the impression of

FIGURE 4.1
The Centrality of Laos in GMS North-South Economic Corridor, Kunming-Bangkok Highway, China-Laos Railway

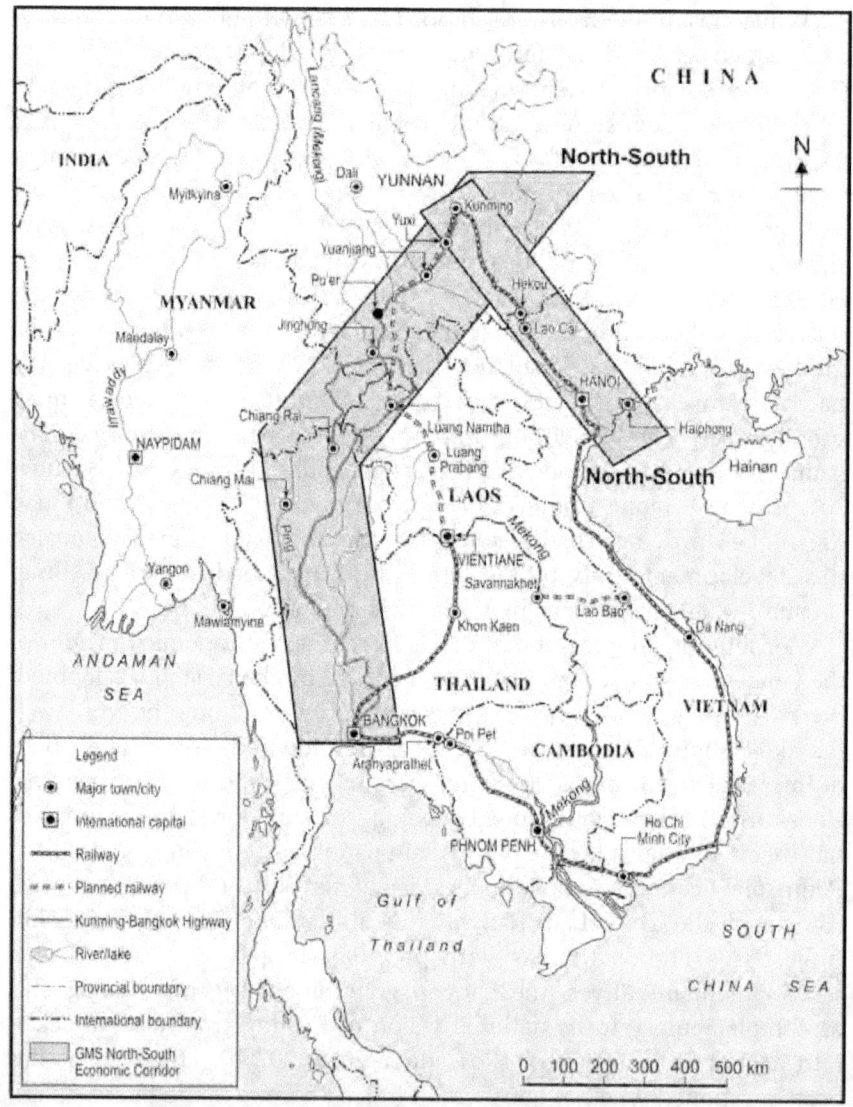

Laos as a passive bystander, boosting its neighbouring markets rather than its own domestic development, solidifies. At a first glance, the road is plied almost exclusively by Thai and Chinese logistics companies (GIZ 2020, p. 33), with Laos risking to "limit itself to 'watching the trucks go by'" (Tan 2014, p. 427).

The implied passive, weak and small position of Laos within larger schemes of regional connectivity is further established in narratives of Laos as an "open" resource frontier (see Rowedder and Tappe, this volume). Like other parts of the country, northern Laos constitutes a site of intensive cash crop cultivation, again mostly backed by Chinese investment and geared towards the ever-growing Chinese market. Besides the well-studied issue of rapidly expanding rubber plantations (Dwyer and Vongvisouk 2017; Lyttleton and Li 2017; Li 2018; Sturgeon 2013; Cohen 2009; see also Suhardiman and Kramp, this issue), large-scale plantations of banana (e.g., Friis and Nielsen 2016; Santasombat 2019) and watermelon (e.g., Lyttleton et al. 2004; Nolintha 2018) are the most prominent examples (for a maize boom in the Lao-Vietnamese borderlands, see Cole's chapter in this volume). Laos' associated developmentalist mantra of "turning land into capital" (Dwyer 2007; Kenney-Lazar, Dwyer, and Hett 2018)—of commodifying land and resources and granting an increasing number of SEZs to mainly external investors—has been analysed as ultimately commodifying Laos' national sovereignty (Laungaramsri 2015) and indicating signs of "soft extraterritoriality" on the part of China (Lyttleton and Nyíri 2011, p. 1256).

Extending Pinkaew Laungaramsri's (2012) notion of "frontier capitalism" beyond its narrow focus on resource extraction, I argue that Laos' path towards development has been generally mapped and imagined through differently produced logics and constellations of the frontier. Besides being a "last frontier" of commodifiable land and natural resources, Laos' geography of interlinked-ness also constitutes an exploitable frontier zone facilitating larger transnational flows of commodities and capital.

The commodity of fruits thus figures prominently in Laos' twofold frontierization (cf. Cons and Eilenberg 2019a) of its abundant land resources and its "geography of peripheral centrality" (Brown 2018), concretely observable in a mainly Chinese-run "shifting plantation production system" (Santasombat 2019) and increased traffic of

Chinese and Thai cargo trucks carrying Thai fruits to China. These two interrelated "fruit frontier" dynamics, operating between the poles of spatially fixed agriculture and cross-border commodity flows, can be understood as constituting "frontier assemblages", demonstrating "the intertwined materialities, actors, cultural logics, spatial dynamics, ecologies, and political economic processes that produce particular places as resource frontiers" (Cons and Eilenberg 2019b, p. 2). However, in Cons and Eilenberg's (2019b, p. 7) understanding of "frontiers as *imaginative*—zones in which the material realities of place are inextricably bound to various visions of and cultural vocabularies for what the frontier is and might be", the cultural vocabularies of imagining the frontier largely seem to be confined to external actors, mainly comprising entangled sets of corporate actors and state agencies, who frame "these spaces as simultaneously critical, open, and in need of intervention" (2019b, p. 9).

TOWARDS AN ETHNOGRAPHY OF THE "FRONTIER FROM BELOW"

Building on Keith Barney's (2009) impulse to include previously rather neglected local agents (not merely passive victims) in his analysis of Laos as a "relational frontier", my study likewise pays closer attention to the social practices and discourses of a wide range of people on the ground differently involved in local productions of the transnational "fruit frontier" between Thailand, Laos and China. In this ethnography of the "frontier from below", I will foreground the central role of small-scale traders in northern Laos (Huay Xai in Bokeo province and the towns of Luang Namtha and Muang Sing in Luang Namtha provinces—an area which is also covered by Ponce's contribution to this volume) in trading Thai fruits to Laos and China, who are otherwise largely invisible in studies and reports on the Sino-Thai fruit overland trade. As Philip Taylor (2016, p. 151) argues in general for processes of "frontier commodization in post-socialist Southeast Asia", "[s]uch small scale flows of commodities and people may not be well covered in national statistics, but their aggregated impacts on local economies and landscapes may be substantial." Hailing from diverse social, economic and ethnic backgrounds, cross-border traders in northern Laos share the "experimentarian ethic" (High 2013, p. 491) of flexibly exploiting the promisingly improved regional connectivity and proximity to China and Thailand. Besides fruits, many of them are also trading a wide portfolio of Chinese and Thai everyday household commodities to supply local marketplaces throughout northern Laos (Rowedder 2020a).

As I will demonstrate in this chapter for the case of the fruit trade, the indispensable role of Lao small-scale traders in the actual everyday workings of this dynamic borderland economy is rooted in their continual discursive and practical reproduction of Laos' frontier constellation of being squeezed between the larger and powerful markets and economies of Thailand and China. They are able to do so because the vernacular discourse central to enabling the transnational flow of Thai fruits revolves around the notion of graded fruit quality. As the notion of quality is inherently comparative, it is well suited to being a device for realizing and rearticulating differences across borders, thereby easily slipping into starkly essentialized national stereotypes.

Drawing on my larger long-term, multi-sited ethnographic research project of accompanying small-scale traders in the Yunnan-Laos-Thailand borderland economy through participant observation, semi-structured interviews and situationally emerging conversations between 2015 and 2019,[1] I will in the following trace in more detail how Thai agriculturalists and Lao cross-border traders engage in these local frontier-making discourses and practices related to and arising from handling fruits both as territorially rooted agricultural products and as highly valued transnational commodities. I start this exploration of the "fruit frontier" in northern Thailand's village of Ban Huay Meng in Chiang Khong district (Chiang Rai province), located by the Mekong River, which has evolved from an ethnic minority village into an important national and regional fruit supplier. I will first dwell upon some considerable detail of Ban Huay Meng's local agrarian history to fully understand the emergence of a discursive "fruit frontier" based on national Thai formulations of high-quality agricultural sophistication and superiority. Gradually crossing over to Laos, I will demonstrate how Ban Huay Meng's Thai discourses on fruit quality, tied to space and soil, are put in cross-border motion and contestation by mobile Lao traders and Chinese buyers.

BAN HUAY MENG: FROM ETHNIC FRONTIER TO THAILAND'S NATIONAL FRUIT FRONTIER

Located along the Mekong River, in Thailand's northernmost Chiang Rai province, Ban Huay Meng is the oldest of three Tai Lue[2] villages in the Chiang Khong district, an area which Thianchai Surimas and Carl Middleton also study in their contribution to this volume. It shares with Ban Sri Donchai and Ban Hat Bai the history of Tai Lue migration from Muang Ou in Sipsongpanna (now located in present-day Phongsaly province in northernmost Laos) into Chiang Khong in the late nineteenth century. It is commonly understood that this Lue migration out of Sipsongpanna first to present-day northwestern Laos was mainly an escape from Chinese oppression (Muang Ou got invaded by Qing troops at that time) and a socio-economically general miserable situation, whereas the subsequent migration out of Laos to present-day northern Thailand needs to be understood against the backdrop of the strengthening regional power of Siam. Muang Sing in northern Laos, the newly established capital of the Lue principality of Chiang Khaeng, eventually got under Siamese suzerainty in the late nineteenth century (Grabowsky and Wichasin 2008, p. 45). Nan, a strengthening tributary state of Siam with Chiang Khong as its strategic "Mekong outpost" (Walker 1999, pp. 29–36), played an essential role in consolidating Siamese influence in the Upper Mekong region. Desperately in need of manpower, Nan troops forced large populations in territories of present northwestern Laos to resettle in northern Thailand. This is also in accord with the village headman (*kamnan*)[3] of Ban Huay Meng who likewise told me that their ancestors' further migration to Chiang Khong was not voluntary, but rather because the ruler of Chiang Khong required more labour. However, one group of Tai Lue villagers managed to settle down in Ban Pung and Ban Tha Fa (also called Ban Sang), in present-day Bokeo province, 30 and 70 kilometres away from Huay Xai, respectively.

Despite the involuntary character of the migration, it is documented that the Lue of Ban Huay Meng quickly managed to maintain good and close relations with the governor of Chiang Khong. Sophida Wirakunthewan (2005, p. 46) argues in her comprehensive study on ethnicity and trade dynamics in Chiang Khong that these early established, close relations to the seat of power (*sunklang khong amnat*) provided critical advantages. Access to plenty of arable land paved the way for a successful agricultural trajectory, which started, besides rice and corn cultivation, with the villagers' investment in tobacco processing. However, the decisive turning point was the beginning of orange cultivation in 1963 which should drastically uplift the economic condition of Ban Huay Meng, constituting the cornerstone for a rapid agro-economic development towards a nationally and regionally well-reputed supplier of oranges and subsequently other fruits.

This intensive agricultural focus of Ban Huay Meng prompted Wirakunthewan (2005, p. 63) to remark that "if one is visiting Ban Huay Meng at present, one might not find the uniqueness of being a Tai Lue community like in Ban Sri Donchai or Ban Hat Bai."[4] Ban Huay Meng is primarily an agricultural village whose Tai Lue cultural background is not visibly practised and lived anymore—unlike the Tai Lue of Ban Sri Donchai and Ban Hat Bai who are still prominently displaying their outstanding traditional weaving techniques. Along with the recent trend of revitalizing, and commodifying, ethnic consciousness and regional identities in northern Thailand and beyond, Ban Sri Donchai opened a "Tai Lue Cultural Centre" (*sun wattanatham thai lue*) in 2018, adding to a burgeoning landscape of newly promoted "Tai Lue Weaving Centres" which simultaneously act as small museums or "study centres" (*sun khwamrianru*) and frequently offer "Tai Lue-style" homestays. Ban Huay Meng's economic development centred on fruit cultivation thus seems to overshadow its perception as a distinctively Tai Lue village. Its narrative of having gradually developed into a model "fruit village" fully integrated into the Thai national and regional borderland economy was also more present in conversations with the villagers of Ban Huay Meng.

As mentioned earlier, Ban Huay Meng's success story as a fruit village started with the cultivation of oranges. With the first harvest in 1968 sold well at several markets throughout Chiang Khong, more villagers became interested in this new, promising agricultural business. The *kamnan* referred to a subsequent group of seven farmers who grew oranges to great success. With the help of the Chiang Rai provincial government, which started to promote the local cultivation of fruits such as oranges and to organize respective fruit festivals and fairs, the oranges of Ban Huay Meng began to be known outside of

Chiang Khong district and Chiang Rai province. This orange boom ended abruptly in 1996 due to an encroaching bacterial infestation, destroying the entire orange harvest and permanently contaminating the water, the soil and the trees. Most of the villagers abandoned orange cultivation altogether and shifted to the marketization of other fruits, which they first bought mainly from markets in Chiang Rai, but subsequently grew by themselves. They increasingly focused on cultivating rambutan, which, by their own accounts, again led to a success story of gaining a regional and national reputation for their highly qualitative agricultural produce. Ban Huay Meng's farmers also started to successfully experiment with growing other fruits while resuming orange cultivation.

Due to the limited scope of this chapter, it should suffice here to sum up that Ban Huay Meng has been continuously portrayed by the *kamnan*, fruit growers and researchers as a site of a hard-earned agro-economic success story of fruit cultivation, with its orchards and produced high-quality fruits as the village's predominant emblem. It is this emerging village identity strongly tied to the entanglement of pride in the agricultural quality and a pronounced sense of Thai (agricultural) national identity that shapes Ban Huay Meng's cross-border fruit trade relations.

OPENING UP TO CROSS-BORDER TRADE

Ban Huay Meng has not only found its place in the Thai economy as an increasingly prominent supplier of fruits for the local and national markets; it has also emerged as a significant supply centre for a thriving regional borderland economy equipped with regionally well-connected, cosmopolitan traders.

The *kamnan* mentioned the year 1996 as the beginning of the village's increased cross-border trade activities with Laos after their main domestic market segment of oranges broke away for the time being. This cross-border trade started indeed as a Tai Lue enterprise, as it was mainly facilitated by cross-border Tai Lue kinship ties. The *kamnan* specifically referred to the Tai Lue of Ban Pung on the Lao side, who also later acted as middlemen between Ban Huay Meng traders and Chinese buyers further afield. However, he was quick in asserting that not long after that initial phase, an increasing number of non-Lue people in Laos became interested in this cross-border fruit trade, their curiosity triggered by the observable increasing wealth of Tai Lue merchants. Attracted by this promising business opportunity, more non-Lue actors came in to participate in cross-border trade with Ban Huay Meng. It seemed to be indeed important to the *kamnan* to repeatedly stress that there was now a wide mix of different actors; therefore, he concluded, their cross-border relations could and should not be understood as primarily or exclusively based on Tai Lue kinship or family relations anymore.

Through the village's informal river port, Thai fruits have been shipped across the Mekong River to the port of Khonekeo in Huay Xai on the Lao side for further distribution to markets in northern Laos and, more recently, to markets in China's Yunnan province (see Figure 4.2). At present, there are six trading households involved in cross-border fruit trade, among whom the *kamnan* and his wife Oy (well known in Chiang Khong and beyond in Laos and Xishuangbanna as "Pa Oy" ["auntie Oy"]) were one of the first established. Besides trading fruits from Ban Huay Meng's orchards, they also trade fruits bought from wholesale markets in the provinces of Chumphon (southern Thailand), Kanchanaburi (western Thailand), Rayong (eastern Thailand) or Bangkok (especially at the largest wholesale market, *talat thai*), thus underlining again their full integration within Thailand's overall national fruit market infrastructure.

Supporting Wirakunthewan's (2005, p. 56) aforementioned point of traditionally close relationships of several Tai Lue groups with the "centre of power" (*sun amnat*), the *kamnan* has been, in his long-standing experience as the village head and, more recently, as the subdistrict *kamnan*, successfully managing a close-knit network with several local state agencies, which enables Ban Huay Meng to run its own river port. This informal but tolerated border-crossing has attracted numerous traders not only from across the border but other places within and far beyond Chiang Khong district due to its reputation for providing a smooth, uncomplicated and affordable handling. Importantly, the latter is possible due to the hiring of exclusively Lao labourers for boat transportation and loading the goods from the boats onto trucks and vice versa—unlike other river ports in Chiang Khong which are

"Only the Best Fruits for China!" 89

FIGURE 4.2
Ban Huay Meng as Centre of Transnational Thai Fruit Trade

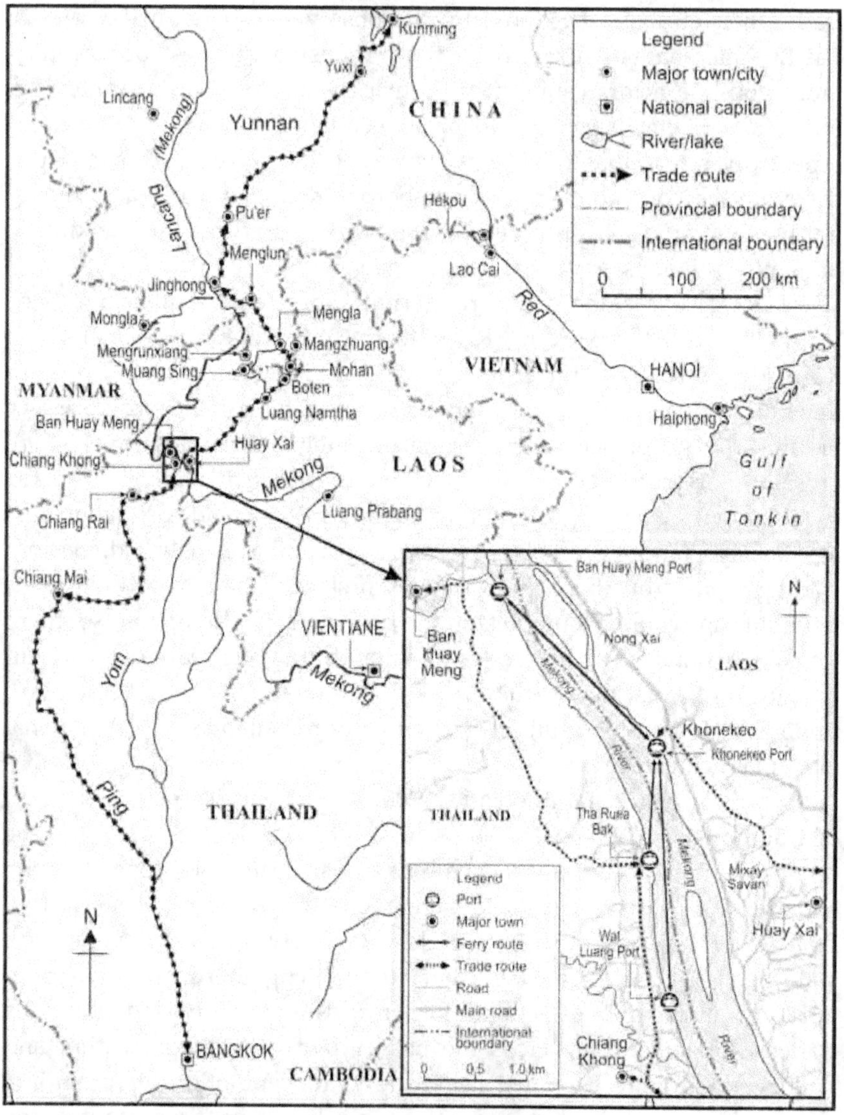

mainly operated by Thai boats. Across the border at the Khonekeo port, Lao traders, and increasingly Chinese buyers themselves, collect fruit orders. Hence, Ban Huay Meng's fruit cultivators and traders constitute the physically least mobile actors in this transnational fruit network. Some of them would only occasionally cross the border to collect payments or to make sure that their empty fruit baskets are returned to them in a timely manner.

EMERGING DISCOURSES OF A TRANSNATIONAL FRUIT FRONTIER

Ban Huay Meng villagers being both agriculturalists and traders, their higher degree of spatial fixity, compared to mobile Lao traders, find expression in an emotional and proud attachment to their cultivated land. My numerous attempts to talk about their cross-border trade endeavours often ended in lengthy, rather technical conversations revolving around their self-grown fruits. Proudly detailing aspects of quality (*khunaphap*), related grade (*kret*), taste (*rotchat*) and appearance (mainly in terms of beauty, *khwamsuaingam*), they made it unmistakably clear that it was their advanced experience, knowledge and skills, embedded in the highly sophisticated agriculture of Thailand in general, that helped them to achieve producing distinctive and inimitable high-quality fruits, ideally suited for international trade. Their discursive self-assuredness is also built on a firm sense of superiority, not only to allegedly mediocre Chinese fruits (mentioning issues of extensive usage of chemicals and "fake fruits" [*phonlamai plom*]), but also to the less developed agricultural economy in neighbouring Laos. The latter is also often tied to the formulation of cultural stereotypes of the "lazy Lao". Notably, this Thai perspective of agricultural superiority in relation to Laos and China was also often mirrored in conversations with sellers, traders and consumers across the Thai border.

In northern Laos, the lack of domestic production of consumer goods, in combination with increased cross-border connectivity, leads by necessity to the inherently transnational character of the local landscape of marketplaces where mainly Chinese and Thai commodities intersect. It is therefore unsurprising that conversations at these sites revolved around comparing them. The common argument in these markets was that Thai commodities were in general of much better, more reliable quality while Chinese commodities were cheaper, but of lower quality. Concerning the latter, many cited probable high toxic contaminations of Chinese vegetables and fruits, which prompted them to express their discomfort about poor food security in China in general. Market women selling vegetables and fruits would also often half-jokingly, half-seriously lament that Lao farmers were simply not able to engage in professional, large-scale agriculture so that they would have no choice but to buy and sell agricultural produce from China or Thailand. One vendor in Muang Sing described the Lao consumers' dilemma that both Chinese and Thai fruits were delicious but full of chemicals. He asserted that Lao agricultural produce would be free of any chemicals; however, as they were only grown on a small scale, their sale prices would be even more expensive than imported products from Thailand and China so that they would not find their way into the markets. He stated lacking expertise and professionalism on the part of Lao farmers as the main reason for the very limited scale of Lao agriculture.

Tot, a trader from Luang Namtha who is together with his wife and his son regularly attending cross-border trade fairs in Xishuangbanna, found clearer words for the status of agriculture in Laos. When I accompanied him and his family to such a trade fair, he explained to me that the "Thai method" (*withikan thai*) of doing agriculture would be much more developed, mature (*toeb to*) and professional (*pen asip loey*). Thus, Thai farmers would generally do better as they carefully studied how to apply specific agricultural techniques and develop products while Lao farmers would rather hastily try to grow something without any prior knowledge, research and experience. This prompted him to further derive a general discussion about the Lao national problem of lacking education, even implying a culture-bound reluctance to gain proper knowledge and skills which would all hinder processes of sustainable professionalization.

The common remarks on the lacking quality and food security of Chinese products overheard at markets and among traders in Laos were in turn also echoed on the Chinese end of the overland supply chain of Thai commodities. Chinese customers and sellers at regional trade fairs and numerous supermarkets specializing in Thai products throughout Xishuangbanna commonly stated their lost trust in Chinese product quality, reliability and safety as one of the main reasons why they preferred Thai commodities.

THAI FRUITS IN MOTION: "BEST FRUITS FOR CHINA, NORMAL FRUITS FOR LAOS"

This tri-national commodity hierarchy directly finds its expression in the transnational trade of Thai fruits. Watching the fruit cargo being loaded onto boats at the river port of Ban Huay Meng (see Figure 4.3), I soon learnt how local actors disassembled the transnational flow of Thai fruits into its national components along the dimension of quality. Curious why I could often overhear the term *thammada* ("normal", "ordinary"), the village traders explained to me that "normal" fruits would go to Laos, but the best and most beautiful ones of premium quality would be assigned to Chinese buyers. Or in the words of Pa Oy, the wife of the *kamnan*:

> You know, there are numerous different quality grades, but for today I can say that these ordinary ones [pointing to one basket of mangosteens] are designated for Lao buyers. Those bigger ones [pointing to another basket of mangosteens], we sell to the Chinese as usual. They like big and beautiful fruits. Of course, these are also more expensive, but the Chinese are willing to pay for this as they can afford it.

FIGURE 4.3
Village port of Ban Huay Meng, Chiang Khong district, Chiang Rai province, Thailand

Source: Photo taken by the author, 2015.

FIGURE 4.4
Loading Thai Fruits on Trucks at Khonekeo Port, Huay Xai, Bokeo Province

Source: Photo taken by the author, 2017.

This bluntly articulated practice of reserving high-quality fruits for the Chinese market and low-quality fruits for the Lao market was constantly reiterated both in Thailand and in Laos. Graded Thai fruit quality thus reproduces in its transnational circulation national borders, invigorating economic, social, cultural and political hierarchies. In other words, Thai fruits, as a transnational commodity, are moving boundary markers. This nationally couched fruit-related quality discourse of supplying Thailand, transiting Laos and receiving and demanding China inevitably leads to instances of conflict, particularly between Thai suppliers and Chinese customers, revealing underlying frictions reflecting "the awkward, unequal, unstable, and creative qualities of interconnection across difference" (Tsing 2005, p. 4). Equipped with their high confidence in the premium quality of their cultivated fruits, the traders of Ban Huay Meng often come directly face to face with the somewhat different and challenging Chinese understanding of fruit quality and aesthetics. I could best observe this during one of my numerous stays at Khonekeo port where I witnessed what I call the "mangosteen incident" (see Figure 4.4).

THE "MANGOSTEEN INCIDENT": CONTESTED FRONTIERS OF FRUIT QUALITY

Amidst the usual bustle at the port where long lines of small trucks were queuing on a narrow road, waiting to be loaded, three baskets of mangosteens drew the attention of a larger crowd, including the traders from Ban Huay Meng with whom I crossed over this time as they planned to collect some payments by themselves. It turned out that Chinese buyers had abandoned those mangosteens as they were dissatisfied with their quality. Chang, one of the Ban Huay Meng traders, whispered to me angrily: "You know, the Chinese are like that. They are too often not satisfied with the goods and just return them. They would refuse to pay as well. This is really not good for the market!" His comments were widely echoed in a broader discussion among other bystanders commonly complaining about too picky Chinese customers. Some of the Lao traders examined the fruits and concluded that most of them were of very good quality, demonstratively eating some of them. They also invited me to taste them and were all the happier when I conceded that they were indeed quite delicious (as far as my layman knowledge was concerned), interestingly prompting them to state, partly proudly, partly jokingly, that even a German researcher knew better about aspects of taste and quality of tropical fruits than their Chinese customers. Although said in a joking manner, the claim of a widespread Chinese unfamiliarity with tropical fruits was serious and repeated several times by most of the Lao and Thai bystanders. In the absence of the Chinese traders in question who had left the scene long since, a sudden sense of unity and solidarity among Lao and Thai traders was seemingly created in the consensus that Chinese buyers were not able to fully understand and appreciate the quality of their tropical fruits. Apart from blaming the Chinese trade participants for lacking knowledge of and familiarity with their goods, the discussion quickly turned to listing further associated negative qualities of the "troublesome" (*yung lambak*) and "annoying" (*chob mi rueang*) Chinese in general: dishonesty, unpredictability, a tendency to cheat, greed, rudeness and arrogance were recited.

What might be understood as a Chinese slight against their proudly articulated belief of guaranteeing unmatched qualities and standards triggered much discontent among traders back in Ban Huay Meng as well. My subsequent conversations there were very much dominated by references to problematic issues with the Chinese, often revolving around complaints about the difficult "Chinese character" (*nisai khong khon jin*) in general and not uncommonly questioning the future of directly trading with the Chinese. I was also told stories of several Ban Huay Meng traders who entirely gave up trading with the Chinese side. Some of them ran into debts due to outstanding payments and lacking profits, which they all attributed to unacceptable business practices involving some cheating practices (*kan kong*) on part of the Chinese buyers.

LAO CROSS-BORDER TRADERS: MEDIATING FRICTIONS, REPRODUCING FRONTIERS

As the "mangosteen incident" shows, the struggle over fruit quality and allegedly different business habits between Thai suppliers and Chinese buyers is largely decided on Lao soil. However, Laos is not merely a passive venue of these frictions, but also a site of their active mediation by Lao traders. Much more mobile than the trading agriculturalists of Ban Huay Meng, whose trading activities mostly end at their river port, Lao fruit traders are more flexible and successful in handling the "troublesome Chinese". Accompanying several Lao cross-border traders, I could observe that they tactically adopted a rather "neutral" and practical position in which the Chinese traders' judgement of low fruit quality does not represent a personal affront against them as it does to Ban Huay Meng traders. They furthermore appear to blend in with this tri-nationally graded quality logic by pragmatically capitalizing on their status of belonging to an allegedly inferior, underdeveloped and low-quality economy. Reminiscent of market vendors in Laos, they often stressed in a self-ironic manner that Lao people were just too lazy and unskilled to establish large-scale and professional agriculture competitive with Thailand or China. They actively sustain their cross-border neighbours' stereotypes of Laos and transform them into an essential engine enabling the transnational flow of Thai fruits. While their view of an underperforming agricultural sector explains the import of Thai fruits for the Lao domestic market, their perception of China's economic supremacy explains the further export of high-quality fruits to China. Lao traders, operating between different quality spheres of traded Thai fruits, are thus in a unique position in this 'qualitatively bordered' transnational trade system. My encounters with Pa Saeng, a locally well-known fruit trader in Muang Sing who regularly buys from Pa Oy in Ban Huay Meng and sells further across the border in China, illustrate this.

"Rambutans from Ban Huay Meng are not that beautiful this year", Pa Saeng explained to me while putting some on a plate with the intent to create a relaxed atmosphere for our first conversation in Muang Sing in early July, which marks the beginning of the rambutan season. She reiterated this point throughout numerous subsequent conversations, stressing that this would potentially impact her sales in China. The proud and self-confident assertions about the premium quality I had heard while talking with fruit growers and traders in Ban Huay Meng were now on the Lao side relativized or already contextualized with anticipated Chinese quality concerns. Pa Saeng then directed the conversation towards her worries about Chinese buyers' recent complaints about the lacking quality of her traded Thai fruits. Several of her Chinese customers also accused the Thai fruit growers of covering low-grade fruits with high-grade fruits. Thus, she had no choice but to tell Pa Oy in Ban Huay Meng about these issues in a "friendly manner" (*wao di di noi*), mainly over the phone. Saying this, she sounded as if she claimed to undertake the diplomatic task to "friendly" mediate Sino-Thai disputes about fruit quality and trade practices.

This "friendly talk", as I could overhear from her phone conversations and directly observe at several gatherings when both Thai and Lao traders met each other, largely relied on negatively stereotyping "the Chinese" in general, similar to the apparent joint Lao-Thai solidarization against the commonly shared problem of handling troublesome Chinese traders as observed during the "mangosteen incident". Especially when alcohol was involved, joyful and exaggerated mocking and mimicking of "the Chinese" knew no limits. Yet, howsoever pejorative their remarks on China were, they rested at the same time on an intimate familiarity, or "agonistic intimacy" (Singh 2011; Saxer and Zhang 2017) of their Chinese counterparts. This was even more the case on the Lao side when the Lao traders were only by themselves. Talks about "the Chinese" were often interspersed with a significant amount of Chinese language phrases and extended knowledge about recent developments in several locations in Yunnan province and beyond, indicating a certain sense of admiration.

Interestingly, this outwardly essentialized, but inwardly intimate engagement with their Chinese counterparts is further coupled with similar joking and exaggerated comments on and performances of "Thai habits" (*nisai khong khon thai*). Although these acts of performing or imitating the "neighbourly Other" (Endres 2015) took place in playful and indeed often alcoholized settings, they still provided useful insights into their distinct intermediary position, equipped with flexibly usable repertoires of national stereotypes. Thus, returning to the Khonekeo port, Lao traders further complemented the aforementioned Lao-Thai solidarization against "the troublesome Chinese" by Lao-Chinese solidarization against "the unreliable Thai". Two days before the "mangosteen incident", I could catch some snippets of a conversation between two Chinese fruit buyers and two Lao middlemen in the Lao language.[5] The latter tried to appease the formers' discontent and concerns about repeated quality failures by showing their understanding and by referring to the general problem of the tendency to cheat among certain Thai agriculturalists and traders, over which they would have no control. I could also hear cultural references to a particular "Thai way" (*withi thai*)[6] of ambivalent and oblique communication. The Lao merchants assured in this connection that they would clearly communicate the quality issue to their Thai suppliers as they would know "how to talk to the Thai" (probably in the spirit of Pa Saeng's notion of "friendly talk" with Pa Oy).

Lao traders skilfully manage to socialize with and cater to both Thai and Chinese actors by invoking national stereotypes about the respectively "Other", thereby responding to and again revitalizing Sino-Thai frictions which in turn are needed to maintain the transnational flow of Thai fruits. This mirrors Anna Tsing's (2005, p. 6) emphasis on the productive and creating dimension of frictions: "Friction is required to keep global power in motion." Lao traders complement their successful attention to frictions with frontier-making practices. By performing their ascribed economic inferiority, they concretely act upon and sustain Laos' frontier status of a land-linked periphery, re-enacting the associated notion of a domestically underdeveloped and backward, but geopolitically significant thoroughfare within geographies of regional connectivity and proximity. Paradoxically, their cross-border trade performance and, by extension, their economic agency and livelihood depend on the prevailing frontier trope of the largely externally driven development of Laos that benefits primarily external actors. In a sense, these small-scale cross-border fruit traders in northern Laos actively reproduce and maintain a frontier dynamic which keeps themselves invisible—namely a booming Sino-Thai overland fruit economy that seemingly leaves no room for local livelihoods in Laos. Friction and frontier are their capital.

OUTLOOK

Keith Barney (2009, pp. 148, 156) argues that "a relational-geographical approach may aid in locating the complex, situated and cumulative nature of local social and environmental transformations which reproduce frontier space, inequality and marginality, sometimes in unexpected ways", adding for the case of Laos that "[r]elational approaches to frontier transformations recognise how Laos, and territories within Laos, are being actively 'peripheralised' in a globalised economy". This chapter has pointed to highly mobile and flexible small-scale traders in northern Laos as conventionally "invisible", but on the ground central actors who reproduce an unequal and hierarchical frontier space through practices of self-marginalization. However, this ingeniously maintained frontier constellation has been operating on shaky grounds, always exposed to rapid and unpredictable change.

Recently, the fruit trade-oriented small-scale frontier livelihoods of Lao traders have been challenged by external, more large-scale factors of China's attempts to compete for and secure access to tropical fruits. Both China's stricter cross-border import regulations and its constant efforts to cultivate tropical fruits domestically run the risk of closing this small-scale fruit frontier economy, potentially impeding the logistics, direction and intensity of the transnational flow of Thai fruits. Lately, increasing numbers of Lao fruit traders complained that it became much more difficult to transport Thai fruits into China, which would be only reserved for licensed large-scale trading companies mainly from China and Thailand.

Additionally, China's dependence on Thailand (and other Southeast Asian countries) to satisfy its ever-rising demand for tropical fruits, which is essential for the local workings of this overland fruit frontier, might dwindle in the future due to China's heavy investment in agricultural research of domestic tropical fruit cultivation, propelled by the Chinese Academy of Tropical Agricultural Sciences (CATA). Currently, tropical fruits—including mango, longan, lychee, dragon fruit and avocado—are already cultivated in China's southern provinces of primarily Guangdong, Guangxi and Hainan, and to a lesser extent Yunnan, Fujian, Sichuan and Chongqing (GIZ 2020, pp. 3–28). There has been even news on the successful cultivation of tropical fruits in greenhouses in the Gobi desert (Xinhua 2020). Moreover, in a quite symbolic gesture to master the most valued and highly demanded tropical fruit, there have been promising experimentations to cultivate durian in Hainan province, which already alerted Thailand's trade authorities, urging Thai agriculturalists to remain competitive (e.g., *Straits Times*, 7 September 2019). Besides pushing the tropical fruit frontier domestically, China could also further build on its already established extraterritorial plantation economy in Laos mentioned above. These highly interrelated two "fruit frontiers"—of transnationally moving and locally (and largely externally financed) growing commodified tropical fruits—intersect in Laos, as concrete manifestations of the aforementioned governmental mantras of "transforming from a land-locked to a land-linked country" and "turning land into capital". These two frontier configurations, of simultaneously frictional and fluid connectivity and spatial fixity, constitute a dynamically shifting, elastic and relational "frontier assemblage" (Cons and Eilenberg 2019a). If further extending the Chinese-backed concession-like fruit plantation model into Laos, the tri-national cross-border trade of Thai fruits, with Lao traders as central actors, might further diminish.

It thus remains to be seen how this possible agrarian shift, largely shaped by agro-economic competition between Thailand and China, will, in combination with already observable cross-border protectionism mainly on the Chinese side, impact local livelihoods previously depending on an unchanged, unrestricted and unlimited flow of Thai fruits into the Chinese market. Eventually, as Antonella Diana (2013, p. 27) points out in her study on China's Tai Lue cross-border traders, "trans-border trade and mobility of ethnic minority border dwellers remain conditional on an unpredictable state mechanism of loosening and tightening", leading to the circumstance that "[s]ome individual's practices are enabled while others' are constrained by politico-economic structures of national and transnational breadth."

However, at least in the case of Lao fruit traders, I do not fully subscribe to her grim conclusion that "[t]heir success as flexible border citizens had been inhibited by a new wave of state authoritarianism entangled with corporate accumulation" (Diana 2013, p. 36). As I show elsewhere for the case of newly aspiring small-scale traders in northern Laos in general (Rowedder 2020a), they display high levels of risk-taking, resilience, flexibility, pragmatism and creative mobility. Their continual attempts to adjust to rapid changes in terms of relocation of marketplaces, patterns of commodity supply and demand, and border regulations lead both to success and failure. Experimenting entrepreneurial newcomers are embedded in a much longer history of appropriating and engaging politically and economically larger (precolonial, colonial, national) powers, acting in what C. Patterson Giersch (2006, pp. 3–4) describes for the Yunnan-Southeast Asian frontier as a "middle ground" of "fluid cultural and economic exchange". Moreover, for the borderlands of Laos, Thailand, China and Burma in general, Andrew Walker (1999) focuses in his "micro-sociology of borders" (p. 112) on the historically rooted notion of regulation as a social practice shared both by "borderlanders" and state agents, leading to "collaborative borderlands" (p. 111) that reveal "complex and subtle collaborations between local initiative and state power" (Walker 1999, p. 112). Regarding Luang Namtha province in particular, Olivier Évrard (1997, p. 12) states that it "has for centuries been a place for trade and movement to and fro. Numerous mule trails, nowadays simply footpaths, once criss-crossed the province linking Siamese, Burmese and Chinese border posts", whereas Nathan Badenoch and Tomita Shinsuke (2013, p. 60) describe Luang Namtha's historical trajectory as a "cosmopolitan space of cultural contention."

Returning to the present state of the fruit trade, I could already observe instances of resilience and flexible economic experimentation. For example, one trading household in Muang Sing, good friends with

Pa Saeng, abolished the fruit trade altogether and shifted to trading textiles. They are now specializing in the trade of traditional Tai Lue textiles, bought from the Thailand-Myanmar borderlands. They mainly sell those in Tai Lue villages throughout Luang Namtha province, especially during larger festivities. Others already flirted with the idea of "renting land to the Chinese" (*sao thi din hai khon jin*), provided they themselves, or relatives or friends, did own land. The latter only demonstrates their potential flexibility to navigate between the two frontier processes in Laos of land-richness and land-linkedness. For the time being, both frontier configurations will impact on, challenge, change, create, and be reproduced and modified by, local livelihoods. My stubborn questions about those challenges and uncertainties have been often answered with a relaxed smile: "No matter what, we will find a way."

Notes

1. The main period of fieldwork was from late February 2015 until early January 2016, covering parts of Yunnan province (Kunming and Xishuangbanna Dai Autonomous Prefecture), northern Laos (Huay Xai in Bokeo province and Luang Namtha and Muang Sing towns in Luang Namtha province) and northern Thailand (Chiang Mai and Chiang Rai provinces). I conducted some follow-up fieldwork in January and February 2017, mainly in Xishuangbanna and Luang Namtha province. Most recently I revisited Luang Namtha and Chiang Rai provinces in March 2018 and August/September 2019. The main findings are published in my recent book *Cross-Border Traders in Northern Laos: Mastering Smallness* by Amsterdam University Press (Rowedder 2022).
2. The Tai Lue, one of the several Tai-speaking groups in the region, originate from Sipsongpanna (before the sixteenth century rather known as Muang Lue, "the polity of the Lue"), which became in 1953 incorporated into the People's Republic of China as the "Xishuangbanna Dai Autonomous Prefecture" of Yunnan province. Besides Xishuangbanna, they are at present scattered across different parts of Yunnan, northern Laos, northern Thailand as well as in eastern Myanmar (mainly in Shan state) and northwestern Vietnam (mainly Lai Chao province).
3. He also serves as the head of Chiang Khong's central Wiang subdistrict (comprising fourteen villages). I will in the following simply refer to him as *kamnan*, using the Thai title of sub-district head with which I usually addressed him during our conversations.

4. Original Thai quote: หากใครเข้าไปเยือนหมู่บ้านห้วยเม็งอาจไม่พบความโดดเด่นของความเป็นชุมชนชาวลื้อ ดังเช่นที่อาจพบเห็นได้ที่หมู่บ้านศรีดอนชัยหรือบ้านหาดบ้าย.
5. This is not particularly strange as I could witness not a small number of Han Chinese in Laos being fluent in Lao language.
6. Compare Tot's remark on the "Thai method" (*withikan thai*) of agriculture mentioned before.

References

Badenoch, Nathan, and Tomita Shinsuke. 2013. "Mountain People in the *Muang*: Creation and Governance of a Tai Polity in Northern Laos". *Southeast Asian Studies* 2, no. 1: 29–67.

Barney, Keith. 2009. "Laos and the Making of a 'Relational' Resource Frontier". *Geographical Journal* 175, no. 2: 146–59.

Brown, Alan. 2018. "Laos's Peripheral Centrality in Southeast Asia: Mobility, Labour, and Regional Integration". *European Journal of East Asian Studies* 17: 228–62.

Cohen, Paul T. 2009. "The Post-opium Scenario and Rubber in Northern Laos: Alternative Western and Chinese Models of Development". *International Journal of Drug Policy* 20, no. 5: 424–30.

Cons, Jason, and Michael Eilenberg, eds. 2019a. *Frontier Assemblages: The Emergent Politics of Resource Frontiers in Asia*. Hoboken: John Wiley and Sons.

———, and Michael Eilenberg. 2019b. "Introduction: On the New Policies of Margins in Asia: Mapping Frontier Assemblages". In *Frontier Assemblages: The Emergent Politics of Resource Frontiers in Asia*, edited by Jason Cons and Michael Eilenberg, pp. 1–18. Hoboken: John Wiley and Sons.

Diana, Antonella. 2013. "The Experimental Governing of Mobility and Trade on the China-Laos Frontier: The Tai Lue Case". *Singapore Journal of Tropical Geography* 34, no. 1: 25–39.

Dwyer, Michael. 2007. *Turning Land into Capital. A Review of Recent Research on Land Concessions for Investment in the Lao PDR*. Vientiane: Land Information Working Group (LIWG).

———, and Thoumthone Vongvisouk. 2017. "The Long Land Grab: Market-assisted Enclosure on the China-Lao Rubber Frontier". *Territory, Politics, Governance* 7, no. 1: 96–114.

Endres, Kirsten W. 2015. "Constructing the Neighbourly 'Other': Trade Relations and Mutual Perceptions across the Vietnam-China Border". *SOJOURN: Journal of Social Issues in Southeast Asia* 30, no. 3: 710–41.

Evrard, Olivier. 1997. "The New Villages of Luang Namtha Province". In *Resettlement and Social Characteristics of New Villages: Basic Needs for Resettled*

Communities in the Lao PDR, edited by Yves Goudineau, pp. 5–46. Vientiane: UNESCO-UNDP.

Friis, Cecilie, and Jonas Østergaard Nielsen. 2016. "Small-Scale Land Acquisitions, Large-Scale Implications: Exploring the Case of Chinese Banana Investments in Northern Laos". *Land Use Policy* 57: 117–29.

Giersch, C. Patterson. 2006. *Asian Borderlands: The Transformation of Qing China's Yunnan Frontier*. Cambridge: Harvard University Press.

GIZ. 2020. *Tropical Fresh Fruit Exporter's Guide to China: A Market Research Report for Local Agri-businesses in Cambodia, Lao PDR, and Vietnam*. Bonn and Eschborn: Deutsche Gesellschaft für Internationale Zusammenarbeit (GIZ).

Grabowsky, Volker, and Renoo Wichasin. 2008. *Chronicles of Chiang Khaeng: A Tai Lü Principality of the Upper Mekong Region*. Honolulu: Center for Southeast Asian Studies, University of Hawai'i.

High, Holly. 2013. "Experimental Consensus: Negotiating with the Irrigating State in the South of Laos". *Asian Studies Review* 37, no. 4: 491–508.

Kenney-Lazar, Miles, Mike Dwyer, and Cornelia Hett. 2018. *Turning Land into Capital: Assessing Ten Plus Years of Policy in Practice*. Vientiane: LIWG (Land Information Working Group).

Kubo, Koji, and Shozo Sakata. 2018. "Chapter 1: Impact of China's Increasing Demand for Agro Produce on Agricultural Production in the Mekong Region". In *Impact of China's Increasing Demand for Agro Produce on Agricultural Production in the Mekong Region*, edited by Koji Kubo and Shozo Sakata. Bangkok: Bangkok Research Center, JETRO Bangkok/IDE-JETRO. https://www.ide.go.jp/library/English/Publish/Reports/Brc/pdf/21_01.pdf (accessed 1 October 2021).

Laungaramsri, Pinkaew. 2012. "Frontier Capitalism and the Expansion of Rubber Plantations in Southern Laos". *Journal of Southeast Asian Studies* 43, no. 3: 463–77.

———. 2015. "Commodifying Sovereignty: Special Economic Zones and the Neoliberalization of the Lao Frontier". In *Impact of China's Rise on the Mekong Region*, edited by Yos Santasombat, pp. 117–46. New York: Palgrave Macmillan.

Lei, Lei. 2018. "A General Review of China's Fruit Import Status". In *Impact of China's Increasing Demand for Agro Produce on Agricultural Production in the Mekong Region*, edited by Koji Kubo and Shozo Sakata, Ch 2. Bangkok: Bangkok Research Center, JETRO Bangkok/IDE-JETRO. https://www.ide.go.jp/library/English/Publish/Reports/Brc/pdf/21_02.pdf (accessed 1 October 2021).

Li, Yunxia. 2018. "In-between Poppy and Rubber Fields: Experimenting a Transborder Livelihood among the Akha in the Northwestern Frontier of Laos". In *Trans-Himalayan Borderlands: Livelihoods, Territorialities, Modernities*, edited by Dan Smyer Yü and Jean Michaud, pp. 243–62. Amsterdam: Amsterdam University Press.

Lyttleton, Chris, and Yunxia Li. 2017. "Rubber's Affective Economies: Seeding a Social Landscape in Northwest Laos". In *Changing Lives in Laos: Society, Politics, and Culture in a Post-Socialist State*, edited by Vanina Bouté and Vatthana Pholsena, pp. 301–24. Singapore: NUS Press.

──────, and Pál Nyíri. 2011. "Dams, Casinos and Concessions: Chinese Megaprojects in Laos and Cambodia". In *Engineering Earth: The Impacts of Megaengineering Projects*, edited by Stanley D. Brunn, pp. 1243–65. London, New York: Springer.

──────, Houmphanh Rattanavong, Bouakham Thongkhamhane, and Souriyanh Sisaengrat. 2004. *Watermelons, Bars and Trucks: Dangerous Intersections in Northwest Lao PDR*. Vientiane: Institute of Cultural Research of Laos and Macquarie University.

Nolintha, Vanthana. 2018. "Lao PDR's Fruit Production for Export: A Case Study of Watermelon in Luangnamtha Province". In *Impact of China's Increasing Demand for Agro Produce on Agricultural Production in the Mekong Region*, edited by Koji Kubo and Shozo Sakata, Ch 3. Bangkok: Bangkok Research Center, JETRO Bangkok/IDE-JETRO. https://www.ide.go.jp/library/English/Publish/Download/Brc/pdf/21_03.pdf (accessed 1 October 2021).

Rowedder, Simon. 2019. "Railroading Land-linked Laos: China's Regional Profits, Laos' Domestic Costs?". *Eurasian Geography and Economics* 61, no. 2: 152–61.

──────. 2020a. "'I Didn't Learn Any Occupation, So I Trade': Untold Stories of Transnational Entrepreneurial Experimentation in Northern Laos". *SOJOURN: Journal of Social Issues in Southeast Asia* 35, no. 1: 31–64.

──────. 2020b. "Understanding China's BRI in Northern Laos". *Business Times*, 13 January 2020. https://www.businesstimes.com.sg/asean-business/understanding-chinas-bri-in-laos (accessed 1 October 2021).

──────. 2022. *Cross-Border Traders in Northern Laos: Mastering Smallness*. Amsterdam: Amsterdam University Press.

Santasombat, Yos. 2019. "Rent Capitalism and Shifting Plantations in the Mekong Borderlands". *Southeast Asian Affairs 2019*, edited by Daljit Singh and Malcolm Cook, pp. 177–91. Singapore: ISEAS – Yusof Ishak Institute.

Saxer, Martin, and Juan Zhang, eds. 2017. *The Art of Neighbouring: Making Relations Across China's Borders*. Amsterdam: Amsterdam University Press.

Singh, Bhrigupati. 2011. "Agonistic Intimacy and Moral Aspiration in Popular Hinduism: A Study in the Political Theology of the Neighbour". *American Ethnologist* 38, no. 3: 430–50.

Straits Times. 2019. "Made-in-China' Durians: Thailand's Trade Office Warns of Future Competition". 7 September 2019. https://www.straitstimes.com/asia/se-asia/made-in-china-durians-thailands-trade-office-warns-of-future-competition (accessed 1 October 2021).

Sturgeon, Janet C. 2013. "Cross-Border Rubber Cultivation between China and Laos: Regionalization by Akha and Tai Rubber Farmers". *Singapore Journal of Tropical Geography* 34, no. 1: 70–85.

Sun, Yun. 2017. "Winning Projects and Hearts? Three Cases of Chinese Mega-Infrastructure Projects in Southeast Asia". *The Asan Forum Special Forum*, September–October 2017. http://www.theasanforum.org/category/special-forum/?dat=September%20%E2%80%93%20October,%202017 (accessed 1 October 2021).

Tan, Danielle. 2014. "Chinese Networks, Economic and Territorial Redefinitions in Northern Lao PDR". In *Transnational Dynamics in Southeast Asia: The Greater Mekong Subregion and Malacca Straits Economic Corridor*, edited by Nathalie Fau, Sirivanh Khonthapane, and Christian Taillard, pp. 421–52. Singapore: Institute of Southeast Asian Studies.

Taylor, Philip. 2016. "Frontier Commoditisation in Post-Socialist Southeast Asia". *Asia Pacific Viewpoint* 57, no. 2: 145–53.

Theparat, Chatrudee. 2020. "China Demand Spiking for Thai Durian". *Bangkok Post*, 27 July 2020. https://www.bangkokpost.com/business/1958175/china-demand-spiking-for-thai-durian (accessed 1 October 2021).

Tsing, Anna L. 2005. *Friction: An Ethnography of Global Connection*. Princeton: Princeton University Press.

Walker, Andrew. 1999. *The Legend of the Golden Boat: Regulation, Trade and Traders in the Borderlands of Laos, Thailand, China and Burma*. Honolulu: University of Haiwai'i Press.

Wirakunthewan, Sophida. 2005. *Chiang Khong: chatiphan lae kankha thi chaidaen*. [Chiang Khong: Ethnicity and Trade at the Border]. Bangkok: The Thailand Research Fund.

Xinhua. 2020. "Across China: Tropical Fruits Grow Ripe on Arid Land". 6 July 2020. http://www.xinhuanet.com/english/2020-07/06/c_139192155.htm (accessed 1 October 2021).

5

COMMODITY FRONTIERS IN MOTION

Tracing the Maize Boom across the Lao-Vietnamese Borderlands

Robert Cole

"If all of you only grow rice, you cannot get out of poverty."—Farmer, Ban Phoukhao (citing maize trader).

INTRODUCTION

We met the *naiban* (village head) on a cool morning near his field hut, at the foot of the hills surrounding Ban Homphou, Houaphan province, Laos. The hut overlooked paddy fields to which the *naiban's* wife was piping water from the nearby stream, a tributary of the *Nam Ma*, enabling them to produce two rice crops per year, as with the handful of other households in the village with paddy land. This provided his family with about 20 sacks of rice for consumption, but much of the limited paddy area in the village had been damaged by heavy erosion further up the mountain slopes during the previous rainy season, resulting from consecutive seasons of monoculture maize. The loss of paddy land had contributed to a general expansion of upland rice and maize in the village, to compensate for lost wet-rice production, signifying the extent to which the commodity crop of maize had become insinuated within formerly subsistence-oriented livelihoods. The first job of the day was to sharpen the *"pa"* (Figure 5.1), hooked machetes we then used to clear a maize field on the hillside above us. The field was covered with thick brush, as the *naiban* planted the land with maize every second year with a one-year fallow, which he found marginally more productive than continuous cropping. As we worked, the *naiban* spoke of how many households in the village had become increasingly reliant on maize: "The main product here is maize now, if people have to stop growing maize, they don't know what to do."

FIGURE 5.1
Sharpening Tools for Clearing a Maize Field, Ban Homphou.

Source: Photo taken by the author, March 2017.

This chapter examines the circumstances behind the initiation of commercial maize in the mid-2000s in two villages near the mountainous border between Houaphan province, Laos and Son La province, Vietnam, upon which the *naiban* and households had come to consider themselves dependent by the time of this research. The analysis that follows was informed throughout by a multi-sited study conducted from 2016 to 2018, comprising a household component in the two study villages, with periods of participant observation throughout the maize production cycle, random-sampled ($n=30$ per village) household surveys, purposive-sampled key informant interviews (nineteen per village) and gender-specific focus group discussions (three per village). The second methodological component focused on the maize/feed production network, including thirty-eight key informant interviews with government agencies, a network of traders, processors and other private sector actors, as well as researchers and non-governmental organizations (NGOs). The network interviews took place in Yen Chau district, Son La province and Hanoi, Vietnam; and Xiengkhor district, Houaphan province and Vientiane, Laos. The research sought to understand: (i) the formation and evolution of the maize network in the Lao-Vietnamese borderlands; and (ii) the social and landscape outcomes of maize among smallholder farmers.[1]

The two villages are referred to under the pseudonyms of *Ban* ("village") *Homphou* ("valley"), a low to midland village with a dominant Tai Daeng ethnic population and Phou Tai and Ksingmul minorities, and *Ban Phoukhao* ("mountain peak"), a Black Hmong village below the peak that creates the watershed shared by the two villages, as well as forming the porous border between Laos and Vietnam. Both villages had experienced rapid livelihood transitions in the decade preceding the study, from primarily subsistence rice farming before 2006, to increasingly commercially oriented livelihoods combining rice with hybrid maize thereafter. The villages cultivated landraces of upland swidden rice (with limited wet rice in Homphou), and traditional glutinous maize varieties for consumption and feeding animals. Limited cash sales of surpluses (along with opium in Phoukhao) and livestock were quickly superseded as maize came to dominate the landscape. In the process, these formerly remote locations became enmeshed within widening market relations, transforming not only local livelihoods but the physical landscape around them.

To understand the beginnings of this transformation it is necessary to consider trends underway in both Laos and Vietnam which created the preconditions for a regionalized agri-food system. The following sections show how the initiation of maize in Houaphan province entailed a convergence of policy- and socio-economic trajectories spanning the Lao-Vietnamese borderlands, extending from the market reforms and state efforts to draw foreign investment while fostering commercial, intensive and sedentary agricultural practices. Notwithstanding historic policy and political influence between the two socialist allies, these trajectories can be viewed as proceeding largely independently of one another up to the early 2000s. At this point, the intersection of policy and market trends in Laos and Vietnam gave rise to the maize network across Houaphan and Son La provinces, including the study sites.

Intrinsic to this policy frame is a broader frontier assemblage, a space in which "the expansive nature of extraction comes into its own" (Tsing 2005, p. 27), where remote uplands are redrawn as zones of commodity production, absorbing marginal landscapes and peoples into expanding spatial networks of accumulation. For Cons and Eilenberg (2019, p. 2), the term "frontier assemblage" is both descriptive and analytic, referring to "the intertwined materialities, actors, cultural logics, spatial dynamics, ecologies, and political economic processes that produce particular places as resource frontiers". The Lao uplands have come to represent an archetypal resource frontier since the 2000s amid a meteoric rise of land- and resource-focused investments, particularly from China, Thailand and Vietnam, covering large tracts of the Lao countryside (Barney 2009; Bouté and Pholsena 2017). It is a frontier that has been actively forged through policies courting foreign investments, on the one hand, to fulfil development objectives of economic growth and modernization, and on the other to control and harness peripheral space into "productive" use (Barney 2009; Hirsch and Scurrah 2015; see also contributions to this volume by Ponce, Rowedder, Suhardiman and Kramp, and Tappe). Mediated by local power geometries and spurred on by the post-2008 land rush and government emphasis on "Turning Land Into Capital", land concessions came to cover more than 1 million ha in Laos, including agriculture, plantations, and operational mining and hydropower (Dwyer 2011; Ingalls et al. 2018). More recently, social and environmental impacts, instances of dispute and political contestations have prompted shifts in policy, including periodic suspensions of concessions, albeit with inconsistent outcomes (MRLG 2017; Cole and Ingalls 2020). Meanwhile, other forms of agribusiness have continued to rapidly expand into the uplands, including cross-border contract farming arrangements, often for large downstream companies (Manorom et al. 2011; Cole 2021, 2022). Swept up in this advancing commodity frontier, the productive potential of the Lao countryside has thus been captured both directly through processes of accumulation by dispossession (notably concessions), and indirectly through accumulation without dispossession, such as contract farming and the promotion of commercial crops (Cole and Rigg 2019), as this chapter explores.

ORIGINS OF THE MAIZE FRONTIER

Understanding the preconditions to initiation of maize at the two study sites in Laos requires as a starting point considering policy and socio-economic trajectories underway at the time of its uptake on both sides of the Lao-Vietnamese border. In Laos, two interlinked policy objectives with particular influence over the uplands were firstly ongoing efforts to foster a transition from subsistence swidden to sedentary and intensive commercial farming, and secondly, sharpening government and international focus on opium eradication at the turn of the millennium. Simultaneously, market reforms magnified the already significant gravitational pull of the Vietnamese economy over Northeast Laos, particularly based on the investment of foreign firms in the industrialization of key agricultural subsectors in Vietnam. This created soaring demand for maize from which a network of enterprising traders sought to profit.

As can be observed throughout Southeast Asia, from the perspective of Lao policymakers, agricultural modernization through the application of new technologies and, following the market reforms, commercially oriented production, has long been viewed as the cornerstone of rural development. In the Lao uplands, the rotational swidden practices relied on by most farmers have been historically at odds with state ideals of a modern agricultural sector due to discursive association with poverty, environmental degradation and "backwardness" (Hirsch 2000; Baird and Shoemaker 2007; Hett et al. 2011). Laos' pursuit of foreign agribusiness investments in its upland frontiers has from this perspective been one element in a wider strategy to promote sedentary, intensive farming as a "way out" of traditional practices deemed to hold back rural development ideals and the improvement of living conditions (GoL 2004). A senior respondent from a Lao research institution depicted the meeting point between state policies and private investment in commodity crops such as maize as follows:

> During the 1990s, the government had a policy to enhance agricultural production in Laos in different ways. They opened [the economy] and they were seeking [investment] ... to promote commodity crops, to enhance economic development, to make people's livelihoods better, and at the same time, they were also thinking about how to make people *produce more* rather than just going to the forest and collecting [timber and non-timber forest products (NTFPs)] .... They also developed national policies to support these activities.

Amid the advancing wave of commercialization, maize had already been given increasing priority in agricultural policies since the late 1990s as the government observed booming demand in neighbouring markets, and began to feature in the five-year National Socioeconomic Development Plans (NSEDP) for the agriculture and forestry sectors. The 6th NSEDP (2006–10) noted a threefold increase in the maize production area in Laos from 2000 to 2005, with hotspots in the northwest (bordering Thailand) and northeast (bordering Vietnam) provinces. The plan also called on state agricultural agencies nationwide to "focus on the plantation of certain industrial crops based on the potential of each region to increase export volumes," including maize, as well as to prioritize the adoption of high-yielding hybrid varieties (CPI 2006, p. 134). Although landrace sweetcorn had previously been a common food and fodder crop among rural households, the adoption of hybrid maize signified a shift towards such an export-oriented industrial crop, with almost all of Laos' targeted maize output intended for neighbouring markets. Export-oriented production was in turn greatly enabled by contract farming arrangements, which have helped to extend commodity crops further into marginal spaces, connecting cross-border traders with farmers, financing conversion to new practices and fulfilling absent supply linkages, as observed by a Houaphan provincial official:

> When [Vietnamese] businessmen came to Samneua to support farmers for [contract] maize production ... it just boomed [and] changed household

production from consumption to commercial purposes ... Since then, we can observe the maize production has highly increased, of course the [area] of forest destruction also rapidly increased at the same time.

These observations capture several key facets of the frontier assemblage that brackets the formation of the maize network: the pivotal role of opportunistic Vietnamese traders crossing into Laos in search of "available" land and labour; the rebalance from semi-subsistence to commercial production by Lao farmers, in some ways meeting policy objectives to sedentarize former "nomadic" practices; and landscape impacts which would later affect the viability of livelihoods as production reached its peak (Cole 2022). At the point of the initiation of the maize network, however, a second policy trend fostered the receptiveness of households at the study sites to a new, and importantly licit, commodity crop. An exemplar of the "lawless" imaginary of frontier regions, the ongoing illicit cultivation of opium was the antithesis of the Lao government's goal of modern, commercial farming in the uplands, viewed by state and international organizations alike as produced and consumed by "the poorest of the poor, living in some of the most remote and under-developed areas of northern Laos" (Chansina 2008, p. 37). Opium was thus wielded in policy discourse as symbolic of "primitiveness and backwardness ... a fetishized cause of poverty" (Cohen 2013, p. 177), and an obstacle to development (Lu 2017). The 1990s intensification of the global "War on Drugs" saw Laos' progressive cooperation with US and UN efforts to suppress opium as part of conditional aid flows (Cohen 2009, 2013), targeting the elimination of opium by 2005 (UNODC 2015).

This gave farmers a few short years to abandon opium before the state started applying punitive measures—a complex task given its entrenched role in the subsistence economy, numerous medicinal uses for humans and livestock, and the common reality of addiction among producing communities (Epprecht 2000; Cohen 2013). Respondents in Ban Phoukhao described how almost all households had at some time produced opium before the ban, and that "men came from other places to buy [opium] here", although the crop provided little income, and many more people consumed it locally than bought it from villagers. A member of a former opium-producing household estimated that "the average income from opium for a household was about VND5 million [US$345 at historic exchange rates] per year at that time [2002–3, the last years of production in the village], which people used to support their families." Public communication and education campaigns had started in 2001 to strengthen awareness of the illegality of opium in all provinces, followed by government raids to seize poppy seeds, order the destruction of crops and impose fines for non-compliance (Chansina 2008; Cohen 2009). The experience of the campaign in Ban Phoukhao, which began in 2001 and finished with the final abandonment of production by 2003, was depicted by a respondent as follows: "By 2001, the government was already stopping opium, so people could not grow it anymore …. Government staff came to this village and cleared the opium fields and destroyed it, but they paid some money to the farmers because they knew we had no other income."

Although the eradication campaign was intended to provide alternative development to support food security and alleviate poverty, this was unevenly delivered, and the impacts of the loss of opium income in Laos included food shortages, migration and livestock stress sales (Cohen 2009; Htun 2018). A joint survey between the Lao government and UNODC in 2005 showed that only 50 per cent of more than 2,000 villages which had produced opium in 1998 received alternative development assistance (Chansina 2008). Respondents in the present research reported that no livelihood initiatives or infrastructure improvements were provided for opium growers with the campaign, highlighting the removal of income with no foreseeable replacement cash crop, and "from 2003 until about 2005 there was no opium and also no road [to the villages], so living conditions were very hard at that time." This finds parallels with Vietnam's opium suppression efforts, succeeding in a 98 per cent decline in production from 1990 to 2001, via a combination of tighter state control over and surveillance of opium-producing regions,[2] and a range of conditional development support including infrastructure and agricultural extension. Coverage was similarly patchy in Vietnam in terms of livelihood support, including the introduction of alternative cash crops, though living conditions and food security were observed to improve in some former opium-producing locations (Windle 2012).

After the final eradication of opium in Phoukhao in 2003, farmers gained what minimal income they could, sometimes only bartering for salt, through the transport of traditional sweetcorn varieties for sale across the border in Vietnam, carried by packhorse and buffalo across the mountains. Retracing the same tracks, the first Vietnamese trader visited the villages shortly thereafter, in 2005, offering a kind of informal alternative development in the absence of official government support, depicted by a respondent in Phoukhao as follows:

> After clearing the opium, nobody had any knowledge about how to do anything else and the government did not show us how to do anything, so it was the Vietnamese who showed us. We learned all the techniques for growing maize from Vietnam, including the spacing, how many seeds to plant, when to plant, when to use fertilizer.

The slopes cultivated by farmers at both study sites provided adequate conditions for hybrid varieties, and the chance of a new income source. Maize thus became not only an opium replacement crop, but the first fully commercial crop through which households in both villages could access stable income, seemingly delivering the commercialization of livelihoods envisioned in policy as the means to absorb frontier populations into a "modern" rural economy. Over the same period in Laos' northern borderlands with China, the shortcomings of official alternative development efforts had been subsumed by China's Opium Replacement Policy in largely similar circumstances, though focused on state-subsidized efforts to introduce commercial rubber to former opium-producing villages (Lu 2017; Htun 2018). Cohen (2009) observes that the resulting take-off of rubber as an opium replacement crop in the Lao-Chinese borderlands in 2003–4 was enabled by the convergence of soaring demand in China and an urgent need for a cash crop to substitute opium income in Laos, as well as a resourceful network of private business actors. The circumstances prior to the initiation of the maize network in Laos' northeast borderlands followed a strikingly comparable path, though without state subsidies as in the Chinese case, and triggered by Vietnam's agricultural restructuring and explosive demand for maize.

THE MAIZE AND ANIMAL FEED COMPLEX IN NORTHWEST VIETNAM

The trajectory of maize expansion in northwest Vietnam embodies the country's parallel market and agrarian transitions, with farmers at the leading edge of reforms in private production that preceded decollectivization, and the rapid commercialization of agriculture that followed under *Doi Moi*. The shift from cooperative to household-based production occurred in tandem with the beginnings of industrialization of certain agricultural subsectors from the late 1980s through the 1990s. These included animal feed, livestock and poultry, as the government sought to catalyse rural growth by opening to foreign investors. Soon after Vietnam's reforms were formally initiated in 1986, a Vietnamese delegation had visited Thailand to call for investments. The Thai agri-food conglomerate Charoen Pokphand Foods (CP) foresaw huge growth in animal feed and livestock on the back of the reforms, establishing a representative office in 1988 to study market potential. Key opportunities were observed in the cultivation of feed crops and feed processing to support the anticipated rise in meat consumption that was likely to accompany wider economic growth. The corporation received a permit to establish its Vietnamese subsidiary, CP Vietnam, in 1993, and followed a sequential investment strategy to track the evolving market, introducing its core business of high-yielding seeds and agricultural inputs, and subsequently expanding into feed production.

This had clear parallels with CP's strategy in its home market of Thailand, fostering maize intensification for its own feed mills and later livestock and poultry, and controlling value enhancement and capture across different production stages amid soaring demand for meat, as economic growth began to take off in the late 1980s (Goss, Burch, and Rickson 2000). A markedly similar scenario was triggered by market reforms and agricultural restructuring in Vietnam. However, for feed production in Vietnam to expand at a similar pace as in Thailand, CP and its initial competitors in the Vietnamese market in the early 1990s were dependent on Vietnamese farmers to significantly intensify maize production and meet the demand for raw materials. As was the case in Laos, landrace sweetcorn had long been cultivated on a household basis in the Vietnamese uplands for human consumption and to support pig and poultry raising. Once *Doi Moi* gathered pace in the 1990s, farmland became increasingly constrained in the more productive lowland regions, such as the Red River Delta, which also continued to prioritize wet rice according to government requirements, and improved domestic maize varieties were introduced to the mountainous Northwest to help increase overall production.

With the initial strategy of introducing high-yielding varieties to stimulate interest in maize among Vietnamese smallholders, thereby achieving the needed critical mass of raw commodities to build a feed industry, CP and other lead firms had a transformative impact on production practices in the early 1990s. Farmers abandoned traditional varieties in favour of new hybrids, up to tripling yields from about 2 tons/ha to 5–6 tons/ha, thereby enabling the rapid growth of the feed sector. From the mid-1990s, according to a seed company representative, "hybrids changed the game of the whole industry [and] totally changed the way farmers produce maize." Commercial maize was adopted throughout northwest Vietnam, and national acreage increased from 600,000 ha in the 1990s to 1.1 million ha at the time of the present study. Son La province quickly became the epicentre of the advancing commodity frontier, and according to a government crop production official, "the [national] capital for maize, and it helped to reduce poverty, especially when people could make profit due to the high price".

As observed by an international researcher, maize proved enticing for farmers in marginal upland areas of Vietnam because of the perception of guaranteed profits, after decades of extreme hardship, and a limitless market: "As long as there is a market the farmers will always go for it, even if there are relatively large capital investment requirements, farmers will find a way to overcome these if there is strong enough demand." The high prices farmers enjoyed during this period were due to short supply in a rapidly expanding feed sector, in which CP gained an increasingly dominant position in the northwest, as observed by an agronomist:

> The big [trigger] was when CP came in Ha Tay town and built this huge processing plant ... it's in Hanoi [but] just on the border with Hoa Binh ... they're positioned there so all major roads to the Northwest where there's maize production, they're all coming and passing there. So they have very good strategic positions there.

The seemingly unquenchable demand and perception of livelihood benefits among farmers, particularly relative to rice production, helped to drive the maize frontier across the northwest, and incrementally towards the border with Laos. A Vietnamese government researcher depicted the progressive conversion to maize as follows:

When the price was really good, the production area in the northwest was already reaching the maximum, because they destroyed 100 per cent of the forest, and [traders] continued to open to Laos ... the collectors, traders, mostly Kinh people from the [Red River] Delta coming to the northwest, and also to the border, Moc Chau, going to Laos ... Xiengkhouang province, Houaphan, they passed the border and they also recommend[ed] the hybrid seeds ... that was about 2005, that means after the boom for maize in Vietnam, but when the area was limited, traders continued to Laos.

Across the Lao-Vietnamese border in Houaphan, a steady flow of Vietnamese investors, some former farmers, others experienced traders in Vietnam, began arriving in neighbouring districts seeking opportunities to invest in maize production.

AGENTS OF FRONTIERIZATION: HOW CROSS-BORDER TRADERS LINKED LAO HOUSEHOLDS TO THE VIETNAMESE FEED SECTOR

Traders are in all senses the lynchpins of the maize/feed network, chasing opportunities and forging connections with new production areas, often where farmers are otherwise physically disconnected from markets, including across borders (see Rowedder, this volume, for the similar central role of cross-border traders in establishing and sustaining a "fruit frontier" in the borderlands of China, Laos and Thailand). Maize traders thus have a unique perspective as the direct, grassroots agents of frontierization amid wider state and regional trends in agri-food systems and rural policy and investment trajectories. Among the respondents of the study, some traders had accumulated experiences of rural change in Vietnam across several generations, their families having moved to the northwest under long-running state efforts since the 1950s to ease population pressures in the Red River Delta, by promoting settlement and cultivation of marginal frontier regions (referred to as "taming the uplands", Hardy 2000). Those with such long-term experiential knowledge identified the switch to commercial maize as following shortly after the end of centralized planning in the agricultural sector in the mid-1980s, before which maize for human and animal consumption could not be sold, but only exchanged for rice. With the gathering pace of *Doi Moi*, as farming became market-oriented, maize spread across Son La during the 1990s–2000s. A trader in Moc Chau district observed that the first step was the rapid increase in productivity from the introduction of hybrids, followed by the expansion of foreign feed companies after the early 1990s. This move in particular shifted the scale of demand in the eyes of traders, though at first the feed mills only bought maize locally, as there were no processing capabilities in the still-isolated mountain districts.

Mr Giang (pseudonym), the maize trader working in Ban Homphou at the time of the research, was part of a later procession of internal migrants to Vietnam's upland frontier; *Doi Moi* economic opportunists "hoping to get rich in a region recently described in the lowlands as a 'promised land'" (Hardy 2000, p. 22). Giang first moved from the Red River Delta province of Hung Yen to Moc Chau district, Son La province, in 1998 where he and his young family struggled for a couple of years selling vegetables and working in a dairy cooperative. As people from his hometown began relocating to Son La in increasing numbers in search of land and opportunities, particularly in Yen Chau district near the border with Laos, Giang and his family decided to follow them. The trader described his early experiences there:

> Many young people were moving from Hung Yen to Son La province then, and a lot of people moved to Yen Chau ... Sometimes people would come to visit Moc Chau and they saw that it was hard to make a living and my family faced many difficulties, so they encouraged me to move to Yen Chau and make a new start. We moved [there] in 2001, but at that time had no land ... to earn a living we transported food from Moc Chau to sell in the market in Yen Chau, and sold food to a construction company that was building the new road to the border, and also Vietnamese soldiers who were based at the border checkpoint with Laos. We were selling food to the border soldiers for about seven years and during this time I made friends with Lao people who invited me to visit Laos ... That is when I saw opportunities to invest and do business [in Laos].

Although yet to be initiated at the study sites in Laos, maize contract farming was already well established in Son La province by the time Giang moved to Yen Chau in 2001, as the Vietnamese feed sector continued to expand. However, in the 1990s, transporting maize from production areas around Son La province was fraught with difficulties due to the poor mountain roads, and many villages could only be reached with durable Soviet-era military trucks (see Figure 5.2). This

FIGURE 5.2
Maize Truck, Ban Homphou

Source: Photo taken by the author, March 2017.

would equally prove to be the case on the Lao side of the border once the network had been extended there.

CP was the favoured buyer among traders as they would purchase any quantity, and the strategic position of the CP feed mill at the intersection of northern trunk routes made it the easiest to reach in the region. Small traders were soon handling hundreds of tons per day in the early 2000s during the peak harvest period in northwest Vietnam, typically between July and August, and some became increasingly interested in investing across the border in Laos. As is central within the frontier imaginary, traders also considered that Laos held advantages due to the relative "availability" of virgin land across the mountainous border, compared to the tightening supply and falling soil productivity in Vietnam, increasing costs of further maize expansion domestically. As traders and processors were often previously farmers themselves, they commonly sought out strategic niches in the transport, supply or processing of maize that were not at the time covered by other competitors, utilizing productive assets or savings to purchase equipment, plug gaps, or otherwise find solutions to production constraints. One such pioneering farmer-cum-trader, who started buying maize across the Lao border in 2000, had been working as a road-building contractor in Houaphan province when he identified the opportunity:

> We built some of the local roads in Laos, so I saw a lot of potential for maize production and trade and started to invest in maize there. People on the Lao side were starting to produce maize on a large scale from about 2000. In each village we invested by providing seeds and loans to help the farmers start growing, then we made contracts with the farmers to produce for us. At first, transport was difficult because the roads to the villages were so bad, so we started building more roads to make it easier to transport the maize.

Before the expansion of a network of maize feeder roads, farmers in some locations of Xiengkhor district on the Lao side, including the study sites, were better connected to the adjacent Vietnamese district of Yen Chau than the neighbouring Lao villages or district centres. A respondent in Ban Homphou noted that maize contracts were initiated later at the study sites, with the first trader visiting in 2005, than in surrounding villages in Xiengkhor district because of the lack of road access, including the absence of a bridge over the Nam Ma at the time, separating the villages from the wider district where maize was quickly expanding from the early 2000s. This is confirmed by Giang's description of his first forays into Laos as a trader, supplying farm tools that villagers were too cut off to conveniently source from markets on the Lao side, before taking on maize contracts from the end of 2007, highlighting the remoteness of the villages at the time:

> It was easy to cross the mountains into Laos, but there was no bridge over the Ma river at that time, so it was easier for the Lao villagers to work with us [than the local district economy in Laos] .... I started by selling fertilizers, chemical sprayers and rice mills, and the farmers would pay with maize production after the harvest, so that's how I started trading maize up to now.

This remoteness gave the traders willing to make the journey a significant power advantage over farmers, and thereby profits at the primary stages of production and processing. A handful of Vietnamese traders divided amongst themselves the different areas they worked in around Xiengkhor and the neighbouring Sopbao district, where they could transport maize directly across the border. The lack of provincial information on areas with suitable growing conditions meant that the traders often visited district authorities directly and requested to make contracts at the village level. Once they achieved district approval, traders would travel to the provincial capital of Samneua to register with various government offices to gain licences to conduct business in Laos and export to Vietnam. Numerous contract systems were initiated throughout Houaphan province in the early 2000s, based on the so-called "2+3" model, in which farmers contribute land and labour, and traders contribute imported inputs, technical advice and connection to the market (Manorom et al. 2011; Higashi 2015; for contract farming schemes in the case of rubber in Laos, see also Suhardiman's and Kramp's contribution to this volume). Vietnamese traders disseminated knowledge on planting techniques including timing and spacing among Lao farmers to help them get started, providing a form of unofficial agricultural extension as detailed above, and introducing the key ingredient of hybrid seeds. The distance of the study sites from a paved road meant that villagers depended on the trader to purchase output and to build and maintain the feeder roads each year, as expressed by the Homphou village committee: "We have to sell to him. [Giang] also lends farmers money so they need to repay him ... the whole village depends on one seven-ton truck that takes the maize to Vietnam, across the border to Yen Chau district." This highlights the reliance of the villagers on the trader in terms of 'plugging in' to the wider maize network, while Giang avoided damaging competition with other traders by working in difficult to reach locations.

THE MAIZE FRONTIER IN BAN HOMPHOU AND BAN PHOUKHAO

Before the arrival of commercial maize, livelihoods in Ban Homphou and Ban Phoukhao were largely subsistence-oriented and separated to some degree from the nearest district economies. Although for the most part operating outside of a cash economy, households would occasionally sell rice surpluses and livestock in the district markets, or in the case of Phoukhao, limited opium production, to provide for their families what they could not produce from the land. As summarized by a Houphan provincial government official, in the mountains where the two villages are located: "Before, farmers were only focused on upland rice, and maybe NTFPs ... there was no commercial production here before maize—none." Put another way, although it would be inaccurate to say that no cash sales were going on at all, these were so infrequent and small as to be essentially invisible to the state. Respondents commonly portrayed the (perhaps in some instances, idealized) abundance of past times, including land that was "free to clear", connecting shrinking land availability to intensifying cultivation and population pressures (see also Ponce, this volume).

In both villages, most respondents described the first trader visiting the village head in 2005, to explain how to produce maize and discuss contract arrangements, who then discussed the system with the villagers to find out who wanted to join. They subsequently relied on the village head to deal with the trader and negotiate contract agreements on their behalf at the start of each growing season. As has been observed in other studies of contract maize in Laos, after gaining approval of the village committee and district authorities, the first practical step towards operationalizing the maize contracts was the construction of dirt access roads to the villages and maize fields, as farmers began to cultivate the crop (Vagneron and Kousonsavath 2015; Castella and Phaipasith 2021). A respondent in Phoukhao recalled that "when the Vietnamese trader came, he told us that 'if all of you only grow rice, you cannot get out of poverty, I would like you to grow maize and I will build a road for you.'" The village head of Ban Phoukhao elaborates on this as follows:

> Before [the road] this village was almost impossible to reach by vehicle, and most people walked up the mountain to get here. As well as the "main road" down to the valley, all the feeder roads around the village to different cultivation areas were cut by Vietnamese investors, and the villagers would then repay this over time with part of the maize harvest. The Vietnamese also invested here in other ways, preparing farmland and also the foundations for the primary school.

Estimates of annual household repayments for the road were inconsistent, but some reported paying around VND200,000 (US$9.09), while it was understood by villagers that road-building had cost around VND20,000,000 (US$909) per km, stretching 7 km from Homphou to

Phoukhao alone. Given that traders had cut and maintained feeder roads to numerous surrounding production areas, the time periods of the contracts seemed likely to extend, and as a village deputy put it, "for five years every household has been required to grow maize to pay for that". Once road access had been achieved, the incentive for the entire village to convert to maize production was strong, as the price doubled during the first three cropping seasons, as explained by the Homphou village committee:

> The [initial] price was 500 kip [LAK in international currency code]/kg (US$62.50/ton), and this increased to 700 kip/kg (US$87.50/ton) the next year, before a fixed price was agreed [after] 2006 of 1,000 kip/kg (US$125/ton). This price did not change regardless of the market. Some farmers could sell outside of contracts for up to 1,200 kip/kg (US$150/ton), but most settled for the stability offered by the contracts.

Similar to Homphou, the maize price offered to farmers in Phoukhao rose from LAK800–900/kg (US$112.50/ton) to LAK1,100/kg (US$137.50/ton) over the first few seasons under contract for Vietnamese traders. The slightly higher prices gained in Phoukhao compared to Homphou may have been due to the exchange rate, as farmers in Phoukhao were commonly paid in Vietnamese currency at VND3,000/kg (US$136/ton), as well as closer proximity to the border than Homphou. To commence production each season, trader Giang explained that he would visit from March to May to renew the contract with the village committees and distribute seeds during planting, and from October to December to collect the harvest and pay farmers, staying at a store he kept in Ban Homphou. He then transported the unmilled maize across the border for primary processing (milling and drying) at his depot in Yen Chau district, around two hours' drive across the mountains, before trucking and selling the bulk grain to feed mills around Hanoi, principally the CP mill which could easily buy all he supplied to them.

Giang was generally well regarded in Homphou, and his approach to the contracts always included additional incentives to "support the village", including providing building materials, tools, furniture and cooking utensils during his visits to renew the annual contracts, as well as machinery for the households such as rice mills which they repaid with the maize harvest. These gestures had come to be expected by the village committee, some of whom stated that the village would not renew the contract unless the trader provided some form of incentive in this way. Asked whether the contract might provide better terms or require less repayment to the trader if the farmers did not insist on being provided with such things, the respondent stated that the terms would be the same irrespective of the provision of 'tools', so they always required this. During his visits, Giang would also throw the occasional lunch, pay for the slaughter of a pig for the committee, and provide monetary donations to the local primary school. "Development contributions" to Ban Phoukhao by Giang's relatives seemed to be more based on accessing practical equipment for various tasks in the village, particularly construction machinery used to maintain feeder roads, dig ponds and prepare land for homes, which was sometimes loaned to the village committee. As with the lack of alternative livelihood support following the eradication of opium, the traders' contributions to the villages highlight the limited reach of state resources to frontier regions, despite the steering influence of state agricultural policies and targets detailed above (Cole 2021). How maize traders stepped in to fulfil such gaps is illustrative of their role as agents of frontierization, in constant pursuit of hidden opportunities that characterize the frontier imaginary, linking processes of extraction and production to incorporate marginal lands into regional circuits of accumulation (Cons and Eilenberg 2019).

CONCLUSION

This chapter has explored the convergence of policy trajectories, structural changes in agricultural production, and composition of actors in Laos and Vietnam which in concert triggered the rapid transition to maize across the Lao-Vietnamese borderlands. From the policy perspective, the chapter has shown how Laos' ongoing drive to commercialize and sedentarize former subsistence livelihoods and targets for export-oriented commodity production meshed with early-2000s anti-opium measures to create a basis for the uptake of a new commodity crop. In parallel, the high demand for maize in Vietnam had been catalysed by the Vietnamese government's pursuit of investment to industrialize key agricultural subsectors alongside the *Doi Moi* reforms, including animal feed, and the introduction of hybrid varieties to boost productivity. Observing major growth potential in animal feed and meat production following the reforms,

CP Vietnam and its competitors, the key arm's length economic actors in the regional system, responded with investment strategies focused on feed production and hybrid seed marketing, to kick-start the necessary maize expansion that would enable the interdependent growth of the feed sector.

Farmers in turn responded to the livelihood gains offered by hybrid varieties with an advancing maize frontier across Northwest Vietnam and towards the Lao-Vietnamese border to generate the needed material flows for the network. Households at the study sites, with very little cash income amid an increasingly market-oriented environment, including the loss of opium income without a replacement crop, reported carrying quantities of local sweetcorn across the mountain tracks to sell or barter in Vietnam. Cross-border traders were meanwhile instrumental agents of frontierization, bridging the "last miles" in the network and forming further localized networks to enrol new sites of extraction and production. In combination then, the maize network was initiated by an assemblage entailing market reforms and rural policies that set the political-economic scene for commercialization; the growth of a demand source in the industrialization of feed production spearheaded by CP Vietnam and its competitors; and the key initiators of cross-border traders linking to farmers in the search for income opportunities. The traders built feeder roads to the previously isolated study villages and production areas under informal contracts, initiating the first fully commercial crop among the formerly subsistence-oriented and primarily swidden farmers in Ban Homphou and Ban Phoukhao.

The roads built by the traders are the physical intersection that enabled the creation of new spaces of commercial production, in connecting the Lao households to the market and wider district, material flows in the form of inputs and harvested maize, and contracts to govern production and extension of credit. Although remoteness placed households at a high degree of dependence on traders, the latter were also reliant on access to commodity production, and engaging remote locations ensured a high level of control over value extraction. In this context, the traders took on quasi-"developmental" roles (Cole 2021) in terms of bringing tools and materials to villages which were previously inaccessible due to isolation; and "extensionist" roles by introducing new crops in the absence of official alternative livelihood support. Conversion to maize also dramatically affected landscapes of production through clearance of forests and degrading impacts of monoculture, though these outcomes were yet to be fully felt at the time (Cole 2022). Finally, the would-be detachment of frontier peripheries and livelihood practices from markets and urban centres was radically transformed by the arrival of contract production of commodity crops ultimately to provide for urban consumption. Maize has had far-reaching socio-economic impacts at the study villages in terms of new income streams for farmers and their families, the shift from former subsistence livelihoods to those governed by market exchange, credit and contract obligations, and the transformations brought about by the integration of frontiers within a regional commodity economy.

Notes

1. This chapter includes various extracts of the authors' doctoral thesis and related publications, in particular Cole (2021).
2. Son La province, bordering Houaphan, was among several high opium-producing provinces during the 1990s (Windle 2012).

References

Barney, Keith. 2009. "Laos and the Making of a 'Relational' Resource Frontier". *Geographical Journal* 175, no. 2: 146–59.

Baird, Ian G., and Bruce Shoemaker. 2007. "Unsettling Experiences: Internal Resettlement and International Aid Agencies in Laos". *Development and Change* 38, no. 5: 865–88.

Bouté, Vanina, and Vatthana Pholsena. 2017. *Changing Lives in Laos: Society, Politics and Culture in a Post-Socialist State*. Singapore: NUS Press.

Castella, Jean-Christophe, and Sonnasack Phaipasith. 2021. "Rural Roads Are Paving the Way for Land-Use Intensification in the Uplands of Laos". *Land* 10, no. 3: 330. https://doi.org/10.3390/land10030330 (accessed 10 October 2021).

Chansina, Kou. 2008. "Lao PDR's Experience of Sustainable Alternative Development and Opium Reduction". Paper presented at the regional seminar of Global Partnership on Alternative Development, Chiang Mai, Thailand, 15–17 December 2008.

Cohen, Paul T. 2009. "The Post-opium Scenario and Rubber in Northern Laos: Alternative Western and Chinese Models of Development". *International Journal of Drug Policy* 20: 424–30.

———. 2013. "Symbolic Dimensions of the Anti-opium Campaign in Laos". *Australian Journal of Anthropology* 24, no. 2: 177–92.

Cole, Robert. 2021. "Cashing in or Driving Development? Cross-Border Traders and Maize Contract Farming in Northeast Laos". *Journal of Agrarian Change* 22: 139–161.

———. 2022. "Prospects and Limitations of 'Responsible Agricultural Investment' for Governing Transboundary Agri-Food Systems in Mekong Southeast Asia: Implications for Upland Maize in the Lao-Vietnamese Borderlands". *Environmental Policy and Governance*.

———, and Micah L. Ingalls. 2020. "Rural Revolutions: Socialist, Market and Sustainable Development of the Countryside in Vietnam and Laos". In *The Socialist Market Economy in Asia: Development in China, Vietnam and Laos*, edited by Arve Hansen, Jo Inge Bekkevold, and Kristen Nordhaug, pp. 167–94. London: Palgrave Macmillan.

———, and Jonathan Rigg. 2019. "Lao Peasants on the Move: Pathways of Agrarian Change in Laos". *Australian Journal of Anthropology* 30, no. 2: 160–80.

Committee for Planning and Investment (CPI). 2006. National Socio-Economic Development Plan (2006–2010). Vientiane: Committee for Planning and Investment of the Lao PDR.

Cons, Jason, and Michael Eilenberg, M. 2019. *Frontier Assemblages: The Emergent Politics of Resource Frontiers in Asia*. Oxford: Wiley.

Dwyer, Michael B. 2011. "Building the Politics Machine: Tools for Resolving the Global Land Grab". Paper Presented at the International Conference on Global Land Grabbing, University of Sussex, 6–8 April 2011.

Epprecht, Michael. 2000. "Blessings of the Poppy: Opium and the Akha People of Northern Laos". *Indigenous Affairs* 4: 16–21.

Goss, Jasper, David Burch, and Roy E. Rickson. 2000. "Agri-food Restructuring and Third World Transnationals: Thailand, the C.P. Group and the Global Shrimp Industry". *World Development* 28, no. 3: 513–30.

Government of Lao PDR (GoL). 2004. National Growth and Poverty Eradication Strategy. Poverty Reduction Strategy Paper. International Monetary Fund, Washington, D.C.

Hardy, Andrew. 2000. "Strategies of Migration to Upland Areas in Contemporary Vietnam". *Asia Pacific Viewpoint* 41, no. 1: 22–34.

Hett, Cornelia, Jean-Christophe Castella, Andreas Heinimann, Peter Messerli, and Jean-Laurent Pfund. 2011. "A Landscape Mosaics Approach for Characterizing Swidden Systems from a REDD+ Perspective". *Applied Geography* 32: 608–18.

Higashi, Satomi. 2015. *Impacts on Regional Land Use from Investment in Banana Contract Farming by Chinese Companies: Case Studies in Oudomxay Province, Northern Laos. Occasional Report.* Tokyo: Mekong Watch.

Hirsch, Philip. 2000. *Underlying Causes of Deforestation in the Mekong Region. Report Presented at Regional Workshop on Forest Management Strategies in the Mekong Region.* Vientiane: National University of Laos.

──, and Natalia Scurrah. 2015. *The Political Economy of Land Governance in Lao PDR.* Vientiane: Mekong Region Land Governance.

Htun, Khun Moe. 2018. *Living with Opium: Livelihood Strategies among Rural Highlanders in Southern Shan State, Myanmar.* Chiang Mai: Chiang Mai University Press.

Ingalls, Micah L., Jean-Christophe Diepart, Nhu Truong, Daniel Hayward, Tony Neil, Chanthavone Phomphakdy, Rasso Bernhard, Sinu Fogarizzu, Michael Epprecht, Vong Nanhthavong, Dang H. Vo, Dzung Nguyen, Phong A. Nguyen, Thatheva Saphangthong, Chanthaviphone Inthavong, Cornelia Hett, and Nicholas Tagliarino. 2018. *State of Land in the Mekong Region. Centre for Development and Environment.* University of Bern and Mekong Region Land Governance.

Lu, Juliet N. 2017. "Tapping into Rubber: China's Opium Replacement Program And Rubber Production in Laos". *Journal of Peasant Studies* 44, no. 4: 726–47.

Manorom, Kanokwan, David Hall, Lu Xing, Suchat Katima, Maria Theresa Medialdia, Singkhon Siharath, and Pinwadee Srisuphan. 2011. "Cross-border Contract Farming Arrangement: Variations and Implications in the Lao People's Democratic Republic". *Greater Mekong Subregion-Phnom Penh Plan for Development Management Research Report Series* 1, no. 2.

Mekong Region Land Governance (MRLG). 2017. *Towards Responsible Large-Scale Agricultural Investments in the Mekong Region.* Vientiane: MRLG.

Tsing, Anna L. 2005. *Friction: An Ethnography of Global Connection.* Princeton: Princeton University Press.

United Nations Office on Drugs and Crime (UNODC). 2015. *Southeast Asia Opium Survey 2015: Lao PDR, Myanmar.* Bangkok: UNODC Regional Office for Southeast Asia and the Pacific.

Vagneron, I., and C. Kousonsavath. 2015. *Analyzing Cross-Border Maize Trade in Huaphanh Province, Lao PDR.* Vientiane: Northern Uplands Development Programme.

Windle, James. 2012. "The Suppression of Illicit Opium Production in Viet Nam: An Introductory Narrative". *Crime, Law and Social Change* 57, no. 4: 425–39.

6

NEW FRONTIER SPACES
Complex Entanglements and Power Relations (Re)shaping Land Governance in Laos

Diana Suhardiman and Jonas Kramp

INTRODUCTION

Land, and the way it is governed in Laos, reflects its central positioning for the country's socio-economic development and how the state views it predominantly as an economic asset and extractive resource. Increasing commodification of land and other natural resources has also manifested in the state's territorialization approach and strategies that have sought to reorder relationships between people, land, and the natural environment in ways that facilitate state aims of political control while also promoting economic development. Since the country's independence in 1975, the state has been focusing on various policies to sustain, expand and strengthen its political control. These policies include internal resettlement (Baird and Shoemaker 2005; Évrard and Goudineau 2004; Ponce, this volume), land use planning and land allocation programme (Lestrelin 2010; Rigg 2005), as well as various forms of land commodification through the granting of state land concession (Kenney-Lazar, Dwyer, and Hett 2018; Kenney-Lazar 2019).

In this chapter,[1] we look at the interplay between the state's territorialization approach and strategies and the (re)shaping of frontier dynamics which (un)make the Lao uplands (Kramp, Suhardiman, and Keovilignavong 2020). Rasmussen and Lund (2018) have advocated for a bifocal perspective of territorialization and frontier dynamics, making visible their interplay in (re)configuring space, property relations and institutional arrangements. Both concepts have been used by scholars to analyse and discuss the transformations of upland areas across Southeast Asia (Barney 2009; Diepart and Sem 2018; Hall, Hirsch, and Li 2011). Scholars have also shown how territorial politics shape institutional structures (Bolleyer 2018; Keating 2018) and public policies (Agnew and Mantegna 2018). In Laos, and the region in general, state's territorialization approaches and the (re)shaping of frontier dynamics are most apparent in how states "divide their territories into complex and overlapping political and economic zones, rearrange people and resources within these units, and create regulations delineating how and by whom these areas can be used" (Vandergeest and Peluso 1995, p. 387).

Building on these works, we identify two venues where new frontier spaces emerged and took shape: policy formulation processes and programme implementation. First, we show how the process of (re)creating space, or the unfolding of frontier dynamics, has entered policymaking arenas drawing on the case of the national master plan on land allocation (NMPLA) formulation process. Viewing the NMPLA both as a state's territorialization strategy and breeding ground for new frontier spaces, we illustrate how its formulation process is (re)shaped by ongoing power struggles driven by sectoral government ministries' development targets and bureaucratic competition between various government agencies. Second, we illustrate how different groups within a local community (re)shape local land use planning processes, how they are rooted in complex entanglements of property relations and access to land, and how this manifested in various forms of contestations, both within and outside state spaces (Kenney-Lazar 2019).

FRONTIER SPACES, STATE TERRITORIALIZATION AND STATE FORMATION

Frontier spaces indicate where new resources and commodities come into being and may thus be described in their basic form as "epistemological, discursive and political operations [that enable] powerful actors to turn nature into economic commodities" (Rasmussen and Lund 2018, p. 391). Anna Tsing has famously described this phenomenon in the Indonesian context of Kalimantan (Tsing 2005, p. 32): "A frontier is an edge of space and time: a zone of not yet mapped, not yet regulated. It is a zone of unmapping: even in its planning, a frontier is imagined as unplanned. Frontiers aren't just discovered at the edge; they are projects in making geographical and temporal experience." In their recent work, building on Tsing (2005), Cons and Eilenberg (2019, p. 12) and colleagues call for an understanding of the frontier as an imaginative zone, i.e., an entanglement "anchored in the imaginative, the material, the known and the unknown" that goes beyond frontiers merely being conceived in terms of resource discovery and exploitation.

In this sense, rather than delineating a geopolitical separation of physical space, frontier spaces construct a contact zone or epistemological and political distinction between civilization and the wild (Rasmussen and Lund 2018). In the Lao upland, the government's[2] reforestation policy, for example, aiming to increase forest cover by 2020 to 70 per cent (MRLG 2019), paired with framing swidden agriculture as destructive have worked among other factors as frontier dynamics conjuring an image of the desired future situation in which "backward" swidden agriculture is stabilized and production is fixed. This legitimizes the demarcation of swidden fallows as state-owned forest land ("degraded forest") rendering them unfit for production under shifting cultivation, i.e., appropriating land and resources for environmental ends (Fairhead, Leach, and Scoones 2012). Moreover, recent economic policies have produced frontier spaces in the Lao upland through concessions and encouragement of foreign investment under the slogan of "turning land into capital"[3] and under the rationale of progress and rural development (Kenney-Lazar, Dwyer, and Hett 2018).

Aligned with Tsing's (2005) understanding of frontiers, Barney (2009, p. 152) describes the Lao upland frontier as unevenly distributed ("striated and patchworked") and produced by legal and extralegal means. Drawing on Rasmussen and Lund (2018), we argue that frontierization processes in Laos and beyond have not only transformed uplanders' property relations but also dissolve other aspects of existing social orders—e.g., customary rights, political jurisdictions and subjectivities. Hence, these two sets of dynamics are co-existent and constitutive as frontier dynamics unmake and territorialization establishes spatial control.

At the heart of this interplay lies a dialectic relation between (political) authority and rights and the ensuing contested (re)production of social contracts of recognition (Lund 2016; Lund and Rahman 2018). The latter is manifested in power struggles over multiple interests across scales. This begs the question of how these struggles centred on actors' (in)ability to produce and/or translate political authority and rights through the (re)shaping of local institutional arrangements. This directs our attention not only to how state territorialization and frontier dynamics have formed an integral part of state formation processes, but also to the agency of institutional actors, including the different groups in local communities, and their capacity to shape the process of state formation. Here, we view national policy formulation processes on land in general, and with regard to the NLMPA formulation in particular as an arena of power struggles, a space in the making, (re)shaped by policy actors' interests, strategies and access to resources. Similarly, local arrangements over access to land and customary land rights regimes in Laos illuminate the complexity of state formation—as the latter is shaped by territorialization and the production of frontier space, which are themselves shaped and reshaped by various actors' (i.e., state actors, private sector actors such as rubber companies, and farmers) multiple and often competing goals and interests.

THE NLMPA AS A NEW TERRITORIAL FRONTIER

Despite the lofty goals of the NMPLA as a technical means to address the country's land governance challenges and serve as the national master plan for land allocation, as outlined in the 2017 Party Resolution on Land, the NMPLA in practice has largely been driven by sectoral ministries' bureaucratic interests to ensure the incorporation of their respective development targets into the plan (Suhardiman, Keovilignavong, and Kenney-Lazar 2019). The NMPLA reflects the Lao government's centralized, socialist planning, similar to the country's national socio-economic development plan produced every five years and, thus, is carried out in a top-down manner. It is more concerned with checking off boxes of state goals rather than fundamentally changing how land use is planned throughout the country. Thus, the NMPLA can be seen as a strategy of state territorialization in that it seeks to incorporate the country's land use planning strategies and approaches under a unified and centralized umbrella.

However, the NMPLA's ability to enhance state territorialization is complicated by institutional fragmentation among different sectoral ministries that conflict over different goals matching their institutional targets and sectoral base of power. While the Ministry of Natural Resources and Environment (MoNRE), where the Department of Land (DoL) resides, is intended to be the coordinating, cross-sectoral ministry for all land-related matters in the country, such as land use planning and land registration, it does not always fulfil this role. Only recently established in 2012, MoNRE was the result of the merging of several environmentally related government agencies, such as the former National Land Management Authority (NLMA) which was established in 2007. Thus, although MoNRE has the mandate to play a coordinating role, the reality is that other ministries still assert strong influence and control over the lands also pertinent to their sector. For example, the Ministry of Agriculture and Forestry (MAF) seeks to maintain its control over agriculture and forestry lands while the Ministry of National Defense (MND) seeks to control borderlands that are viewed as critically important for national security (see as well Tappe's contribution to this volume for a related discussion on Lao mining legislation).

As a result of these centralizing dynamics of land use planning combined with institutional fragmentation, the NLMPA process has largely become a process of negotiating different targets for different types of land, with different underlying frontier imaginaries, and within an overarching ratio which aims to fix land uses throughout the country. Here, land classification is reduced to categorizing various types of land use (e.g., forest land, agricultural land) in pursuit of respective government ministries' and departments' political agendas and development targets. For example, one of the most powerful targets for land use planning is that of increasing forest cover to 70 per cent of the country's land area, pursued by the Department of Forestry (DoF). In practice, however, achieving this target seems impossible due to the overlapping boundaries of agriculture and forest land. A DoL/MoNRE official explained that "while DALaM and DoF respectively define 4.5 million ha of agricultural and 70 per cent forest cover as their development target, in practice, the distinction between forest and agricultural land is not always clear" (Interview with DoL/MoNRE official, August 2017). Overlapping boundaries between forest and agricultural land have their roots in the way the government delineates farmers' swidden agricultural land and forest land, relying mainly on its objective to eradicate shifting cultivation and thus categorizing upland farms as areas for forest rehabilitation. This is done even though swidden cultivators often lack any other access to land for their farming activities. Theoretically, NLMPA can only be applied and implemented if overlapping boundaries between forest and agricultural land are sorted out. In practice, however, the mapping of these lands alone is hampered by the physical challenges of seasonal fluctuations and yearly rotation of swidden fields. The latter means that a piece of land that is classified as forest land this year can technically be an agricultural land in the next year if farmers decide to do swidden cultivation on that land. Similarly, a piece of swidden land can turn into forest land over time when farmers cultivate elsewhere.

Consequently, the overlapping boundaries of agricultural and forest land show not only how land relations are politically contested but also reveal the re-shaping of the Lao frontier at the policy formulation level, as the latter is (re)shaped by various government agencies' competing interests and visions. In this context, we argue that while the state's land-use planning could impose on existing land uses and significantly reduce farmers' customary land use rights, the way land use planning has been applied in Laos, on the ground, rather reveals that such interventions are often a contested terrain.[4] Our case study of NLMPA shows how different interests are rooted in and entangled in complex property relations on land and how the state aims to (re)shape the latter to sustain and strengthen its political and economic control with severe policy implications. Even though land categorization has become a political process, driven by competing bureaucratic interests, NLMPA merely reflects underlying contestations and power struggles, with little or no prospect for policy implementation.

OVERLAPPING TERRITORIAL ORDERS AND INTERNAL POWER STRUGGLES

In the Namai upland, Luang Prabang province, overlapping territorial orders and internal power struggles created an internal momentum for rubber expansion on a smaller scale, exacerbating land scarcity, while also reducing the actual significance of land-use planning processes. Over a period of four to five decades (from the early 1970s until recently), territorial aspirations and frontier dynamics have come together in shaping the upland landscape in a contemporaneous effort. Customary land rights occupy in this regard a central role in villagers' decision-making as they are used as a means to secure land holdings and in consequence work to defy state territorialization. The conversion of upland land into rubber gardens feeds on the other hand into the broad-scale project of turning land into capital (e.g., specifically the promotion of rubber as a modern cash crop and a form of forest cover), while also reaffirming the government's misrecognition of claims to swidden land. Even though such conversions are primarily made to secure access to land locally,[5] they reinforce state authority over land by contributing to, rather than challenging, overarching structures. Moreover, by producing rubber independently or as contract farmers, villagers enter into a relationship of mutual recognition in which villagers "breathe life" (Lund 2016) into the Sino–Lao Chilan Rubber Development Company by recognizing its political authority while indirectly lodging a claim (to be recognized by the government) to their land.

Apart from turning land into rubber gardens, some Tai-Lue and Khmu upland holders have also actively engaged in making territory, for example by clearing upland plots, and planting crops on them (e.g., upland rice, maize, mangos), fencing them or by providing use rights to other people. In the local scramble for land, such efforts impeding the defined land-use plan of The Agro-Biodiversity Initiative (TABI) (and its associated mechanism to unmake spatial control of villagers) are often based on subsistence ethics,[6] aiming to maintain customary land (use) rights that ensure access to farmland for upland rice and the production of other crops for consumption. Customary tenure, based on reciprocity, family (and/or former village) ties and traditionalism, in that sense works as a sort of homeostasis in the spatial organization of the Namai upland. However, as discussed in the earlier section, customary land tenure in the immediate proximities of the village has been increasingly transformed by powerful upland holders who preserve land rental arrangements and plant rubber as a territorial strategy with implications for social as well as labour relations, land use and land control.

While labour relations among Khmu relatives are still based on reciprocity, wage labour has become prominent after Khmu resettlement to Namai village as Khmu settlers had to compensate for their lack of access to farmland or the poor quality of the soil of their plots. Khmu settlers, for example, clear and prepare upland plots for Tai-Lue rubber gardens and tap trees to harvest the latex in return for land or payment in cash or kind. Yet, working as a wage labourer on the plantation of the Sino–Lao Chilan Rubber Development Company is more attractive for Khmu villagers as the salary is higher compared to that of working for Tai-Lue employers. Moreover, many of our Khmu informants stated that they preferred tapping rubber compared to cultivating upland rice on rented plots from Tai-Lue as the latter was very labour intensive. During a focus group discussion some of our Tai-Lue informants agreed that despite the current competition over resources, the positive aspect of Khmu resettlement was that the previous shortage of labour was now solved. Khmu informants described labour relations between Khmu and Tai-Lue villagers as more distant than those among Khmu settlers. However, as described by Bouté (2018), these relations between employer and employee are based on certain conditions for example visits of the Tai-Lue to their employees' homes to celebrate Khmu festivities.

The assemblage of state and non-state institutional actors in Namai village has co-produced a complex patchwork of territorial projects. In this fragmented landscape, uncolonized interstitial spaces have been strategically exploited by villagers to secure their customary land rights (Kramp, Suhardiman, and Keovilignavong 2020). For example, by starting small-scale rubber plantations. TABI does not differentiate on their maps between different categories of rubber production such as agro-industrial rubber plantations, contract farms and independent smallholdings. The general category "rubber" used by TABI thus does not make explicit and thereby does not "expose" which land belongs to independent smallholders, contract farmers or the company. TABI's generalization has in that sense allowed those villagers with enough resources to secure their landholdings as rubber gardens, as stabilized rubber cultivation as opposed to rotating swidden farming has been tolerated and has met no opposition by government authorities or TABI so far. Rubber expansion and TABI's land use planning process in this regard overlap as rubber spills into the land use plan's reserved area for swidden cultivation.[7]

CONCLUSION

Our national policy and local case studies have shown how frontier spaces are (re)shaped in policy and local arenas. Furthermore, they illuminated across scales how power relations, different legal orders, and accumulation processes intertwine and are shaped by key stakeholders (e.g., sectoral ministries to sustain and increase their bureaucratic power and villagers to secure their access to land). We have also shown how a rubber frontier space has unmade local land tenure, but more recently has been used as a means to secure farmers' upland plots. Integrating frontier dynamics with a territorialization lens thus allowed us not only to better understand state's and farmers' strategies to secure their respectively bureaucratic power and access to land, but also to unpack the rationales behind these strategies and how they are rooted in views of their customary land rights vis à vis external policy interventions.

Resources such as land or rubber and the dynamics surrounding them have profound consequences on the governance of people and places, as they reshape space and its state-society relations. Frontier dynamics, in our case study, take an ambiguous role in the overall production of authority and rights as the commodification of upland space has become a strategy by both local cash crop farmers, to secure their land tenure, and by the Government of Laos, in its plan to "turn land into capital".[8] Baird (2019) has in this regard recently pointed to the GoL's changed understanding of land which is now to a greater extent treated as an economic asset and to a lesser degree as a building block of national sovereignty. Within the GoL's increasingly neoliberal economic agenda, land concessions have become a crucial component and have, as we have shown, provided a channel for smallholders to turn their land into capital and their customary rights over it into a territorial strategy to secure their land tenure. This process of neoliberalizing nature (Bakker 2005) took shape within a larger spatial-territorial configuration (Dwyer 2013) involving other modes of governance (e.g., coercive resettlement, controlling swidden agriculture by delineating resource use, patronage and rent-seeking of villagers and subsistence ethics). What is interesting in this development is that farmers who have historically faced difficulties in getting government institutions to recognize their land tenure were able to secure the latter through rubber cultivation following a process of territorialization from the ground up. Local rent-seeking of villagers in their scramble for land has in that sense worked together with a neoliberal mode of governance that has established a market for rubber and has allowed for an increasing influence of the Sino–Lao Chilan Rubber Development Company over local resource use. Looking at the process of state formation and the intensification of capitalist relations from below has shown how new social contracts among non-state actors have crystallized giving rise to new configurations of recognition on the local level.

Subsistence ethics and the existing institutional setup have in this process undergone a capitalist transformation with implications for the village's social structure, prompting an increasing social differentiation between villagers. Ethnic minorities in particular take on a disadvantaged position due to their ethnic, educational, political, social and geographical resources. Social inequality of ethnic minority groups within the Laotian process of state formation has become more pronounced as the reconfiguration of spatial relations engendered exclusionary effects. In this paper, we have tied this unequal development to the sectoral ministries' competition for bureaucratic power and to the resulting institutional impasse that cements an imaginative project (see Tsing 2005) rendering swidden farmers as backward and destructive and leaving upland farmers' swidden plots, at best, in legal limbo. Land use policies and planning interventions seeking to transform upland regions, therefore, need to take into account more carefully local power relations, customary land rights and the dynamic nature of swidden cultivation.

Notes

1. Key findings from the chapter are derived from authors' earlier work (Suhardiman, Keovilignavong, and Kenney-Lazar 2019; Kramp, Suhardiman, and Keovilignavong 2020). Jonas Kramp's field work for this article was undertaken previous to his joining the GIZ's Land Governance Team in Germany. The views expressed in this paper are those of the authors and do not reflect the positions of the GIZ.

2. Department of Forestry (DOF).
3. The umbrella policy phrase "Turning Land into Capital" that was coined at the 8th Party Congress in 2006 (Kenney-Lazar, Dwyer, and Hett 2018; Dwyer 2007). Since 1986 and Laos's transition towards a market economy, the government has promoted various forms of land commodification, especially land titling and the granting of state land concessions. New territories of commodified land, especially in the form of concessions, were created through widespread land dispossession, whereby companies acquired farmers' land and communal forest as part of their land concession agreement (Kenney-Lazar, Suhardiman, and Dwyer 2018; Suhardiman et al. 2015; Schumann et al. 2006).
4. While the issue of overlapping agriculture and forest land could in principle be sorted out from the perspective of different government agency's defined development targets, this is not so straightforward with regard to land titling. The idea is that with the new land law the government will push for rapid land titling to reach 100 per cent coverage in 2025. In practice, however, different agencies are still discussing as to whether people living in the protected forest can also be given land titles. This highlights that while the land-titling program could in principle increase some farmers' land tenure security, it can also reduce others' especially those whose lands are located in national protected forest.
5. Baird (2008) similarly showed how ethnic minorities in northeastern Cambodia planted cashew trees to protect land from external intervention.
6. Drawing on Scott's (1976) idea of subsistence ethics, Rehbein (2007, p. 26) writes, "[p]easants' interests are focused on having enough until the next harvest, not on having as much as possible. They achieve this by mutual aid (reciprocity) and by reinforcing family ties and traditionalism. They aim at survival and security, not at affluence and profit. Reciprocity, family orientation and traditionalism, subsumed under the term subsistence ethics, characterize village society in Laos."
7. PAFO and TABI staff underlined that one of the primary goals of the joint venture is to promote food crops such as rice and livestock farming to tackle food insufficiency.
8. See note 3 above.

References

Agnew, John, and Agostino Mantegna. 2018. "Territorial Politics and Economic Development". In *Handbook of Territorial Politics*, edited by Klaus Detterbeck and Eve Hepburn, pp. 306–18. Cheltenham: Edward Elgar Publishing.

Baird, Ian G. 2008. "Various Forms of Colonialism: The Social and Spatial Reorganization of the Brao in Southern Laos and Northeastern Cambodia". PhD dissertation, University of British Columbia.

———. 2019. "Changes in Understandings of Land in Laos: From State Sovereignty to Capital Mobilization". *Kyoto Review of Southeast Asia* 25. https://kyotoreview.org/issue-25/land-in-laos-from-state-sovereignty-to-capital-mobilization/ (accessed 10 October 2021).

———, and Bruce Shoemaker. 2005. "Aiding or Abetting? Internal Resettlement and International Aid Agencies in Laos". *Development and Change* 38, no. 5: 865–88.

Bakker, Karen. 2005. "Neoliberalizing Nature? Market Environmentalism in Water Supply in England and Wales". *Annals of the Association of American Geographers* 90, no. 3: 542–65.

Barney, Keith D. 2009. "Laos and the Making of a Relational Resource Frontier". *Geographical Journal* 175, no. 2: 146–59.

Bolleyer, Nicole. 2018. "Challenges of Interdependence and Coordination in Federal Systems". In *Handbook of Territorial Politics*, edited by Klaus Detterbeck and Eve Hepburn, pp. 45–60. Cheltenham: Edward Elgar Publishing.

Bouté, Vanina. 2018. "New Paths of Work at the Lao-Chinese Border: From Subsistence Agriculture to Wage Labor". In *Searching for Work: Small-Scale Mobility and Unskilled Labor in Southeast Asia*, edited by Matteo Alcano and Silvia Vignato, pp. 23–53. Chiang Mai: Silkworm Books.

Cons, Jason, and Michael Eilenberg eds. 2019. *Frontier Assemblages: The Emergent Politics of Resource Frontiers in Asia*. Chichester: John Wiley & Sons Ltd.

Diepart, Jean-Christian, and Thol Sem. 2018. "Fragmented Territories: Incomplete Enclosures and Agrarian Change on the Agricultural Frontier of Samlaut District, North-West Cambodia". *Journal of Agrarian Change* 18, no. 1: 156–77. https://doi.org/10.1111/joac.12155 (accessed 8 October 2021).

Dwyer, Mike. 2013. "Building the Politics Machine: Tools for 'Resolving' the Global Land Grab". *Development and Change* 44, no. 2: 309–33. https://doi.org/10.1111/dech.12014 (accessed 8 October 2021).

Évrard, Olivier, and Yves Goudineau. 2004. "Planned Resettlement, Unexpected Migrations and Cultural Trauma in Laos". *Development and Change* 35, no. 5: 937–962. https://doi.org/10.1111/j.1467-7660.2004.00387.x (accessed 8 October 2021).

Fairhead, James, Melissa Leach, and Ian Scoones. 2012. "Green Grabbing: A New Appropriation of Nature?". *Journal of Peasant Studies* 39, no. 2: 237–21. https://doi.org/10.1080/03066150.2012.671770 (accessed 8 October 2021).

Friis, Cecilie, Anette Reenberg, Andreas Heinimann, and Oliver Schönweger. 2016. "Changing Local Land Systems: Implications of a Chinese Rubber Plantation in Nambak District, Lao PDR". *Singapore Journal of Tropical Geography* 37, no. 1: 25–42. https://doi.org/10.1111/sjtg.12137 (accessed 8 October 2021).

Hall, Derek, Philip Hirsch, and Tania Murray Li. 2011. *Powers of Exclusion: Land Dilemmas in Southeast Asia*. Singapore: National University of Singapore Press.

Keating, Michael. 2018. "Rescaling the European State: A Constructivist and Political Perspective". In *Handbook of Territorial Politics*, edited by Klaus Detterbeck and Eve Hepburn, pp. 17–29. Cheltenham: Edward Elgar Publishing.

Kenney-Lazar, Miles. 2019. "Neoliberalizing Authoritarian Environmental Governance in (Post)Socialist Laos". *Annals of the American Association of Geographers* 109, no. 2: 338–48. https://doi.org/10.1080/24694452.2018.1537842 (accessed 8 October 2021).

———, Mike Dwyer, and Cornelia Hett. 2018. *Turning Land into Capital: Assessing Ten Plus Years of Policy in Practice*. Vientiane: LIWG – Land Information Working Group.

———, Diana Suhardiman, and Mike Dwyer. 2018. "State Spaces of Resistance: Industrial Tree Plantations and the Struggle for Land in Laos". *Antipode* 50, no. 5: 1290–310. https://doi.org/10.1111/anti.1239 (accessed 8 October 2021).

Kramp, Jonas, Diana Suhardiman, and Oulavanh Keovilignavong. 2020. "(Un)Making the Upland: Resettlement, Rubber and Land Use Planning in Namai Village, Laos". *Journal of Peasant Studies* 47: 1–23. https://doi.org/10.1080/03066150.2020.1762179 (accessed 8 October 2021).

Lestrelin, Guillaume. 2010. "Land Degradation in the Lao PDR: Discourses and Policy". *Land Use Policy* 27, no. 2: 424–39. https://doi.org/10.1016/j.landusepol.2009.06.005 (accessed 8 October 2021).

Lund, Christian. 2016. "Rule and Rupture: State Formation Through the Production of Property and Citizenship". *Development and Change* 47, no. 6: 1199–228. https://doi.org/10.1111/dech.12274 (accessed 8 October 2021).

———, and Noer Fauzi Rahman. 2018. "Indirect Recognition. Frontiers and Territorialization Around Mount Halimun-Salak National Park, Indonesia". *World Development* 101, 417–28. https://doi.org/10.1016/j.worlddev.2017.04.003 (accessed 8 October 2021).

McAllister, Karen E. 2015. "Rubber, Rights and Resistance: The Evolution of Local Struggles Against a Chinese Rubber Concession in Northern Laos". *Journal of Peasant Studies* 42, no. 3–4: 817–37. https://doi.org/10.1080/03066150.2015.1036418 (accessed 8 October 2021).

MRLG. 2019. "Land Tenure Security in 70 Percent Forestland Policy of the Lao PDR". Discussion Note, Vientiane, Mekong Region Land Governance.

Rasmussen, Matthias, and Christian Lund. 2018. "Reconfiguring Frontier Spaces: The Territorialization of Resource Control". *World Development* 101: 388–99. https://doi.org/10.1016/j.worlddev.2017.01.018 (accessed 8 October 2021).

Rehbein, Boike. 2007. *Globalization, Culture and Society in Laos*. London: Routledge.

Rigg, Jonathan. 2005. *Living with Transition in Laos: Market Integration in Southeast Asia*. London: Routledge.

Schumann, Gunda, Pheuiphanh Ngaosrivathana, Bouakham Soulivanh, Somboun Kenpraseuth, Khamdeng Onmanivong, Khamthanh Vongphansipraseuth, and Chithasone Bounkhong. 2006. *Study on State Land Leases and Concessions in Lao PDR*. Land Policy Study no. 4 under LLTP II. Vientiane: GIZ.

Scott, James. 1976. *The Moral Economy of the Peasant: Subsistence and Rebellion in Southeast Asia*. New Haven: Yale University Press.

Suhardiman, Diana, Oulavanh Keovilignavong, and Miles Kenney-Lazar. 2019. "The Territorial Politics of Land Use Planning in Laos". *Land Use Policy* 83, 346–56. https://doi.org/10.1016/j.landusepol.2019.02.017 (accessed 8 October 2021).

———, Mark Giordano, Oulavanh Keovilignavong, and Touleelor Sotoukee. 2015. "Revealing the Hidden Effects of Land Grabbing through Better Understanding of Farmers' Strategies in Dealing with Land Loss". *Land Use Policy* 49: 195–202. https://doi.org/10.1016/j.landusepol.2015.08.014 (accessed 8 October 2021).

Tsing, Anna L. 2005. *Friction: An Ethnography of Global Connection*. Princeton: Princeton University Press.

Vandergeest, Peter, and Nancy Peluso. 1995. "Territorialization and State Power in Thailand". *Theory and Society* 24, no. 3: 385–426. https://doi.org/10.1007/BF00993352 (accessed 8 October 2021).

7

MOVING AWAY FROM THE MARGINS?

How a Chinese Hydropower Project Made a Lao Community Modern and Comfortable

Floramante S.J. Ponce

INTRODUCTION

In December 2018, some days after interviewing Pho ("Father") Tha, he invited me, my research partner, and Pho Keo (his friend) for a lunch and drinking session at his home. Pho Keo and Pho Tha are both Theravada Lao Buddhists in their fifties. Comparing their socio-economic status, Pho Keo was comparatively prosperous because he was a successful businessman in their old village; he also managed to send all his children to college. After the relocation, Pho Keo has been running some lucrative businesses powered by electricity and receiving financial support from his unmarried children. Now Pho

Keo and Pho Tha are no longer neighbours as they live in the new settlement's different zones.

> *Chon* (my nickname in Laos), you should study not just electricity, but also the other new things here. We have now roads going to bigger markets and hospitals, schools and a big health centre nearer to us; the Internet. The government and the company already provided for our needs here. We're now "modern" (*thansamai*); it's more comfortable (*sabay kouaa*) here than before," Pho Keo told us, with conviction.
>
> "Comfortable (*Sabay*)? Perhaps for you, but not for me, *siao* (buddy)," Pho Tha responded, and then he took a swig of his beer. As the old man resumed lamenting:
>
> "How can I feel comfortable like you if I don't have money to buy a sack of rice and medicine? I have no work here; I lost my gardens; I couldn't catch fish here because the river has a low water level. I couldn't do swidden because I haven't received the promised land from the company ... The forest is also far from here. *You ni you lala!!* [Literally: Here just living; it means "doing nothing"] ... How can I feel comfortable like you if I'm always worried about my son illegally working in Thailand to provide for our needs? ... Perhaps we're both modern now because we have electricity and roads here, but still, we're different because you're comfortable here; I am not."
>
> Then Pho Tha excused himself for a while to go to the toilet. "He's already drunk; he already talked a lot," Pho Keo told me. After that, he proposed a toast to me.

The conversation between Pho Tha and Pho Keo orients us about the difference between the resettled in their possessed economic wealth and how they view their relocation experiences. The most striking insight is their disagreement on the notion of comfort (*sabay*) after the relocation. Unlike Pho Keo whose idea of comfort in the new settlement was primarily connected to the advantage of infrastructures, Pho Tha separated his views of being comfortable from being modern by citing other materials (i.e., money to purchase basic needs; food and livelihood sources; among others) and non-material aspects of comfort (specifically when he mentioned his feelings about his child illegally working abroad). Thus, Pho Tha's statement suggests that the new infrastructures in the resettlement community may distribute opportunities to become modern to many, but may circulate comfort to only a few.

The chapter's main objective is to investigate the villagers' ideas of comfortable and modern life after the relocation as prisms through which to understand how frontierization through hydropower development and its impacts have been experienced, internalized and interrogated from below. Recent studies have utilized frontierization to analyse how special economic zones, concessions and other enclosure and development projects have transformed marginal areas into frontier spaces (Arnold 2012; Bach 2011; Levien 2011). Social scientists have usually used frontiers or frontier spaces as either metonyms or metaphors for borderlands or edges that become part of the global capitalist system (Donnan and Wilson 1994; Eilenberg 2012). In this chapter, I adopt Jason Cons' and Michael Eilenberg's conceptualization of frontierization as the extractive project or process of making resource frontier spaces not just to produce capital, but also to incorporate isolated zones into "new territorial formations" (Cons and Eilenberg 2019, p. 2). Although I will discuss briefly the other processes involved in facilitating hydropower projects in Laos, I will give the lion's share of my attention to the resettlement community as a frontier space created by hydropower development. Focusing on this aspect of frontierization also enables me to listen to various stories of how the resettled villagers have become integrated and disintegrated due to the relocation.

Since the implementation of its economic reforms in the 1990s, the Lao state has always emphasized the importance of hydropower and other megaprojects in developing the country's "empty or underpopulated wilderness" (Barney 2009, p. 151)—the prevailing view of Laos as a resource frontier. Apart from globalizing the Lao economy, such development through creating frontier spaces could also address the absolute poverty of many remote people (Baird and Shoemaker 2007, 2008; Barney 2009; Rigg 2018). The Lao state and its development patron banks, as influenced by contemporary mainstream development practitioners, have strongly linked the existence of poverty to the physical isolation of rural riparian and upland populations. To address their "pre-existing state of marginality" (Rigg et al. 2016, p. 63) or "old poverty" (Rigg 2005, p. 25), they should be integrated into the market and state services by relocating to resettlement communities. Thus, for the state and other development players, the production of resource frontier spaces provides opportunities for remote people to move away from the margins, thereby escaping poverty.

This chapter investigates the ways in which hydropower projects' facilitators have imposed some frontier discourses and implemented frontierization processes, and how the resettled villagers in turn have encountered, embraced and contested such frontier dynamics. This investigation might contribute to recent frontier studies that examine how megaprojects' resource frontier making has furthered capital accumulation (Cons 2016; McDuie-Ra 2016) and reorganized risk (Anderson 2019; Paprocki 2019) and sovereignty (Dunn and Cons 2014; Eilenberg 2014; Woods 2011). This chapter aims to extend that scope by exploring how hydropower development's frontierization processes have also unevenly spread opportunities to become modern and comfortable among the displaced people[1].

I start by briefly discussing how and why the Lao state, international financial institutions and hydropower facilitators have adopted and imposed resource frontier discourses. Then, I will investigate the resettled villagers' encounters with the new physical infrastructures, which serve as the reason for resettling and for initially embracing the frontier discourses. After that, I will present how numerous villagers contest frontier discourses by analysing their various experiences of (dis)integration in the resettlement community. Here I will also discuss how they reflect upon their market integration. Finally, I provide some concluding comments assessing the NNua1's frontierization processes by looking at the villagers' experiences and views of comfort and modern life after the relocation.

FRONTIER DISCOURSES AND HYDROPOWER DEVELOPMENT IN LAOS

After the introduction of the New Economic Mechanism (locally known as *Kônkai Sétthakit Mai*) in 1986, the post-socialist Lao state has exerted relentless efforts to boost foreign direct investments (FDIs) related to hydroelectric dams, mining industries, and monoculture plantations (OECD 2017). Under the auspices of major international financial institutions in Southeast Asia, particularly the World Bank and the Asian Development Bank (ADB), the Lao state has implemented structural adjustment reforms based on the Washington Consensus' neoliberal prescriptions (Rigg 2005; Stuart-Fox 2008). These new economic policies were formalized in the country's first constitution in 1991 (Yamada 2018). Since the mid-1990s, the Lao government has also pursued strategies aiming to simplify and ease the processes of doing business in Laos, such as by removing unnecessary prerequisites and by accelerating the approval and release of business permits (Stuart-Fox 2008). All these new capitalist market principles adopted by the state thus aim to make Laos a business-friendly country.

The World Bank and the ADB were aware that such a depiction of Laos was a hard sell to foreign investors. The reasons for that were linked to the country's poor human capital and physical infrastructures, inefficient government bureaucracy and opaque governance (OECD 2017, p. 55). To attract more FDIs, the aforementioned development banks have reimaged the land-locked country as being "the last frontier for intra-regional business opportunities and for environment conservation programming" (Barney 2009, p. 150; see also Rowedder and Tappe's introduction to this volume). They have also portrayed Laos as an "underpopulated wilderness, which holds the promise for high rates of return on investment" (Barney 2009, p. 151). This line of argument also echoes the developmental visions of recent infrastructure projects under China's Belt and Road Initiative (BRI) in Laos—for example, among others, the Vientiane-Boten high-speed railway connecting to the Yuxi-Mohan railway in Yunnan Province, China, and the Nam Nua 1 (NNua1) Hydropower Project (a pseudonym). The Chinese developers of these projects assert that they could materialize the Greater Mekong Subregion's (GMS) half-finished goal for Laos: to transform Laos from being a *land-locked* to a *land-linked country* (Sidaway et al. 2020; World Bank 2020; Rowedder, this volume).[2] The potential of Chinese infrastructure projects to remove spatial constraints and (re)connect Laos to its neighbouring countries might also create opportunity and prosperity for the Lao people, including the most remote rural villagers.

Since then, the Lao state has adopted extensively the foregoing resource frontier discourses. In its investment profile and development plans, for instance, the Lao state often presents itself as the "last frontier" in mainland Southeast Asia with plenty of resources and underdeveloped lands, but with limited technical capacities to develop what it has (see, e.g., Creak and Barney 2018; Lu and Schönweger 2017). These limitations might be overcome by allowing foreign investors of large-scale development projects to make new resource frontiers in Laos and by accepting the guidance offered by the ADB and the World Bank. The assistance includes not just financial aid but also the technical skills of so-called "international experts". In this sense, the resource frontier discourses have also served as an ideological function for foreign investors and international financial institutions to legitimize their presence and development interventions in Laos.

The state officials from the Ministry of Mines and Electric (MEM) and *Électricité du Laos* (EDL) who I had interviewed often reiterated that the transformation of "underused/unproductive spaces" into "productive resource frontiers" through hydropower development (and other megaprojects) was necessary to bring national economic progress. How the Lao state has applied this development principle could be observed in how hydropower projects in Laos have proliferated since the 1990s (see Figure 7.1).

FIGURE 7.1
Number of Dams Commissioned in Laos by Decades

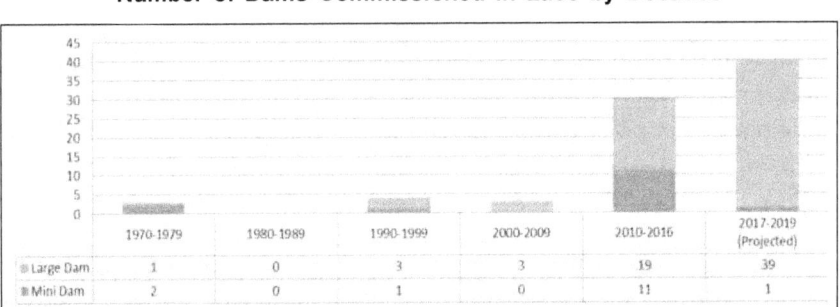

Source: Figure created by the author based on the Ministry of Energy and Mines' Vision 2030; Development Plan 2025; and Five-Year Development Report (2016–2020) (MEM 2017).

Recent mainstream development practitioners in Laos, as elsewhere in the Global South, have described the remote people living in these "underused/unproductive spaces" or "empty/underpopulated wilderness" as poor for two interrelated reasons. First, they imagined that these isolated populations had meagre and simple livelihoods due to the lack of physical infrastructures, so they were disconnected from the local and global market (Rigg 2005, p. 25). This view also resonates with the widely criticized "Frontier Thesis" of Frederick Jackson Turner (1920) arguing that the "wild west" frontiers in North America had abundant resources and backward populations which were always available and open for exploitation. Taming these spaces of wilderness could bring national progress and could also pacify and civilize its remote inhabitants. Second, some mainstream development discourses argue that poverty is prevalent among the populations who lived out of the state's control. They highly emphasized the state's function in delivering poverty alleviation programmes and making adequate service provisions for the isolated people. These difficult-to-reach areas beyond the state's supervision somehow echo Lord Curzon's (1907) notion of "unruly frontier": A space "that is once ungovernable and in urgent need of government" and "territorial incorporation" (Cons and Eilenberg 2019, p. 8; Rowedder and Tappe, this volume).

The Lao state, international financial institutions, and hydropower project developers have also foregrounded a similar line of reasoning to justify the making of resource frontiers through hydropower development. Apart from increasing the national income, globalizing the Lao economy, and turning the country into "the battery of Southeast Asia" (Giovannini 2018), the aforementioned actors argued that the frontier dynamics of hydropower projects could also address the previous marginality and poverty of isolated riparian villagers. By relocating these people to resettlement communities, they might be mainstreamed (Rigg 2018). The new experiences of infrastructures—electrification, access roads, the Internet, etc.—might also integrate them into the market and state services (MEM 2016). This logic of poverty alleviation could be also noticed in the typical script of the Lao state and hydropower companies to encourage the project-affected villagers to be relocated (Whitington 2019).

The Nam Nua 1 (NNua1) Hydropower Project—the facilitator of the Banmai resettlement—has also adopted such discourses/scripts. According to the majority of villagers I interviewed (115 out of 128), the officials and staff of the provincial and district government as well as the NNua1 always emphasized during village meetings and consultations that they were impoverished due to the absence of infrastructures in their former villages. These staff and officials also often pointed up how the resettlement could serve as a panacea for all ills of being *lasamai* (backward) and being *bannok* (being country bumpkins) as well as being *thoukgnak* (poor). In addition, they reiterated that they could easily build infrastructures and provide more economic support in the new settlement, such as new houses, food support, livelihood reconstruction programmes and free electricity. In what follows, I will discuss how the displaced villagers experience and reflect upon the new infrastructures and various promised compensations.

MODERNITY AT THE MARGINS?

Based on the company's profile and reports, the NNua1 Hydropower Project is the largest single hydropower-induced resettlement project in Lao history. The company has relocated an estimate of 1,750 households or 10,000 people from thirty-seven villages of Bokeo and Luang Namtha Province. This is relatively large for a country that has just more than seven million population or almost 31 people per square kilometre (World Bank 2021). Located in Bokeo Province, my primary field site, Banmai (a pseudonym), is the NNua1's biggest resettlement site that has more than 3,100 inhabitants or 566 households. The NNua1 Project compressed ten former villages into this new settlement. According to many villagers, the company had started the displacement in late July 2015 and finished the relocation in the Banmai resettlement in the last quarter of 2016.

Before the relocation, many resettled villagers I spoke with considered themselves relatively indigent, especially when they compared their living conditions to the inhabitants of urban/peri-urban places in Laos or Thailand that had access to roads, better public health centres and schools, 24/7 electricity, Internet signal, and other physical infrastructures. For this reason, it was quite inaccurate to describe that they had an "original affluence" before (Sahlins 1974). In the resettlement community, numerous villagers highly valued the new physical infrastructures—which were constructed and maintained by the NNua1 Company in coordination with the Lao state—primarily because these were their objects of desire in the older settlements. Moreover, 87 out of 128 interlocutors mentioned that their new experiences made them feel, *thansamai* (modern) and *sabay gay* (literally, "comfortable/happy body"; it means that the infrastructures make some of their physical tasks less time-consuming or less tiring).

Within all ten villages displaced by the NNua1 Project in Bokeo, motorboats served as the only available mode of transportation going to Houayxay, Bokeo's provincial capital. Many villages I interviewed—especially those whose former villages were close to the boundary of Luang Namtha—emphasized how the presence of new access roads has reduced their travel time. It has also made their journey more convenient, and it has significantly increased the frequency of their travels going to more urban areas of Laos and Thailand.

Numerous villagers also recognize the benefits of the new big public health centre (*souksala*) in Banmai (Figure 7.2). Of the ten displaced villages, only the three largest villages had small *souksala* before. When the inhabitants of the other seven villages felt sick, they needed to ride boats to go to the health centres of bigger villages. The villagers who had subsistence livelihoods usually did not have money to pay boat fees, constraining them to consult their medical problems. Some relatively poor villagers just relied on "spirit doctors" for addressing their health issues.[3] Further, many women usually delivered their babies at home. Both the resettled villagers and the medical workers I interviewed admitted the lack of health facilities in older settlements. As one villager put it: "It was difficult to find treatment before. Many villagers died due to simple accident, fever, and giving birth."

FIGURE 7.2
Inside the Banmai Resettlement's *Souksala*

Source: Photo taken by the author, 2019.

In the resettlement community, there has been a development in the delivery of public health programmes and health facilities. Owing to their proximity to the *souksala*, the villagers can now receive more prompt first-aid treatment when they get injured or suddenly become ill. The interviewed health workers also claim that there has been a decline in the child mortality rate after the relocation because of two reasons. One, maternal health has generally improved due to more accessible medical assistance for women before and after their childbirth; the other, vaccination programmes for children have been effectively monitored. The villagers also acknowledge how the *souksala*'s health workers have successfully implemented various reproductive health and family planning programs, e.g., distributing condoms and contraceptive pills and providing sex education. During the second quarter of 2020, some friends from Banmai informed me through a Facebook messenger video call that the health workers also organized seminars on preventing some tropical diseases (i.e., malaria, dengue fever, and HIV/AIDS) and COVID-19.

Numerous resettled villagers I talked to also think that the quality of learning and access to schools have become better in Banmai. Although all ten displaced villages had primary schools (kindergarten level to grade five) three years before the relocation, there was only one village that had lower secondary schools (first-year to fourth-year levels). When the students of the other nine villages wanted to pursue their lower secondary education, they needed to commute by boat going to the sole lower secondary school in the area, or to study in Phaoudom District, Houayxay, or nearby provinces, such as Luang Namtha and Oudomxay. In the former villages, many interviewed villagers and students disclosed that their classroom environment was unconducive to learning mainly because the classes of two or more grade levels were merged into one class. Apart from the school facilities, the student-classroom ratio has also improved from more than sixty students per classroom to less than thirty students per classroom. The teachers are quite satisfied with the new computers and printers provided by the company because now they can encode their lesson plans, student records, and examinations (Figure 7.3). The students and teachers I worked with both surmise that all these improvements could have a positive impact on the quality of education.

FIGURE 7.3
A Secondary Teacher Encoded His Lesson Plan and Class Record Using the Common Computer in the Teachers' Room

Source: Photo taken by the author, 2019.

Many villagers I spoke with also appreciate the importance of the new electric grid connection to the resettlement community in general, and to their everyday lives in particular. The health workers mention the advantage of 24/7 electricity in storing vaccines and other medicines in refrigerators and freezers as well as in running some electronic medical equipment, such as nebulizers and digital sphygmomanometers. Without stable electricity, the lights, electric fans, and water dispensers with hot and cold options in schools could not be turned on. Many school teachers and health workers also emphasize the convenience of producing monthly and quarterly reports and other documents using computers and printers powered by electricity.

Some years before the relocation in 2015, the families of relative affluence—whose businesses were "buying and selling" forest products and unhusked rice, big retail stores, and motorboat rental business—as well as those households that managed to save some money from selling their crops and teak woods had already bought machines generating electricity, such as portable gasoline generators (*chakpanfai*), dynamo-electric machines (*daifanfai* or *dainam*), and/or solar panels (*phalangsèng*). However, the indigent villagers who had no savings just used oil/gasoline lamps or sometimes firewood as their main light source at night. In the Banmai resettlement, the company installed electricity and fluorescent lights in all houses that they provided. Many villagers surmise that by dint of their brighter and more stable electric lights, many activities that they do during the day, they can also do them now in the evening. As Pho Keo explained, "The new electric lights in the resettlement can illuminate our place at night as if we are in broad daylight."

As a consequence of their new light sources, some villagers also claim that they can carry out domestic chores (e.g., cooking and cleaning); they can weave and make handicrafts in the evening. For others, looking after sick people, puerperal mothers, and newborn babies at night is more comfortable now. In the new settlement, they can also regularly visit each other's houses as well as accommodate friends and visitors even after dusk. Apart from creating a more festive atmosphere during celebrations, the new electric lights have also enabled the villagers to revel in festivals, weddings, or after *baci/soukhouan* gatherings until dawn. In general, due to the 24/7 electricity, the villagers—especially those who are comparatively wealthy—can use now many appliances, which were impossible to run before.[4] The more stable electricity and stronger Internet connection in Banmai have been also appreciated by many villagers, especially the younger generation (Figures 7.4 and 7.5). Now they can use smartphones and tablets not just to entertain themselves (watching videos and listening to songs on YouTube; and playing online mobile games), but also to become more connected to their relatives and friends within Laos and abroad (usually in Thailand, China and Vietnam) as well as to global news, trends and fads. The chapter's limited space restricts me to discuss in detail the other new electric gadgets and appliances in Banmai.

The electric grid connection has also enabled new livelihood activities in the resettlement community. For example, Pho Keo's main businesses now are enabled by a 24/7 electricity supply: producing ice, selling

FIGURE 7.4
The Mobile Internet Signal Tower in Banmai

Source: Photo taken by the author, 2018.

FIGURE 7.5
The Lao Telecom's Advertisement Poster Highlighting the Importance of Internet Connection in Learning

Source: Photo taken by the author, 2018.

frozen meat and cold drinks in his retail store, husking rice (using an electric-powered milling machine), and printing documents. The electric machines and appliances needed for these new livelihoods could not be used in his former village because there he had to rely on unstable electricity generated by solar panels. They could only use lights and TV for less than two hours per day and even less during the rainy season. He said his new businesses are more convenient because they require less physical work and travelling (*sabay gay*). He just stays at home waiting for his customers. As a result, he now has more time to rest, be with his wife, and look after his grandchildren. "I don't have much problem here. I earn money from my businesses; I also get financial help from my children ... I can retire happily here", Pho Keo claimed. Moreover, he reiterated that his "heart is happier" (*sabay chai lay kouaa*) in Banmai than before.

Table 7.1 reveals the list of new livelihood activities powered by the electric grid connection. This is based on the census of rural non-farm economic activities I carried out in all three zones of the Banmai resettlement from June to July 2019. Many owners regard their new business activities as "modern" (*thansamai*) not simply because they utilize "high-tech" electrical appliances and machines, but because they think their businesses enabled by 24/7 electricity give their rural settlements an air of urbanity (*khu naimuang*). "Now we have many retail stores, hair salons, furniture shops, a tavern with karaoke … It is as lively here as it is in a town", Pho Keo told me. This capacity of electric grid connection to allow the rural villagers to have an urban and modern experience resonates with the findings of Winther (2008, 2013) and Wu (2008) in their studies on the impacts of using electric appliances. After discussing how some villagers have experienced modernity after moving to the resettlement community, I will present in the next section how the NNua1 Hydropower Project's frontier dynamics have (dis)integrated the villagers in various ways.

TABLE 7.1
Livelihood Activities Enabled by the Electric Grid Connection

Livelihood Activities	Electric Appliances / Machines / Gadgets	Banmai Resettlement			
		Zone A	Zone B	Zone C	Total
Rice Milling Shop	Electric-powered milling machine	4	2	2	8
Ice Factory	Electric-powered ice machine	3	0	1	4
Furniture Shop	Electric wood cutter / Air compressor for spray painting	0	2	2	4
Making Ice Cream / Shake	Blender / Big freezer / Electric-powered ice cream machine	3	1	0	4
Retail Store	Refrigerator / Freezer / Lights	15	19	12	46
Lao Lottery Outlet	Portable printer for printing receipts and tickets/ Android tablet (for inputting bet numbers and knowing the winning combination)	1	0	1	2

(*con't*)

TABLE 7.1 (con't)

Livelihood Activities	Electric Appliances / Machines / Gadgets	Banmai Resettlement			
		Zone A	Zone B	Zone C	Total
Night Tavern	Disco lights / TV, speaker, and amplifier (for Karaoke)	2	0	0	2
Brothel	Lights/ Electric fan / Electric heater in the bathroom	1	0	0	1
Hair Salon	Rotating infrared ring orbits (for hair spa and color) / Hair blower	2	0	0	2
Barbershop	Electric razor / TV (for customers)	0	1	0	1
Printing Shop	Printer / Computer or laptop	1	1	0	2
Tire Repair	Electric-powered tire inflator and air compressor	4	0	0	4
Tailoring Shop	Electric-powered sewing machine	1	0	0	1
Eatery	Freezer / Refrigerator / Electric hotpot / Rice cooker	2	2	4	8
Pharmacy	Refrigerator to store medicines	3	1	0	4
Gas Station	Portable fuel dispenser and pump/ Lights	1	0	1	2
TOTAL		43	29	23	95

Source: Compiled by the author, 2019.

(DIS)INTEGRATION AFTER THE RELOCATION

In the Lao state's and hydropower facilitators' frontier discourses, all displaced villagers are considered marginalized, including Pho Keo—even if his family has been relatively wealthy compared to an average Lao family since before his relocation. The successful integration of Pho Keo into the resettlement community fits the Lao state's and the NNua1 Company's frontier narratives. Focusing on his case alone may leave us with a positive impression of development-induced resettlement projects. For this reason, the Lao state and the NNua1 Company often highlight his successful resettlement story.

Sometime in October 2018, the Chinese company interviewed Pho Keo to compare and contrast his experiences both in the former and new settlements. When I asked the NNua1 Company's two Lao staff (who also became my friend) about the interview's purpose, they said that they would use it to create a documentation video about the relocation's impacts. They presented it to the hydropower company's head office in southern China.[5] Pho Keo—like his statements when I interviewed him, and whenever he discussed his resettlement experiences in ordinary conversations—also emphasized during his interview with the company how the new physical infrastructures had integrated him into the market and the state, making him modern and comfortable. As I overheard some of his statements during the shoot of his video interview:

> Now it's also easier to go to other places due to roads. We can go now to bigger markets to buy the things we need for our businesses. It's more convenient for many villagers to sell their handicrafts and other products outside Banmai. We are now near to the district and provincial government offices, so it's easier for them [the local state officials] to reach us, to help us … Because of the new electricity, our lives and many businesses here are like in town. The schools and the health centre are nearer here. We can connect now to our relatives and friends outside Banmai and even abroad due to the Internet and stronger mobile phone signal. If we didn't move here, maybe we wouldn't become *thansamai* [modern]; maybe we wouldn't become *sabay* [comfortable].

As I discussed in the previous section, Pho Keo's notions of *sabay* after the relocation include both the comfort of the body (*sabay gay*) and heart (*sabay chai*). Apart from his above statements, his new businesses—which make him feel more comfortable retiring in Banmai and closer to his family—are also his reasons for having a *sabay chai* ("comfortable/happy heart"). The consistency of Pho Keo in reiterating how the relocation provided him with the opportunity to be modern and to feel more comfortable is emblematic of how the Lao state's and the NNua1's frontier discourses related to hydropower-development-induced resettlement have been internalized and embraced from below. Pho Keo's relocation story, however, represents just less than 1 per cent of total households in Banmai (see Table 7.2, particularly column A).

As mentioned earlier, there were 87 out of 128 interlocutors (column A+B [8+79]) who told me that they experienced becoming *thansamai* and

TABLE 7.2
Participants' Ethnicity and Comfort in Banmai

Ethnic Identification		Comfort in the new settlement				Total
		(A) "Comfortable body, comfortable heart" (*Sabay gay, sabay chai*)	(B) "Comfortable body, poor heart" (*Sabay gay, thouk chai*)	(C) "Poor body, poor heart" (*Thouk gay, thouk chai*)	(D) Refused to answer	
	Lao Buddhists	8	44	15	1	68
	Rmeet	0	30	17	2	49
	Khmu	0	5	6	0	11
Total		8	79	38	3	128

Note: The author did not conduct a survey, but tabulated the responses of 128 participants about their notions of comfort after the relocation.

Source: Compiled by the author, 2019.

sabay gay due to the new physical infrastructures in Banmai. Unlike Pho Keo who felt *sabay chai*, 79 out of these 87 interlocutors told me that after the relocation, they felt *sabay gay* but *thouk chai* (literally: "poor heart"). *Thouk chai* is their strong feeling of sadness that is rooted not just in the loss of previous livelihood and food sources, but also in the disillusionment with the unprovided compensations and with the alleged corruption issues of some Lao staff of the NNual Company and some local state officials. (For more about these corruption issues, see Ponce 2022.)

In the past, many villagers reminisced how the forest and the river near their houses provided them with plenty of natural resources for food and livelihood. They could catch many fish and crustaceans in the river because of the normal water level. In less than twenty minutes, they would be able to reach the dense forest by walking. Apart from wild edibles like bamboo and rattan shoots and wild mushrooms, they could also collect forest products, such as palm fruits, *koktiang/peuakmeuak* (*Debregeasia hypoleuca*), wild cardamom, among others. They could also go hunting for game. They even merged with other households to increase their productivity and to exceed their annual targets in collecting forest products. These were sold to itinerant merchants from nearby villages or provinces. They claimed that they saved almost 90 to 95 per cent of their income because they had lower expenses in their older settlements. They could even exchange their surplus wild edibles, game and fish for gasoline (used for lamps), MSG (monosodium glutamate), body soap, detergent, and cooking oil, among others. Moreover, they asserted they had abundant land around their houses that they could use for shifting cultivation, for grazing their cows and buffaloes, and for planting fruits, *miang* tea, teak woods and rubber trees. Despite such claims of material plenty, I would like to reiterate they still considered themselves relatively poor in the former villages due to the absence of physical infrastructures.

They maintain that after the relocation, abundant natural resources and land have become scarce. Catches have fallen because of the river's low water level induced by the dam construction and drought. Now they also need to walk for more than three hours to reach the dense forest and available swidden areas (Ponce 2022, p. 16). Due to land shortage around the new settlement, they cannot graze their ruminants; they also cannot create big gardens like before. Aside from these changes, some of the NNua1 Company's and the Lao state's unfulfilled promises also made the villagers' hearts poor (*thouk chai*). They insisted that during village meetings in the former villages, the company and the district government promised them three years of food support and free electricity, livelihood reconstruction programmes, and swidden land. Some villagers claimed that they had free electricity for just one year; others received food support three times only. The food aid package contained some kilograms of rice; two packs of noodles, a dozen eggs and a can of sardines per family member; and a quarter kilogram of MSG per household. A few villagers, however, asserted they failed to receive any food support at all (see Ponce 2022, pp. 12-13).

At the time of my research, which was already three years after the resettlement, many villagers were still waiting for the promised swidden land and livelihood programmes. Some staff of the NNua1's outsourced company—which was responsible for distributing livelihood support and providing training related to agriculture—had just surveyed some indigent villagers on the livestock that they wanted to raise in Banmai. Few villagers told me that they already obtained twenty chickens; some were also given a hundred frogs; many did not receive anything. In general, numerous villagers thought that the NNua1 and the district and provincial governments implemented ineffective measures for reconstructing their livelihoods. On top of these, some villagers felt disappointed when they heard that some parts of their financial compensations—especially the compensation for the loss of gardens and tree crops—were purportedly siphoned off by some Lao staff of the NNua1 company and the district government. How few individuals—who have good connections to some Lao state officials and the NNua1's staff—received preferential treatment, especially in obtaining swidden land and other entitlements, also caused disillusionment among many villagers.

The relocation to the resettlement community has undoubtedly integrated the formerly remote villagers into the market. The meanings of market integration, however, vary depending on the displaced villagers' socio-economic background. For Pho Keo, such integration means being modern and finding more convenient ways of doing profitable businesses. Conversely, for the majority of the resettled villagers—specifically those who possess no material wealth to become entrepreneurs—it only leads them to sell their labour power to the market in exchange for subsistence wages. Those villagers who have financial resources, relatives and friends, and/or academic degrees (secondary or college education) have usually migrated to Vientiane and Luang Phrabang or to bigger cities in Thailand to find low-skilled or middle-skilled jobs. Some able-bodied young men have been employed as part-time construction workers by the small Chinese dam near Banmai. However, many poor villagers together with their family members have just worked on Chinese plantations outside Banmai (i.e., banana, bean or rubber plantations).

Numerous villagers I interviewed who worked in plantations disclosed that they had appalling working conditions. They said that it was rare to find kind and considerate Chinese employers. Like many Lao employers and wage labourers from Phongsaly province interviewed by Vanina Bouté, some villagers I spoke with also felt that their labour force was just "eaten" by Chinese entrepreneurs (Bouté 2018, p. 46). Many workers also wear no proper protective gear when using strong herbicides and fertilizers, particularly in some banana plantations. Few villagers I interviewed blamed such exposure to strong chemicals for their recurring headaches and stomachaches and even miscarriages. Oftentimes, their wage payment was given late; their overtime work was unpaid. A few workers also complain that they have not received permanent contracts from their employers, even if they have already worked for more than a year on the plantations. Further, the absence of health insurance and social security worsens their insecure employment.

These new precarious work experiences of many villagers in various plantations prove how the frontier dynamics of hydropower projects have reproduced an emerging "relative surplus-population" or "reserve army" whose "labour power" (*Arbeitskraft*) is readily exploitable to valorize capital (Marx 2002, pp. 1815–55). Put it differently, applying David Harvey's (2005) accumulation by dispossession, the production of resource frontier spaces through hydropower development—including the resettlement communities—dispossessed the displaced villagers' former livelihood sources. Such loss has compelled them to sell or commodify their labour in the market to survive, allowing other capitalists (i.e., the owners of Chinese plantations) to accumulate more capital by exploiting their cheap *Arbeitskraft*. In sum, the relocation to the Banmai resettlement (a frontier zone made by the NNua1) has just transformed the villagers who just relied before on subsistence swidden farming, hunting, gathering, and/or fishing into exploitable commercial farmers or wage labourers—a proletarianization process that is necessary for accumulating and valorizing capital (Marx 2002, pp. 2205–206). Such proletarianization has likewise been observed by Ian Baird (2011) in the resource frontiers of rubber plantations in southern Laos. My findings have also confirmed Cons' (2016) and McDuie-Ra's (2016) arguments about how the resource frontier spaces engendered by megaprojects have facilitated capital accumulation (see also Cons and Eilenberg 2019).

Not all villagers can transmute their bodies into *Arbeitskraft* or can commodify their labour in the market, however. This is not because these members of the relative surplus population are unwilling to sell their labour. Pho Tha, for instance, wanted to work on a Chinese banana plantation in Houayxay. Unfortunately, the Chinese employers told him that they could not employ old men above fifty years. The same goes for the disabled. A few plantations do not hire women. Some villagers surmised that perhaps the Chinese employers thought the aforementioned groups are less productive compared to the able-bodied young men.

For this reason, it is usually the children of the older villagers who work outside Banmai to support the family. This large-scale migration of the young working population is somehow connected to why many grandparents now serve as housekeepers and guardians of children in many households. As I presented in the introductory vignette, Pho Tha's only son has been working illegally in Thailand since 2016. He has been worried about his child. Pho Tha and many elderlies I spoke with feel that the loss of livelihoods after the relocation has disintegrated many families in the new settlement: "If we had good sources of income here, perhaps the young people would have not left Banmai; perhaps many families would have worked together quite happily", Pho Tha mused.[6]

At the time of my fieldwork, Pho Tha did not do swidden farming because he was still waiting for the promised land. Whenever they did not receive remittance from their son, Pho Tha and his wife claimed that they walked for almost four hours going to the dense forest to gather some wild edibles and rattan. They usually sold the latter to handicraft makers in Banmai. When they earned some money, Pho Tha's wife bought threads to weave Lao skirts. Some merchants from the district or provincial capital usually purchased their products.

Like many villagers, Pho Tha was also grateful for their new physical infrastructures; he agreed that these somehow made them modern. However, these could be only fully enjoyed by people who have money. As he lamented:

> If you don't have money here, you can't buy appliances; you can't pay for electricity; you can't go to big markets and hospitals. Some medicines are not free in the *souksala*; you need to buy them. If you don't have money, you can't buy smartphones; you can't buy Internet load ... I don't have money because I don't have livelihoods here. *You ni you lala!* ["doing nothing"]. *Thouk gay, thouk chai* [literally: "Poor body, poor heart"].

Unlike those who mentioned the phrase, "Comfortable/happy body, poor heart" (*Sabay gay, thouk chai*), the thirty-eight villagers who felt having a "poor body, poor heart" (*thouk gay, thouk chai*) after the relocation did not equate the modernity and the air of urbanity brought by the new physical infrastructures with the comfort of the body (see Table 7.2). Similar to Pho Tha, these villagers mentioned that what could mainly make their hearts and bodies *sabay* were the stable sources of income and food, rather than improved access to electricity, roads, public health institutions, markets, or the Internet. They were also very vocal in their dissatisfaction with their relocation experiences. They asserted that their livelihoods in older settlements were much better; the resettlement had made them poorer.

The majority of these villagers whose bodies and hearts became poorer after the relocation were ethnic minorities (twenty-three out of thirty-eight). As Table 7.2 shows, there are no ethnic minorities who feel comfortable like Pho Keo. These data concur with the findings of Bader et al. (2017) that the greater connection to infrastructures, market, and state services—the magic cure-all promoted by the proponents of frontier discourses—might be insufficient to eradicate the poverty of ethnic minorities in Laos. The Lao ethnic minorities could not utilize such connections to secure sustainable livelihoods. This is somehow related to why many of them leave the new settlement, and illicitly go back to their old villages.[7] They disclose that they feel happier in their decisions to illegally return to their former villages not only because of the material plenty provided by nature there but also because they do not need to work with insensitive Chinese bosses anymore.

During the interviews, these villagers who feel *thouk gay, thouk chai* were too outspoken in their criticisms of the purported corruption of local state officials and the NNua1's staff. Many of them also mentioned that the aforesaid actors just deceived them about the promises of progress after the relocation. As Pho Tha put it: "Their promises about improving our lives were just lies, so that they could convince us to move ... We had no choice; we just needed to follow them because they're 'big people' (*phou nyai*)." All the above statements somehow evince how the villagers with a "poor body, poor heart" contest the Lao state's and the NNua1's frontier narratives that the relocation to the resettlement communities might alleviate the isolated people's impoverishment.

MAKING THE MARGINALIZED MODERN BUT NOT COMFORTABLE?

This chapter has investigated the resettled villagers' notions of modern (*thansamai*) and comfort (*sabay*) after the relocation in order to understand how they experience, internalize and contest the Lao state's and the NNua1's frontier discourses and dynamics. In general, the frontier discourses have ideological functions for the Lao state and other key players of hydropower development in Laos. On the macro-scale, the portrayal of Laos as the last frontier "which hold the promise for high rates of return of investment," (Barney 2009, p. 151) helps the Lao state to attract more FDIs related to megaprojects, including hydropower. It also enables the international project developers and funders of hydropower projects to justify their presence and development interventions in Laos. They argue that the development of "underused/unproductive spaces" through hydropower development could increase the national income, globalize the Lao economy, and turn the land-locked country into "the battery of Southeast Asia" (Giovannini 2018).

On the micro-scale, the Lao state and the NNua1 have utilized the frontier discourses to legitimize the resettlement of the remote people living in "empty or under-populated wilderness". The Banmai resettlement community—which is one of the resource frontier spaces produced by the NNua1 Hydropower Project—provides new physical infrastructures to the displaced rural riparian populations, mainstreaming them and connecting them to the market and the state.[8] The Lao state and the NNua1 also believe that these frontierization processes move the isolated villagers away from the margins, alleviating their absolute poverty.

How the resettled villagers embrace or challenge the frontier discourses are contingent on their socio-economic background. During the interviews, the villagers of relative affluence—or those who have huge pre-resettlement savings and who have been running good businesses since before the relocation—usually echo the Lao state's and the NNua1's frontier discourses. They always emphasize how the new physical infrastructures and market integration have made them modern and comfortable. They also feel that improved access to electricity, roads, bigger markets and public health institutions, and the Internet not only provides their rural settlements with an air of urbanity, but also makes some of their everyday physical tasks less time-consuming or less tiring. These comparatively wealthy villagers reiterate that they are happier in Banmai than in the former settlements. However, these villagers who have both "comfortable/happy bodies and hearts" (*sabay gay, sabay chai*) are very few.

Many resettled people (79 out of 128 interlocutors) associate the new physical infrastructures with the experiences of being modern and having comfortable bodies (*sabay gay*); however, not with the happiness of the hearts. They say that their hearts become poorer after the relocation due to three main reasons: first, the loss of previous livelihood and food sources; second, the inadequate compensations; and third, the purported corruption issues of some Lao staff of the NNua1 Company and some local state officials. Their new survival strategies to confront difficult situations also make them feel *thouk chai*. Since most of them have insufficient capital to run convenient and lucrative businesses, they have just sold their labour power in the market. Few villagers go for jobs in more urban/peri-urban areas of Laos and Thailand; many of them work in various Chinese businesses (various plantations and the small Chinese dam) in exchange for subsistence wages. Their current precarious work experiences as commercial farmers or wage labourers demonstrate how the resource frontier spaces produced by hydropower projects have furthered "accumulation by dispossession" (Harvey 2005).

Not all villagers equate the modernity and the air of urbanity brought by the new physical infrastructures with the comfort of the body. These villagers (thirty-eight interlocutors) say straightforwardly that after the relocation, their hearts and bodies become poorer (*thouk chai, thouk gay*). Many of them are either those who cannot commodify their labour due to their biological features (i.e., some elderlies, people with disabilities, and women), or those ethnic minorities who illicitly return to former villages. They thought their lives would have been better if the government had allowed them to stay in their old settlements. Their negative views of the relocation thus manifest how the Lao state's and the NNua1's frontier discourses are being challenged from below.

Notes

1. The chapter is based on my PhD project on modernity, market integration, and (*im*)mobilities facilitated by Chinese BRI Hydroelectric Project in northwestern Laos. I draw on twelve months of ethnographic fieldwork undertaken between 2018 and 2019 in the Banmai Resettlement, Bokeo Province. I conducted participant observation in all three zones of the resettlement community. I also carried out over 250 conversational interviews and 128 semi-structured interviews not just with Lao-Buddhist villagers but also with all ethnic minorities of the new settlement, such as Khmu and Rmeet [or Lamét]. In addition, I interviewed some national and district state

officials as well as some staff of the hydropower company. To secure their anonymity, I deliberately changed the names of the hydropower company, the resettlement village and all research participants.
2. For more information about the Greater Mekong Subregion (GMS), the subregional cooperation programme spearheaded by the Asian Development Bank (ADB), see Matthews and Geheb (2015).
3. Local terms in the resettlement: *mo phi, mo môn, mo nyao*.
4. The common appliances and gadgets in the new village are electric fans, televisions (TVs), satellite dishes to watch TV, ordinary cellphones and smartphones and small and big speakers. The more affluent participants usually possess refrigerators, big freezers, electric pots, electric water boilers, rice cookers and washing machines with dryers. The richest participants have more fancy appliances such as water-cooled portable air conditioners, water dispensers with cold and hot options and water heaters for taking a bath.
5. The video is, however, not publicly available, alas.
6. Apart from economic reasons, there are also overlapping socio-cultural and political factors why young rural villagers of Laos in particular, of Southeast Asia in general, left their "agricultural past" and are motivated to join the urban and global labour force. Some of these include the notions of good life in urban areas, desires to be modern like urbanites; etc. The brevity of this chapter precludes me to tackle these issues. For more information about this topic, see, e.g., Holly High (2014) and Mary Beth Mills (1997, 1999).
7. All the houses in the former settlements were inundated, but the mountain ridges there were not flooded and are still habitable. The provincial and district government, however, restricts them from returning there. This prohibition will avoid any casualties in the future in case the dam collapses unexpectedly.
8. The other frontier spaces include the NNua1 hydropower dam and reservoir, the hydropower power plant, the transmission lines connecting Laos and Thailand.

References

Anderson, Zachary. 2019. "Mainstreaming Green: Translating the Green Economy in an Indonesian Frontier". In *Frontier Assemblages: The Emergent Politics of Resource Frontiers in Asia*, edited by Jason Cons and Michael Eilenberg, pp. 83–98. Oxford: Wiley.

Arnold, Dennis. 2012. "Spatial Practices and Border SEZs in Mekong Southeast Asia". *Geography Compass* 6, no. 12: 740–51.

Bach, Jonathan. 2011. "Modernity and the Urban Imagination in Economic Zones". *Theory, Culture and Society* 28, no. 5: 98–122.

Bader, Christoph, Sabin Bieri, Urs Wiesmann, and Andreas Heinimann. 2017. "Is Economic Growth Increasing Disparities? A Multidimensional Analysis of Poverty in the Lao PDR between 2003 and 2013". *Journal of Development Studies* 53, no. 12: 2067–85.

Baird, Ian G. 2011. "Turning Land into Capital, Turning People into Labour: Primitive Accumulation and the Arrival of Large-Scale Economic Land Concessions in Laos". *New Proposals: Journal of Marxism and Interdisciplinary Inquiry* 5, no. 1: 10–26.

———, and Bruce Shoemaker. 2007. "Unsettling Experiences: Internal Resettlement and International Aid Agencies in Laos". *Development and Change* 38, no. 5: 865–88.

———, and Bruce Shoemaker. 2008. *People, Livelihoods, and Development in the Mekong River Basin, Laos*. Bangkok: White Lotus.

Barney, Keith. 2009. "Laos and the Making of a 'Relational' Resource Frontier". *Geographical Journal* 175, no. 2: 146–59.

Bouté, Vanina. 2018. "New Paths of Work at the Lao-Chinese Border: From Self-Sufficient Agriculture to Wage Labor". In *Searching for Work: Small-Scale Mobility and Unskilled Labor in Southeast Asia*, edited by Silvia Vignato and Matteo Carlo Alcano, pp. 23–53. Chiang Mai: Silkworm Books.

Cons, Jason. 2016. *Sensitive Space: Fragmented Territory at the India-Bangladesh Border*. Seattle: University of Washington Press.

———, and Michael Eilenberg. 2019. "Introduction". In *Frontier Assemblages: The Emergent Politics of Resource Frontiers in Asia*, by Jason; Cons and Michael Eilenberg, pp. 1–24. Oxford: Wiley.

Creak, Simon, and Keith Barney. 2018 "Conceptualising Party-State Governance and Rule in Laos". *Journal of Contemporary Asia* 48, no. 5: 693–716.

Curzon, Lord. 1907 *Frontiers: The Romanes Lectures*. Oxford: Clarendon Press

Donnan, Hastings, and Thomas Wilson. 1994. *Border Approaches: Anthropological Perspectives on Frontiers*. Lanham: University Press of America.

Dunn, Elizabeth Cullen, and Jason Cons. 2014. "Aleatory Sovereignty and the Rule of Sensitive Spaces". *Antipode*. 46, no. 1: 92–109.

Eilenberg, Michael. 2012. *At the Edges of States: Dynamics of State Formation in the Indonesian Borderlands*. Leiden: Brill.

———. 2014. "Frontier Constellations: Agrarian Expansion and Sovereignty on the Indonesian-Malaysian Border". *Journal of Peasant Studies* 41, no 2: 157–82.

Giovannini, Gabrielle 2018. "Power and Geopolitics along the Mekong: The Laos-Vietnam Negotiation on the Xayaburi Dam". *Journal of Current Southeast Asian Affairs* 37, no. 2: 63–93.

Harvey, David. 2005. *The New Imperialism*. Oxford: Oxford University Press.
High, Holly. 2014. *Fields of Desire: Poverty and Policy in Laos*. Singapore: NUS Press.
Levien, Michael. 2011. "Special Economic Zones and Accumulation by Dispossession in India". *Journal of Agrarian Change* 11, no. 4: 454–83.
Lu, Juliet, and Oliver Schönweger. 2017 "Great Expectations: Chinese Investment in Laos and the Myth of Empty Land". *Territory, Politics, Governance* 7, no. 1: 61–78.
Marx, Karl. 2002 [1890]. *Das Kapital, Volume I*, edited by Hans G. Ehrbar. 4th ed.
Matthews, Nathanial, and Kim Geheb. 2015. "On Dams, Demons and Development: The Political Intrigues of Hydropower Development in the Mekong". In *Hydropower Development in the Mekong Region: Political, Socio-Economic, and Environmental Perspectives*, edited by Nathanial Matthews and Kim Geheb, pp. 1–16. New York Routledge.
McDuie-Ra, Duncan. 2016. *Borderland City in New India: Frontier to Gateway*. Amsterdam: Amsterdam University Press.
MEM (Ministry of Energy and Mines). 2016. "Policy Guidelines for the Implementation of Policy on Sustainable Hydropower Development in Lao PDR 2016". Vientiane.
———. 2017 ວິໄສທັດ ຂອງປີ 2030, ຍຸດທະສາດການພັດທະນາ 2025 ແລະ ແຜນພັດທະນາພະລັງງານ ແລະ ບໍ່ແຮ່5 ປີ ຄັ້ງທີ VIII (2016–2020) [Ministry of Energy and Mines' Vision 2030; Development Plan 2025; and Five-Year Development Report VIII (2016–2020)]. Vientiane.
Mills, Mary Beth. 1997. "Contesting the Margins of Modernity: Women, Migration, and Consumption in Thailand": *American Ethnologist* 24, no. 1: 37–61.
———. 1999. *Thai Women in the Global Labor Force: Consuming Desires, Contested Selves*. Brooklyn: Rutgers University Press.
OECD. 2017. "Trends in Foreign Investment and Trade in Lao PDR". In *OECD Investment Policy Reviews: Lao PDR*. Paris: OECD Publishing. https://doi.org/10.1787/9789264276055-6-en
Paprocki, Kasia 2019. "All That Is Solid Melts into the Bay: Anticipatory Ruination on Bangladesh's Climate Frontier". In *Frontier Assemblages: The Emergent Politics of Resource Frontiers in Asia*, edited by Jason Cons and Michael Eilenberg, pp. 25–39. Oxford: Wiley.
Ponce, Floramante S.J. 2022. "'Eating with the People': How a Chinese Hydropower Project Changed Food Experiences in a Lao Community". *Social Anthropology/Anthropologie sociale* 30, no. 1: 1-23.
Rigg, Jonathan. 2005. *Living with Transition in Laos: Market Integration in Southeast Asia*. London: Routledge.
———. 2018. "Rethinking Asian Poverty in a Time of Asian Prosperity". *Asia Pacific Viewpoint* 59, no. 2: 1–14.

———, Katie Oven, Gopi Basyal, and Richa Lamichhane. 2016. "Between a Rock and a Hard Place: Vulnerability and Precarity in Rural Nepal". *Geoforum* 76: 63–74.
Sahlins, Marshall. 1974. *Stone Age Economics*. London: Tavistock.
Sidaway, James D., Simon C. Rowedder, Chih Yuan Woon, Weiqiang Lin, and Vatthana Pholsena. 2020. "Introduction: Research Agendas Raised by the Belt and Road Initiative". *Environment and Planning C: Politics and Space* 38, no. 5: 795–802.
Stuart-Fox, Martin. 2008. *Historical Dictionary of Laos*. Lanham: Scarecrow Press.
Turner, Frederick Jackson. 1920. *The Frontier in American History*. New York: Holt.
Whitington, Jerome. 2019. *Anthropogenic Rivers: The Production of Uncertainty in Lao Hydropower*. Ithaca and London: Cornell University Press.
Winther, Tanja. 2008. *The Impact of Electricity: Development, Desires and Dilemmas*. Oxford, New York: Berghahn Books.
———. 2013 "Space, Time, and Sociomaterial Relationships: Moral Aspects of the Arrival of Electricity in Rural Zanzibar". In *Cultures of Energy: Power, Practices, and Technologies*, edited by Sarah Strauss, Stephanie Rupp, and Thomas Love, pp. 164–76. Walnut Creek: Left Coast Press.
Woods, Kevin. 2011. "Ceasefire Capitalism: Military-Private Partnerships, Resource Concessions and Military-State Building in the Burma-China Borderlands". *Journal of Peasant Studies* 38, no. 4: 747–70.
World Bank. 2020. "From Landlocked to Land-Linked: Unlocking the Potential of Lao-China Rail Connectivity". https://openknowledge.worldbank.org/handle/10986/33891
Wu, Xiujie. 2008. "Men Purchase, Women Use: Coping with Domestic Electrical Appliances in Rural China". *East Asian Science Technology and Society* 2: 211–34.
Yamada, Norihiko. 2018 "Legitimation of the Lao People's Revolutionary Party: Socialism, Chintanakan Mai (New Thinking) and Reform". *Journal of Contemporary Asia* 48, no. 5: 717–38.

8

FRONTIER CAPITALISM IN COLONIAL AND CONTEMPORARY LAOS
The Case of Tin Mining

Oliver Tappe

INTRODUCTION

When France seized control of the Lao territories on the east bank of the Mekong from Siam in 1893, the sparsely populated country remained a colonial "backwater" that received only little administrative and commercial attention (Gunn 1990; Ivarsson 2008). However, as Laos was rich in minerals, not only gold and silver but also tin and copper, it evoked imaginaries of a "Klondike Indochinois and New Bolivia" (Deloncle [1930] 2011, p. 116) and attracted numerous entrepreneurs and venturers. Taking the tin mining area in the Nam Phathaen valley (Khammouane Province, central Laos; see Figures 8.1 and 8.2) as an example, this chapter investigates the contingent processes of (capitalist) frontierization—processes of uneven and combined development on the ground—in past and present Laos.

The image of a resource frontier has certainly shaped the perception of Laos until the present day. Still in the 2000s, the Asian Development Bank depicted the country as a "new frontier" (Barney 2009, p. 147) and promoted transnational investment into mining, energy and agribusiness, which was a striking echo of colonial discourses on underdeveloped and underpopulated Laos. Both under colonial capitalism and in the context of present-day "market socialism with neoliberal characteristics" (Hann and Endres 2018), the vast, forested uplands of Laos (80 per cent of the state territory with only half of the country's population of 7 million), in particular, have been envisaged as a resource-rich frontier awaiting exploitation. This imaginary translated into extractive practice that produced considerable social and environmental costs among the fifty different ethnic groups of Laos and their largely subsistence-based

FIGURE 8.1
Province Khammouane, Lao PDR

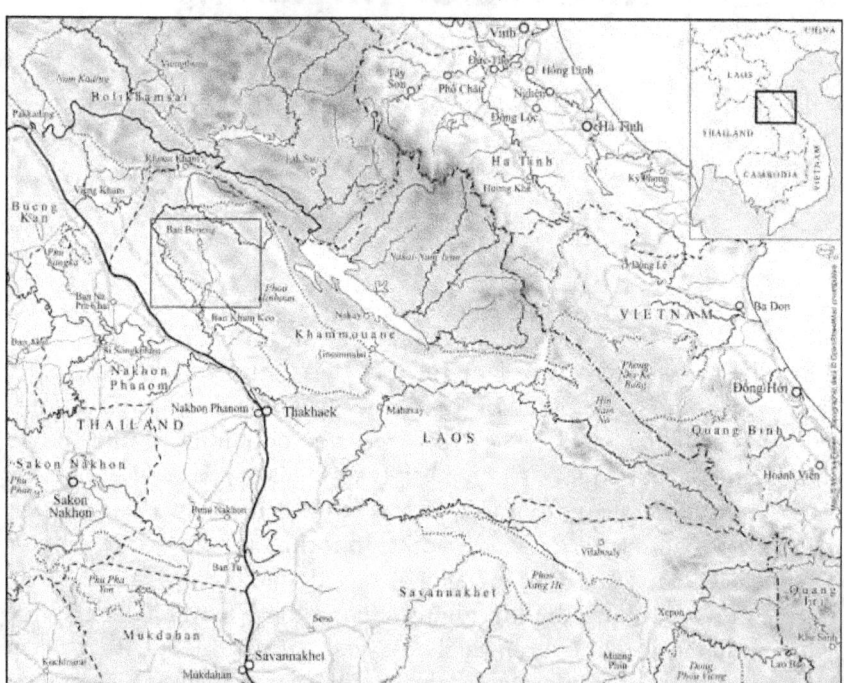

FIGURE 8.2
Nam Phathaen Valley in Khammouane Province, Lao PDR

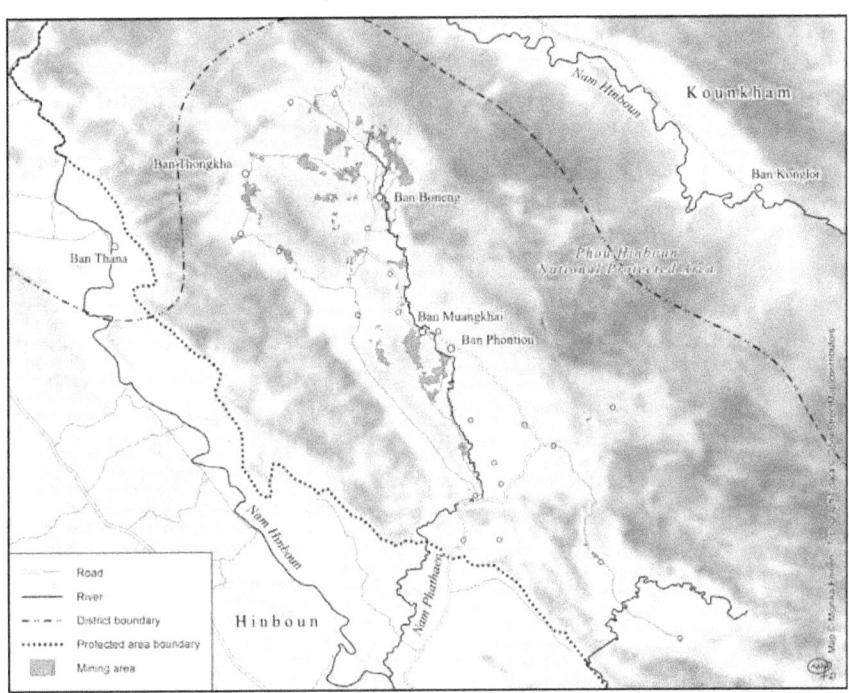

economies (see, e.g., Kenney-Lazar 2018; Rigg 2005; Laungaramsri 2012; Dwyer and Vongvisouk 2017; Ponce, this volume).

As several authors have noted (Tsing 2005; Li 2014; Cons and Eilenberg 2019), the concept of the (resource) frontier can be used as a heuristic device to examine the interwoven social, economic, political and environmental dynamics and transformations at the margins of global capitalism (see as well the introduction to this volume by Rowedder and Tappe). In particular, the relationship between global capital and indigenous communities, processes of exclusion, and increasing inequalities can be examined through the lens of the frontier. Shifts in local subsistence strategies and labour relations under conditions of frontier capitalism and rudimentary industrialization constitute a key aspect to be discussed in this chapter.

Processes of frontierization in colonial and present-day Laos are intertwined with discourses of backwardness with both economic and racial connotations (Ivarsson 2008; Goscha 2012; Barney 2009). This makes Laos a fruitful arena to investigate trajectories of uneven and combined development through old and new processes of spatially and temporally incoherent capitalist expansions (and contractions), resulting in economic and social contradictions and ambiguities (see van der Linden 2007; Allinson and Anievas 2009; Kasmir and Gill 2018; Strümpell and Hoffmann forthcomimg). Those dialectics arguably shape the Lao frontier and reproduce it—not as a linear process of enclosure but as fragmentary recasting (see Nyíri 2012 for the case of Special Economic Zones in the Lao-Chinese borderlands; Rowedder, this volume). The persistence of Lao miner-peasant livelihoods calls for a closer examination of the historical contingencies of frontier capitalism.

Against this backdrop, one key problem in the context of mining in Laos is the precarious coexistence of artisanal and small-scale mining (ASM) and industrial large-scale mining (LSM) operations, a pattern that has been characterizing the Lao tin mining area in Khammouane for the past hundred years. This pattern includes shifting labour relations between agriculture and industry that correspond with processes of uneven and combined development, arguably grounded in the complex frontierization processes that shape the Nam Phathaen valley.

Taking the tin mining area in Khammouane as a test case, I will address the following questions:[1] How did and do processes of frontierization play out on the ground, shaping local subsistence strategies within shifting frontier assemblages? How is frontier capitalism linked to the question of (unfree) labour, especially in sparsely populated regions? How does the reproduction of the frontier (instead of a closure) correspond with processes of uneven and combined development? My historical perspective aims to illustrate the dynamics of frontier capitalism in Laos from the French colonial *mise en valeur* policy to the Chinese Belt and Road Initiative—both targeting allegedly "untapped" resource frontiers.

MINING THE LAO FRONTIER: A BRIEF HISTORICAL OVERVIEW

Early French accounts highlight the local mining practices in the river valleys of Laos, in particular, artisanal gold mining (e.g., Pavie 1900; Gosselin 1900; Raquez 1902). Precious metals constituted important tax and tribute commodities for centuries. A constant flow of gold, silver, copper and tin connected upland societies to the Lao principalities along the Mekong (and further to the Siamese court). This was part of an encompassing exchange cycle linking upland and lowlands in mainland Southeast Asia through complex movements of goods and people (Grabowsky and Wichasin 2008).

The French took advantage of this existing mining system and began systematic explorations by the turn of the twentieth century. This happened at a time when the colonial government heavily invested in infrastructures and met French capitalist interests through state contracts, monopolies, and subsidies, not least to dismantle Chinese commercial dominance in Indochina (Brocheux and Hémery 2009; Sasges 2015). New roads connecting the Lao towns by the Mekong with the Vietnamese ports also aimed at redirecting flows of revenue and trade away from neighbouring Siam (Goscha 2012). However, transport across the rugged Lao hinterland remained slow and costly in comparison to the route across the Mekong to Siam, often controlled by Chinese merchants.

Even more challenging for the fledgling frontier capitalism in colonial Laos, however, was the question of labour. In the case of the Lao tin mines, local villagers only practised small-scale mining for two months during the dry season. The French resorted to Vietnamese migrant labour, using the newly built roads and existing networks of coolie recruitment. With modern mining technologies, Western know-how and separate workers' compounds, the mining area of the Nam Phathaen became the first sizeable industrial agglomeration in the country (and remained so after national independence in 1953).

While the enthusiastic anticipation of a railroad linking the Mekong with the Vietnamese coast and corresponding exaggerated hopes of economic development had been disappointed, the tin mines remained a stable industrial enterprise, best represented by the *Société des Études et Éxplorations Minières de l'Indochine* (Mouscadet 2013). By the start of the mineral boom in the 1920s, local tin mining in the villages around the French mines seemed to have proceeded as well: "*une petite industrie indigène*" with basic mining techniques and simple earthen ovens to melt the mineral.[2]

The tin mining area in Laos remained an only rudimentary industrialized frontier, though. After national independence and later in the context of the Second Indochina War, the tin mines—still under the direction of French engineers, and in lack of alternative notable industries—were important for the revenues for the Royal Lao Government (in cooperation with the ally Thailand, see CIA 1967). After the communist revolution of 1975 and the resulting exodus of the educated class to Thailand (including many skilled Vietnamese workers; see Evans 2002), the mines—like other economic sectors—fell into decline. The American "secret war" in Laos, a sideshow of the war in Vietnam, had left the country heavily bombed and with destroyed infrastructures (including many roads to Vietnam). Most critical was perhaps the closure of the border to Thailand that made trade across the Mekong difficult (ibid.).

The villagers in the Nam Phathaen valley returned to their fields and occasionally dug for minerals in the abandoned mines. In the 1980s, Russian (and later North Korean and Chinese) engineers were running the mines on a modest level (Lahiri-Dutt, Alexander, and Insouvanh 2014). The valley faced increasing mechanization and environmental degradation (e.g., deforestation due to charcoal production) while local communities continued their specific subsistence strategy combining agriculture with ASM in both abandoned and active mines.

After decades of war and revolutionary struggle, the Lao People's Democratic Republic was basically an agrarian subsistence economy, with the only revenues resulting from mineral and timber export. In the 1990s, the World Bank identified mining as a key sector for socio-economic development and revenue generation. Since then, the mining and energy sector has attracted a large share of foreign direct investment (FDI)—especially from the economic regional powerhouses China, Thailand and Vietnam—and generates important state revenue. The Lao Ministry of Energy and Mines estimates more than 150 mineral reserves in the country, including gold, copper, tin, iron, bauxite, lignite and potash (Mottet 2013; Tappe 2021).

Perceptions of the Lao mining sector used to be dominated by the "big two" gold and copper mining areas: Phu Bia mine in Xaysomboun province; and Xepon mine in Savannakhet province, extractive enclaves in the mountains. Established by Australian mining companies under World Bank guidance, the mines were later purchased by Chinese enterprises. Until both mines reduced production to a minimum in 2020 (as planned even before the pandemic), they generated more than 90 per cent of state revenues earned from mining (ibid.; Barney 2018). However, several smaller mining operations currently explore the remaining gold reserves and other rare metals in these areas, taking advantage of existing infrastructures and new technologies.

Smaller mining areas such as the tin mines of Khammouane are today marked by Chinese or Vietnamese concessions (investment from both countries accounts for more than 80 per cent of FDI in the Lao mining sector; Mottet 2013). While ASEAN integration fosters transnational trade and migration (in particular with Thailand and Vietnam), the legacy of the Chinese Go Out policy of the 1990s and the recent Belt and Road Initiative (BRI), in combination with the legal reforms in Lao PDR, has resulted in a massive increase of Chinese investment (Tan 2014; see Nyíri and Tan 2017 for broader tendencies of Chinese involvement in Southeast Asia). Chinese infrastructure investment in the context of the BRI adds a new dynamic to the sector, linking upland peripheries to the "economic corridors" already envisaged before by World Bank and ADB (Dwyer 2020).

These tendencies in the resource-driven economic development strategies have not translated into job opportunities for a great part of the local populations, though. As in the case of Vietnamese- and Chinese-run plantations in Laos (see, e.g., Baird et al. 2019), and recent infrastructure projects, most mining companies prefer a Chinese and/or Vietnamese workforce, especially (but not only) with regard to skilled labour. The reason for this tendency within the Lao labour market is manifold (see ibid.; Molland 2017; Tappe 2019a) and will be discussed in more detail below.

Artisanal and small-scale mining has for long been neglected, sometimes as "informal" or even "illegal", by policymakers (Lahiri-Dutt 2014, p. 17). Amidst reports of closure and perhaps fragmentation of the two big mines, and a growing uncontrolled ASM sector, the latter shifted into focus and received more political attention. For the moment, we witness a more differentiated view of the mining sector that includes various practices of artisanal and small-scale mining, the different actors involved, and state attempts at control and formalization (Barney 2018; Moretti and Garret 2018; Keovilignavong 2019).

Thus, in most mining areas in Laos we can identify (uncontrolled) processes of frontierization, sometimes encouraged by legal frameworks—business-friendly ones initiated by World Bank—sometimes hampered by legal uncertainties and political chaos on the ground. The focus on resource extraction—and the disconnection from other sectors of the Lao economy, prevent the development of a skilled local workforce and reproduce the frontier situation with its characteristic power imbalances and contradictions.

ARTISANAL, SMALL-SCALE AND LARGE-SCALE MINING: FRONTIER DYNAMICS AND CONTESTED LIVELIHOODS

This is the curious situation today in the Nam Phathaen valley: local artisanal miners digging in open pits overshadowed by Chinese excavators, sometimes using tools leased from the foreign companies, precariously balancing the mineral along the muddy slopes (Tappe 2019b). Chinese and Vietnamese concessions cover most of the land in the valley, often overlapping with local land rights, with a dozen mining operations ranging from medium-scale ad hoc businesses to large-scale enterprises. In the Nam Phathaen valley as elsewhere in the mineral-rich Lao uplands, such concessions blossomed after the World Bank encouraged reforms towards market capitalism since the 1990s to develop the largely agrarian Lao economy.

Luning and Pijpers (2017) describe the coexistence of industrial mining companies and local mining communities as (more or less voluntary) "cohabitation", shaped by uneven power relations and with often unresolved questions of illegality and resource governance (see Hilson 2009; Bryceson and Geenen 2016 for African ASM contexts). Local villagers certainly operate in a legal grey zone, sometimes tolerated by the companies, as will be discussed in more detail below. Even if ASM produces income opportunities, the villagers suffer from the side effects of resource extraction such as environmental degradation and pollution that negatively affect agrarian subsistence.

Processes of dispossession and exclusion on the Lao resource frontier date back to colonial times when French entrepreneurs could easily claim concessions through the colonial administration and/or military force (Gunn 1990). However, with French operations only punctual and limited, local ASM communities could easily move elsewhere to secure their livelihoods (that relied on flexible upland swidden cultivation, anyway). Meanwhile, ASM was included in the colonial economy through a newly established tax system that targeted the non-monetarized upland societies with requirements for *corvée* labour and commodities such as minerals, opium and valuable forest products (ibid.).

Environmental degradation began to be an issue under colonialism when the French enterprises intensified the production of charcoal to run the melting ovens that previously were only used on a minimal scale. Mechanized open-pit mining under French and Russian direction later turned large tracts of arable land along the Nam Phathaen into wastelands that have not recovered until the present day. On the contrary, farmland has been continuously reduced, and the reliance on ASM increased (Lahiri-Dutt 2014; Lahiri-Dutt, Alexander and Insouvanh 2014).

ASM in the Nam Phathaen valley includes mining with simple tools in abandoned mines or running concessions, as well as panning in the rivers that contain the sewage of the mining operations further upstream. More than 95 per cent of the working-age population practise ASM which accounts for an estimated 70 per cent of the average household income (interviews in Ban Muangkhai, February 2019). ASM is largely a family business with gendered labour divisions between male diggers and female panners, often drawing labour away from what remains of the agricultural sector in the valley.

What are the consequences for local livelihoods? Agrarian subsistence has become increasingly precarious, with cultivation and livestock suffering from the polluted environment. The local economy has been commercialized, and a number of traders are active in the valley, either buying minerals from the villagers or selling goods for daily needs to them (including drinking water as the water sources are by and large contaminated). The landscape and society of this remote village certainly carry the marks of a century of resource extraction (Lahiri-Dutt 2014; Earth Systems and BGR 2019; Tappe 2019b).

What historian Geoffrey Gunn (1990, p. 35) has identified as a "localized agromineral sphere" in colonial Laos, can still be observed today. The historical vicissitudes of colonialism, socialism and recent globalization tendencies in Laos notwithstanding, the Nam Phathaen valley population (approx. 12,000 people) demonstrates a specific miner-peasant identity that Kuntala Lahiri-Dutt (2014, p. 3) describes as "mining by peasants", even though some households in the valley do not cultivate the land at all—while still insisting on living from the resources of the valley's earth. Arguably, the moral economy of the local villages is still shaped by subsistence ethics that combines remnants of agriculturally based livelihoods with resource extraction.[3]

PROBLEMS OF LAO MINING LEGISLATION

A discussion of legal issues in the mining sector will further illustrate the ambiguities of "mining encounters" (Pijpers and Eriksen 2018) on the Lao resource frontier. Tin mining in the Nam Phathaen valley is regulated by the Ministry of Energy and Mines, primarily through the Law on Minerals (2017). Yet other ministries are also involved in the whole process between concessions and impact assessments (Ministry of Natural Resources and Environment, Ministry of Planning and Investment, Prime Minister's Office; see Earth Systems and BGR 2019). Poor communication and competition between ministries and different administrative levels of the respective ministries (national, provincial and district) is a major problem in Laos. This produces challenges for resource (frontier) governance and legal frameworks for investment (Lu and Schönweger 2019; Keovilignavong 2019; Suhardiman, Keovilignavong, and Kenney-Lazar 2019; Baird 2011).

A recent advisory report (Earth Systems and BGR 2019) notes a lack of commitment to the enforcement of core legislation throughout the approval process, exploration and mining from the responsible ministries and their provincial and district counterparts. Moreover, district and provincial authorities are highly dependent on financing from mine operations to conduct monitoring. Not surprisingly, only limited funding is provided. Obviously, local ASM communities are caught in the crossfire of competing and contradicting legal regulations on different and arguably disparate scales.

What exactly counts as ASM remains an ongoing debate. The Law on Minerals clearly distinguishes between artisanal mining and small-scale mining. Artisanal mining mainly means panning for alluvial gold and tin, practised by using "primitive tools, mechanized equipment with fewer than five horsepower and no more than ten laborers". It is considered a communal, non-permanent operation, "and shall not be regarded as a business". Throughout Laos we find villages holding customary rights to practise artisanal mining while others operate in a legal grey zone (Lahiri-Dutt 2014; Barney 2018; Keovilignavong 2019; Tappe 2021, pp. 4–6).

For small-scale mining, the law appears more complicated. Small-scale mining includes "digging, drilling, blasting, and sorting of mineral from the surface, underground and under water where it is not appropriate for industrial mining within an area not to exceed ten hectares". Again, this mining activity is only permitted "for Lao entities" such as village communities or single households. They are entitled to obtain official permissions and legal rights to do small-scale mining. And yet, larger mining concessions granted to foreign companies are often superimposed on such communal rights (ibid.).

The specificities of ASM in the Law on Minerals make it also difficult to legally reckon with recent trends of mechanization and intensification in ASM and the rise of domestic and foreign small-to-medium-scale mining activities that escape such categorizations. Many mining operations in Laos outside the relatively well-monitored LSM, thus navigate in legally ambiguous waters. Increased mechanization, migration and other, unintended effects of mining development entail a variegated pattern of ASM which poses considerable challenges for effective legislation and governance, as Keith Barney (2018, pp. 354–55) has pointed out.

Most of the mining concessions in the valley were granted before the aforementioned regulations were introduced, or during the process. In consequence, there is a number of legal community or family-run artisanal mining operations which found themselves on concession grounds or, rather, investors realized that there were already legal mining activities, even if only small scale, operating at the local level. Although artisanal mining within a concession is de facto illegal, exploiting a concession without proper land titles is legally ambiguous as well. What looks orderly at the macro level of ministerial planning is thus more complex on the ground, the whole process yielding unexpected, contingent results depending on mining sites.

The interaction of artisanal miners and mining companies is certainly complex; it can be conflictual or mutually beneficial. Only a few mining enterprises try to block entry of ASM miners on their concession grounds, while the majority tolerate ASM activities on concession grounds either by taking advantage of local informal labour (see below), acknowledging local customary rights, or just realizing their own legally dubious concession acquisition (in cases when such concessions were granted without the required consultations at district or village level; interviews February 2019). Mining companies are usually not held accountable for pollution even if the law calls for sustainability and post-closure rehabilitation. This is so far hardly ever enforced. Increased LSM activities result in vast stretches of degraded land and limited agricultural options. Local communities suffer a lot from land degradation, pollution, noise and other side effects of mining. As already indicated above, arable land is either minimized by open mining pits, dumps and other mining facilities or affected by pollution; deforestation entails the reduced availability of non-timber forest products and timber forest products for community harvest; water pollution threatens local fishery, livestock and drinking water reserves (Earth Systems and BGR 2019, pp. 10–16). Therefore, villagers carry the risks of mining opportunities, often ignorant of laws that can protect them.

As Keith Barney (2018, pp. 354–57) notes, the recent decade has witnessed another environmentally detrimental development: medium-scale mechanized mining that operates with backhoe excavators, pump dredges and sluices blurs the boundaries between LSM and ASM as fixed in the Law on Minerals. This emerging field draws in workers, operators and investors from China and Vietnam who negotiate permissions with local authorities, usually without any governmental control or monitoring. Local villagers lease farmland to those mining operators for some easy money but then see their land being irreparably damaged. This development and increased, uncontrolled use of chemicals have been identified in ASM contexts throughout Laos (cf. Keovilignavong 2019) including the Nam Phathaen valley.

Adding to environmental and health issues, the fact that the local villagers have to buy fish, rice and drinking water (unlike the average Lao village community) for consumption, puts the income opportunities of mining in a more questionable light. This aspect is also critical for the understanding of labour relations in the tin mining area of the Nam Phathaen valley, in particular concerning the exclusion from regular employment and the preference for informal ASM activities. The next section traces questions of labour back to colonial times.

LABOUR RELATIONS IN LAO TIN MINING

At the turn of the twentieth century, the French travel writer Alfred Raquez (1902, pp. 499–503) provided detailed descriptions of local mining practices: The villagers dug narrow vertical shafts in the ground, between 10 and 20 metres deep with a diameter of 80 and 150 centimetres. Then they dug out tunnels, extracted the ore, crashed it with stones and washed it in wide bowls or coconut shells (techniques still used today). Finally, the miners melt the mineral in small earthen ovens and produced small nuggets to sell in the Mekong towns or to give to Chinese merchants in exchange for textiles, salt, dried fish, and sometimes rice in cases of local famine (cf. Laurent 1907).

When I visited the valley more than a hundred years later, the parallels between ASM practices in past and present struck me. In an abandoned mine near the former headquarter of the French *Société des Études et Explorations Minières de l'Indochine* and, decades later, of a short-lived Lao–North Korean joint venture, I watched local villagers climbing into narrow shafts with rickety bamboo ladders. They used basic tools to produce the ore while their wives and daughters washed it with simple pumps. The more thorough the processing, the higher the concentration of the mineral and, thus, the profit when selling the mineral to traders or the mining companies operating in the vicinity (see Figure 8.3).

FIGURE 8.3
Artisanal Tin Miners in the Nam Phathaen Valley

Source: Photo taken by the author, February 2019.

In this section, I will discuss the different labour relations that mark the tin mining industry in the Nam Phathaen valley. Both in colonial times and the present, Vietnamese work migrants constitute the main workforce in the industrial mining operations (actually, in all labour-intensive sectors of the Lao economy; see Tappe 2019a). Local Lao villagers are by and large excluded from regular employment and operate in a legal grey zone between illicit ASM activities and informal work for the mining companies.

Exclusion from regular employment and the precarious cohabitation patterns echo labour regimes under colonialism: a local Lao village population with mixed livelihoods consisting of ASM and agriculture (and, in the past, of foraging in the forest), and small industrialized mining enclaves relying on a temporary migrant workforce from Vietnam. The ratio may change, and overlaps happen during periods of waxing and waning local employment in response to diverse external forces (border policy, legislation, economic crisis, etc.).

In the Lao uplands and elsewhere, indigenous labour was considered insufficient and unreliable (Goscha 2012; Tappe 2016). Indeed, the local peasants in the Nam Phathaen valley only practised tin mining in the dry season, for both practical and cosmological reasons. During the monsoon the spirits of the water may become aggressive, causing floods and landslides.[4] Mining work was certainly more dangerous in the rainy season, and wet rice cultivation required labour for most of the year, so mining was just more practicable in the agriculturally slack winter months.

As in all labour-intensive sectors of the Indochinese economy, the recruitment of Vietnamese labourers, the so-called "coolies", appeared more convenient to the colonial enterprises. The tin mining area in Laos attracted thousands of Vietnamese from the impoverished coastal areas of northern Annam.[5] This migration was more spontaneous in comparison to the state-orchestrated recruitment campaigns on behalf of the newly established enclaves of colonial capitalism in southern Indochina, most notably the rubber plantations on the high plateaus of Cambodia and Cochinchina (Brocheux and Hémery 2009; Aso 2018).

As I have discussed elsewhere (Tappe 2016), "coolie" labour constituted a kind of hybrid between wage labour and coerced labour—politically institutionalized and legitimized. According to the law, it was possible to leave the contract when advances and other costs were paid off. However, it was difficult for the labourers to do so given the low salaries and deductions for food and accommodation in the isolated compounds. They rather accumulated more debts and their systematic exploitation of the (often heavily guarded) workplace continued (see Klein 2012).

In the Lao tin mining area and elsewhere in Indochina's resource frontiers, the impoverished population of coastal northern and central Vietnam constituted a veritable reserve army of labour. For the year 1932, Geoffrey Gunn (1990, p. 48) counts a workforce of 1,157 in the tin mines (down from 6,000 in 1929, prior to the world economic crisis), 921 of them Vietnamese, 156 Lao. This ratio indicates the Vietnamese dominance in the labour sector, but also the fact that at least seasonal work in the colonial mines had become a part of local Lao livelihoods, perhaps parallel to agriculture and fishing.

Frontier capitalism's Vietnamese workforce—unlike the Lao miner-peasants—showed gradual tendencies of proletarianization, however, interrupted by political crises and spontaneous (re)migrations. The 1930s witnessed the emergence of the first communist cells in the Lao mines, agitating against colonial exploitation and hard working conditions (Gunn 1988). The economic crisis and corresponding salary cuts fuelled workers' unrest, and the mines became the arena of the first labour struggles in the country (with only a few Lao participating, though). In 1946 and 1975, many Vietnamese moved back or further to Thailand. Together with the miner-peasant subsistence ethics that blur the distinction between pre-capitalist and capitalist modes of production, these developments mean that the Lao tin mining area never experienced full proletarianization.

Moreover, present-day employment patterns resemble the colonial labour regime, an efficient means to prevent labour organization (Derks 2010). Since Lao labour laws largely ignore ASM labour and the contract labour in the foreign enclaves, neither Vietnamese migrants nor local villagers can expect protection from this side (and neither from the Lao trade union, under strict control of the Party-State). Therefore, the tin mining context implies precariousness for both groups of mining workers.

Today, Vietnamese work migrants in Laos take advantage of border arrangements, efficient recruitment networks and networks among local Lao-Viet communities. However, lacking legal security in Laos, they depend on the goodwill of their employers and local authorities (Baird et al. 2019; Tappe 2019a). Working (illegally) on a thirty-day tourist visa, they used to cross the bridge between Thakhaek (Laos) and Nakhon Phanom (Thailand) for monthly "visa runs"—a practice now complicated by Thai authorities.[6] Thus, cases of visa overstay and corresponding insecurity are increasing among the Vietnamese migrant community.

In the mines, Vietnamese labourers earn less than the official minimum wage in Laos (LAK1,200,000; US$128). Given the extreme poverty in some regions of Vietnam and the favourable exchange rate of the Vietnam dong to the Lao kip, working in Laos remains an opportunity for impoverished and mobile parts of the Vietnamese population. Due to better roads and efficient communication networks cultivated by Lao-Vietnamese middlemen, seasonal work migration to Laos is convenient for both employers and employees. Therefore, a transregional perspective is key to understanding labour relations in mining and other labour-intensive economic sectors of past and present Laos.

While Vietnamese (and Chinese) companies find it more efficient to recruit migrant labour, local Lao seem to prefer freelance artisanal mining to employment under a fixed contract. Low salaries and hard working conditions make formal jobs in the mining sector less attractive, anyway. Since the job skills of the Lao miner-peasants are considered insufficient for better-paid jobs (e.g., engineer), the Lao rarely obtain regular work contracts. Accordingly, ASM miners lack even the little work security that Vietnamese formal workers have.

Unskilled workers earn hardly more than the minimum wage of LAK1.2 million in the mines while skilled workers, such as excavator operators and mechanics, can earn up to LAK3 million (US$320). Regrettably, hardly any local Lao can get one of these well-paid jobs due to a lack of skills and the preference of Chinese and Vietnamese companies for their countrymen. Interestingly, Lao artisanal miners often refuse unskilled jobs in the mines because they can earn more than the minimum wage by doing ASM. In addition, young Lao rather prefers to accept precarious working conditions in neighbouring Thailand where salaries are higher. Remittances are an important factor for household incomes.

More than 90 per cent of the working population in the Nam Phathaen valley is active in freelance artisanal and small-scale mining, either in closed mines or operating concessions. Artisanal mining may generate up to US$200 per month depending on the amount of ore and its tin concentration. On bad days it may be half of that and without the small benefits such as insurance which direct employment provides. Artisanal miners enter the pits without protective gear and other means of work security. Accidents occur very often but health risks are exempt from the equation when people talk about income opportunities (interviews in Ban Muangkhai, February 2019).

An interesting phenomenon is local Lao ASM communities that constitute an informal workforce tied to the mining operations through leasing contracts of tools and machines. One Chinese company had made such arrangements with several households in the village Ban Boneng. Those "freelancers" lease jack-hammers and pumps to produce and process the ore as described above, and are obliged to sell the ore at a fixed price to the company. This holds advantages for both parties: The company can outsource labour and circumvents labour laws, and the local villagers enjoy more security (not work security, though) and stability. Illicit sale to itinerant metal traders occurs as well, to the discontent of the companies, yet another aspect of the precarious cohabitation.

Unlike the Vietnamese migrant workers, the Lao seem to maintain more distance from the industrial workplace and rely on the moral economy of the village instead. They constitute a casual, temporary and largely unskilled workforce that is separated from the Vietnamese migrant workers both socially and physically (Parry 2018). While the Vietnamese often live in compounds in the workplace (e.g., mine, plantation or infrastructure project) and spend their leisure time after long working days among themselves (often gambling and singing karaoke), the Lao workers resent long working hours with regard to their social obligations in the household and village. There are certainly overlaps (for instance, intermarriage and respective celebrations of Lao/Thai and Chinese/Vietnamese New Year) but the pattern remains valid.

We can identify a division of the workforce in the mines between more or less regular company workers and "a penumbra of insecure casual and temporary labour" as Jonathan Parry (2018, p. 1) puts it.

The Vietnamese coolies on the colonial mines, and the Vietnamese labour migrants of today, both examples of coerced immobilization in the workplace, constitute a convenient workforce for frontier capitalism. Yet also the local miner-peasants help to reproduce the frontier by shifting between the household economy and the industrial workplace along a continuum of informal ASM variants and casual employment.

The capitalist frontier in Laos seems to co-produce specific labour relations, either informal/unregulated (in ASM contexts) or unfree ones (the coolies in the colonial enclaves and, arguably, also the contract workers of today; see Derks 2010; Damir-Geilsdorf et al. 2016). Addressing the question of labour from a historical perspective thus offers new perspectives to understanding processes of frontierization and extractivism on the margins of global capitalism (see Banaji 2011).

CONCLUSION

Laos is a frontier in the sense of Anna Tsing's (2003, p. 5100) notion of "not yet". Incomplete processes of industrialization and proletarianization mark key sectors of the economy. The extractive industries in past and present Laos merely constitute enclaves in shifting frontier contexts where processes of uneven and combined development play out on the ground. Such enclaves may have only limited direct effects on local labour relations due to the preference for migrant labour, but certainly have indirect effects on local socio-economic configurations with regard to environmental degradation, changing local subsistence strategies, and increasing precariousness due to contested land use regimes (see Suhardiman and Kramp, this volume).

Factors for the persistence of the Lao resource frontier are, until today, the constant labour reserve from Vietnam, the low labour costs of extractive industries, opportunities for investors, but also ambiguities and precarity. The reproduction of local miner-peasant subsistence strategies in the Nam Phathaen valley also illustrates the uneven development and inequalities on the mining frontier (not least when adopting a regional perspective, with Laos occupying a "peripheral centrality" (Brown 2018) in the economically dynamic ASEAN region, increasingly linked to China).

What Philip Taylor (2016) has described as "frontier commoditization" in post-socialist Southeast Asia, appears rather as recommoditization (or just reproduction?) of a colonial frontier through a combined neoliberal and frontier capitalist agenda today.

Current frontierization implies uneven development, especially through the spatial and institutional separation of resource extraction from other sectors of the economy. Global capital—in the case of Laos mainly from China, Vietnam and Thailand—requires such allegedly "underdeveloped" resource frontiers.

The Lao economy has hitherto never developed beyond resource extraction—not only because the French did not build industries that could compete with industries in the metropole but also because a broad alliance of international agencies and investors from neighbouring countries supported resource-based economic growth in Laos. Not surprisingly, Laos never witnessed the evolution of a skilled and organized working class (let alone a labour aristocracy). Given the availability of a mobile and cheap Vietnamese reserve labour army, capitalist entrepreneurs on the Lao frontier do not need a local working class, anyway (at least that was the case before COVID-19 disrupted the transnational mobilities in Southeast Asia).

Meanwhile, the Lao Party-State benefits from the alleged "privilege of historical backwardness"—to quote Leon Trotsky—in that they can cash in the revenues from mining concessions and other forms of resource extraction while leaving investment in infrastructures and technologies to the "more developed" neighbouring countries. Investors from China, Vietnam and Thailand co-produce the Lao frontier through their competition with each other for influence in Laos, revealing both economic and geopolitical aspects of capitalist expansion in Southeast Asian peripheries (Myanmar constitutes another case in point; see Kenney-Lazar and Mark 2021; Mierzejewski, this volume). The political elite in Laos is reaping the benefits of frontier capitalism while leaving economic, social and environmental risks to foreign investors and local communities. Frontier capitalism thus reproduces one of the last communist regimes in the world. Interestingly, the regime aims to legitimize this kind of frontier capitalism as a necessary step towards socialism. The question remains if the local communities living on the contested resource frontiers will buy the message.

Notes

1. This paper is part of an ongoing project on the history and anthropology on tin mining in Laos, financed by the German Research Foundation. Previous field research in Laos and archival research in France have been kindly supported by the Competing Regional Integrations in Southeast Asia (CRISEA) interdisciplinary research program (funded by the European Union's Horizon 2020 Framework Program), and through the Small Grants Program of the German Society for Asian Studies.
2. Archives nationales du monde du travail (Roubaix, France), Fonds Belugou 176 AQ 23, *Copie de l'Option sur les Mines d'étain de Pak–Hin–Boun* (March 1926).
3. The socio-cosmological dimension of tin mining in Laos will be a central issue for my future research in the Nam Phathaen valley, following the example of key anthropological works in South American (Nash 1979) and central Asian (High 2017) mining contexts.
4. Ritual practice aimed at protection against malevolent ghosts are still crucial for the Lao ASM communities in the Nam Phathaen valley. Integrated into a general animist belief system that shapes the lifeworlds of both Buddhist Lao and non–Buddhist ethnic minorities (Sprenger 2016), the tin miners address specific water spirits that may cause landslides and flooding—crucial for work security (interviews in Ban Muangkhai, February 2019).
5. Vietnamese migration resulted in massive demographic changes in the Mekong River towns such as Thakhaek, where the Vietnamese constituted 85 per cent of the urban population, the highest percentage of Vietnamese among all Lao towns (Pietrantoni 1957, p. 230). This was an effect desired by many French administrators who considered the allegedly more "industrious" Vietnamese "race" as key to the development of sparsely populated Laos (Goscha 2012).
6. Under the current pandemic, transnational migration patterns between Thailand, Laos and Vietnam are changing for the time being. It remains to be seen if the labour regime in Laos will move back to the status quo ante, with Vietnamese workers again dominating the labour-intensive sectors in Laos, and Lao workers preferring employment in Thailand—movements currently restricted after decades of relaxed border arrangements.

References

Allinson, Jamie C., and Alexander Anievas. 2009. "The Uses and Misuses of Uneven and Combined Development: An Anatomy of a Concept". *Cambridge Review of International Affairs* 22, no. 1: 47–67.

Aso, Michitake. 2018. *Rubber and the Making of Vietnam: An Ecological History, 1897–1975*. Chapel Hill: University of North Carolina Press.

Baird, Ian G. 2011. "Turning Land into Capital, Turning People into Labour: Primitive Accumulation and the Arrival of Large-Scale Economic Land Concessions in Laos". *New Proposals: Journal of Marxism and Interdisciplinary Inquiry* 5, no. 1: 10–26.

———, William Noseworthy, Nghiem Phuong Tuyen, Le Thu Ha, and Jefferson Fox. 2019. "Land Grabs and Labour: Vietnamese Workers on Rubber Plantations in Southern Laos". *Singapore Journal of Tropical Geography* 40: 50–70.

Banaji, Jairus. 2011. *Theory as History: Essays on Modes of Production and Exploitation*. Chicago: Haymarket Books.

Barney, Keith. 2009. "Laos and the Making of a 'Relational' Resource Frontier". *Geographical Journal* 175, no. 2: 146–59.

———. 2018. "Reassembling Informal Gold-Mining for Development and Sustainability? Opportunities and Limits to Formalisation in India, Indonesia and Laos". In *Between the Plough and the Pick: Informal, Artisanal and Small-Scale Mining in the Contemporary World*, edited by Kuntala Lahiri-Dutt, pp. 335–70. Canberra: ANU Press.

Brocheux, Pierre, and Daniel Hémery. 2009. *Indochina: An Ambiguous Colonization, 1858–1954*. Berkeley, CA: University of California Press.

Brown, James A. 2018. "Laos's Peripheral Centrality in Southeast Asia: Mobility, Labour, and Regional Integration". *European Journal of East Asian Studies* 17: 228–62.

Bryceson, Deborah F., and Sara Geenen. 2016. "Artisanal Frontier Mining of Gold in Africa: Labour Transformation in Tanzania and the Democratic Republic of Congo". *African Affairs* 115, no. 459: 296–317.

CIA. 1967. "Intelligence Report. Geographic Brief on Laos". February 1967. https://www.cia.gov/readingroom/docs/CIA-RDP84-00825R000100680001-1.pdf (accessed 10 October 2021).

Cons, Jason, and Michael Eilenberg, eds. 2019. *Frontier Assemblages: The Emergent Politics of Resource Frontiers in Asia*. Hoboken: Wiley and Sons.

Damir-Geilsdorf, Sabine, Ulrike Lindner, Gesine Müller, Oliver Tappe, and Michael Zeuske, eds. 2016. *Bonded Labour: Global and Comparative Perspectives (18th–21st Century)*. Bielefeld: transcript.

Deloncle, Pierre. 2011. "The Development of Laos". In *Laos in the 1920s: The Gods, Monks and Mountains of Laos*, edited by Jean Renaud, pp. 103–21. Bangkok: White Lotus. First published 1930.

Derks, Annuska. 2010. "Bonded Labour in Southeast Asia: Introduction". *Asian Journal of Social Science* 38, no. 6: 839–52.

Dwyer, Mike B. 2020. "'They Will Not Automatically Benefit': The Politics of Infrastructure Development in Laos's Northern Economic Corridor". *Political Geography* 78: 102–18.

———, and Thoumthone Vongvisouk. 2017. "The Long Land Grab: Market-Assisted Enclosure on the China-Lao Rubber Frontier". *Territory, Politics, Governance* 7, no. 1: 96–114.
Earth Systems and BGR. 2019. *Impacts of Tin Mining in the Hinboun District, Lao PDR.* Vientiane: Ministry of Energy and Mines.
Evans, Grant. 2002. *A Short History of Laos: The Land in Between.* Crow's Nest: Allen and Unwin.
Goscha, Christopher E. 2012. *Going Indochinese: Contesting Concepts of Space and Place in French Indochina.* Copenhagen: NIAS Press.
Gosselin, Charles. 1900. *Le Laos et le Protectorat Francais.* Paris: Didier Perrin.
Grabowsky, Volker, and Renoo Wichasin. 2008. *Chronicles of Chiang Khaeng: A Tai Lü Principality of the Upper Mekong Region.* Honolulu: Center for Southeast Asian Studies, University of Hawai'i.
Gunn, Geoffrey C. 1988. *Political Struggles in Laos (1930–1954): Vietnamese Communist Power and the Lao Struggle for National Independence.* Bangkok: Editions Duang Kamol.
———. 1990. *Rebellion in Laos: Peasant and Politics in a Colonial Backwater.* Bangkok: White Lotus.
Hann, Chris, and Kirsten Endres, eds. 2018. *Socialism with Neoliberal Characteristics.* Halle: Max Planck Institute for Social Anthropology.
High, Mette. 2017. *Fear and Fortune: Spirit Worlds and Emerging Economies in the Mongolian Gold Rush.* Ithaca: Cornell University Press.
Hilson, Gavin. 2009. "Small-Scale Mining, Poverty and Economic Development in Sub-Saharan Africa: An Overview". *Resources Policy* 34: 1–5.
Ivarsson, Søren. 2008. *Creating Laos: The Making of a Lao Space between Indochina and Siam, 1860–1945.* Copenhagen: NIAS Press.
Kasmir, Sharrin, and Lesley Gill. 2018. "No Smooth Surfaces: The Anthropology of Unevenness and Combination". *Current Anthropology* 59, no. 4: 355–77. https://doi.org/10.1086/698927 (accessed 10 October 2021).
Kenney-Lazar, Miles. 2018. "Governing Dispossession: Relational Land Grabbing in Laos". *Annals of the American Association of Geographers* 108, no. 3: 679–94.
———, and SiuSue Mark. 2021. "Variegated Transitions: Emerging Forms of Land and Resource Capitalism in Laos and Myanmar". *Economy and Space* 53, no. 2: 296–314.
Keovilignavong, Oulavanh. 2019. "Mining Governance Dilemma and Impacts: A Case of Gold Mining in Phu-Hae, Lao PDR". *Resources Policy* 61: 141–50.
Klein, Jean-François. 2012. "Esclavages, engagismes et coolies, histoire des sociétés coloniales au travail (1850-1950)". In *Sociétés impériales en situations coloniales. Afrique, Asie, Antilles (années 1850 – années 1950),* edited by Jean-François Klein and Claire Laux, pp. 163–82. Paris: Ellipses.
Lahiri-Dutt, Kuntala. 2014. "Extracting Peasants from the Fields: Rushing for a Livelihood?". *ARI Working Paper Series* 216.

———, Kim Alexander, and Chansouk Insouvanh. 2014. "Informal Mining in Livelihood Diversification: Mineral Dependence and Rural Communities in Lao PDR". *South East Asia Research* 22, no. 1: 103–22.

Laungaramsri, Pinkaew. 2012. "Frontier Capitalism and the Expansion of Rubber Plantations in Southern Laos". *Journal of Southeast Asian Studies* 43, no. 3: 463–77.

Laurent, Louis. 1907. *Les productions minérales et l'extension des exploitations minières*. Marseille: Barlatier.

Li, Tania M. 2014. *Land's End: Capitalist Relations on an Indigenous Frontier*. Durham: Duke University Press.

Lu, Juliet, and Oliver Schönweger. 2019. "Great Expectations: Chinese Investment in Laos and the Myth of Empty Land". *Territory, Politics, Governance* 7, no. 1: 61–78.

Luning, Sabine, and Robert J. Pijpers. 2017. "Governing Access to Gold in Ghana: In-Depth Geopolitics on Mining Concessions". *Africa* 87, no. 4: 758–79.

Molland, Sverre. 2017. "Migration and Mobility in Laos". In *Changing Lives in Laos: Society, Politics, and Culture in a Post-Socialist State*, edited by Vanina Bouté and Vatthana Pholsena, pp. 327–49. Singapore: NUS Press.

Moore, Jason W. 2000. "Sugar and the Expansion of the Early Modern World-Economy: Commodity Frontiers, Ecological Transformations, and Industrialization". *Review* 23: 409–33.

Moretti, Daniele, and Nicholas Garrett. 2018. "Artisanal and Small-Scale Mining Governance: The 'Emerging Issue' of 'Unregulated Mining' in Lao PDR". In *Between the Plough and the Pick: Informal, Artisanal and Small-Scale Mining in the Contemporary World*, edited by Kuntala Lahiri-Dutt, pp. 311–34. Canberra: ANU Press.

Mottet, Éric. 2013. "Au Laos, la nouvelle aventure minière pourra-t-elle se dérouler sans conflits?". *Les Cahiers d'Outre-Mer* 262. http://journals.openedition.org/com/6862 (accessed 10 October 2021).

Mouscadet, Marc. 2013. *L'exploitation des ressources du sous-sol au Laos à l'époque coloniale de 1893 à 1940*. Mémoire, Paris: INALCO.

Nash, June. 1979. *We Eat the Mines and the Mines Eat Us: Dependency ad Exploitation in Bolivian Tin Mines*. New York: Columbia University Press.

Nyíri, Pál. 2012. "Enclaves of Improvement: Sovereignty and Developmentalism in the Special Zones of the China-Lao Borderlands". *Comparative Studies in Society and History* 54, no. 3: 533–62.

———, and Danielle Tan, eds. 2017. *Chinese Encounters in Southeast Asia: How People, Money, Ideas from China Are Changing a Region*. Seattle and London: University of Washington Press.

Parry, Jonathan. 2018. "Introduction: Precarity, Class, and the Neoliberal Subject". In *Industrial Labor on the Margins of Capitalism: Precarity, Class, and the Neoliberal Subject*, edited by Chris Hann and Jonathan Parry, pp. 1–38. London: Berghahn.

Pavie, Auguste. 1900. *Mission Pavie, Indo-Chine, 1879-1895*: Géographie et voyages. Paris.

Pietrantoni, Eric. 1957. "La population du Laos en 1943 dans son milieu géographique". *Bulletin de la Société des Etudes Indochinoises* 32: 223–43.

Pijpers, Robert J., and Thomas H. Eriksen, eds. 2018. *Mining Encounters: Extractive Industries in an Overheated World*. London: Pluto Press.

Raquez, Alfred. 1902. *Pages laotiennes*. Hanoi: F.H. Schneider.

Rigg, Jonathan. 2005. *Living with Transition in Laos: Market Integration in Southeast Asia*. London: Routledge.

Sasges, Gerard. 2015. "Scaling the Commanding Heights: The Colonial Conglomerates and the Changing Political Economy of French Indochina". *Modern Asian Studies* 49: 1485–525.

Sprenger, Guido. 2016. "Graded Personhood: Human and Non-human Actors in the Southeast Asian Uplands". In *Animism in Southeast Asia*, edited by Kai Århem and Guido Sprenger, pp. 73–90. London: Routledge.

Strümpell, Christian, and Michael Hoffmann, eds. Forthcoming. *Industrial Labour in an Unequal World: Ethnographic Perspectives on Uneven and Combined Development*. Berlin: De Gruyter.

Suhardiman, Diana, Oulavanh Keovilignavong, and Miles Kenney-Lazar. 2019. "The Territorial Politics of Land Use Planning in Laos". *Land Use Policy* 83: 346–56.

Tan, Danielle. 2014. "Chinese Networks, Economic and Territorial Redefinitions in Northern Lao PDR". In *Transnational Dynamics in Southeast Asia: The Greater Mekong Subregion and Malacca Straits Economic Corridor*, edited by N. Fau, S. Khonthapane and C. Taillard, pp. 421–52. Singapore: Institute of Southeast Asian Studies.

Tappe, Oliver. 2016. "Variants of Bonded Labour in Precolonial and Colonial Southeast Asia". In *Bonded Labour: Global and Comparative Perspectives (18th–21st Century)*, edited by Sabine Damir-Geilsdorf et al., pp. 103–31. Bielefeld: transcript.

———. 2019a. "Patterns of Precarity: Historical Trajectories of Vietnamese Labour Mobility". *TRaNS: Trans-Regional and -National Studies of Southeast Asia* 7, no. 1: 19–42.

———. 2019b. "Lao Labour: Arbeitsverhältnisse am Beispiel des Zinnbergbaus in der Provinz Khammouane". *Südostasien* 1/2019. https://suedostasien.net/lao-labour- arbeitsverhaeltnisse-am-beispiel-des-zinnbergbaus-in-der-provinz-khammouane/ (accessed 10 October 2021).

———. 2021. "Artisanal, Small-Scale and Large-Scale Mining in Lao PDR". *ISEAS Perspective*, no. 2021/44, 15 April 2021. https://www.iseas.edu.sg/

articles-commentaries/iseas-perspective/2021-44-artisanal-small-scale-and-large-scale-mining-in-lao-pdr-by-oliver-tappe/ (accessed 10 October 2021).

Taylor, Philip. 2016. "Frontier Commoditisation in Post-Socialist Southeast Asia". *Asia Pacific Viewpoint* 57, no. 2: 145–53.

Tsing, Anna L. 2003. "Natural Resource and Capitalist Frontiers". *Economic & Political Weekly* 38, no. 48: 5100–6.

———. 2005. *Friction: An Ethnography of Global Connection*. Princeton: Princeton University Press.

van der Linden, Marcel. 2007. "The 'Law' of Uneven and Combined Development: Some Underdeveloped Thoughts". *Historical Materialism* 15: 145–65.

9

CHINESE INVESTMENTS AND RESOURCE FRONTIERS IN CAMBODIA

Systemic Transformation

Vannarith Chheang

INTRODUCTION

China's overseas investments have significantly shaped resource frontiers in Cambodia. Resource frontiers here refer to "spaces of capitalist transition, where new forms of social property relations and systems of legality are rapidly established in response to market imperatives" (Barney 2009, p. 146). Exploiting new frontiers of land and natural resources are the key sources of economic development. The process of economic development is not just about allocating scarce resources but also about obtaining and developing new frontiers of natural resources. In this connection, "frontier-based development is the process of exploiting or converting new sources of relatively abundant resources for production purposes" (Barbier 2011, p. 7). Extractive and productive transformations are the makings of new Asian resource frontiers called "frontier assemblages", referring to "the intertwined materialities, actors, cultural logics, spatial dynamics, ecologies, and political-economic processes that produce particular places as resource frontiers" (Cons and Eilenberg 2019, p. 2).

Systemic transformation is defined as the drastic changes in social, economic, natural, political and governance landscapes. This chapter provides an initial qualitative assessment of the impacts of Chinese investments on systemic transformation in Cambodia. The chapter has three main sections, namely, enabling factors, perceived impacts of the Chinese investments, and local governance issues. Sihanoukville is used as a case study to demonstrate the impacts of Chinese investments on local governance. It argues that the influx of Chinese investments to Cambodia—in both extractive and productive sectors—over the past decade has shaped resource frontiers in many ways as they generate cross-sectoral impacts on the Cambodian economy, society, environment, politics and governance. Agriculture, manufacturing, infrastructure and tourism are the main investment sectors. While Chinese investments present huge material opportunities, they also disrupt local livelihoods and the environment and transform local governance at varying speeds and magnitude.

ENABLING FACTORS

Foreign direct investment (FDI) plays a critical role in socio-economic development in Cambodia. Peace, macroeconomic stability, political predictability, resource endowment, relatively cheap labour forces, and gradual improvement of investment climate together with governance reforms and gradual economic diversification have enabled Cambodia to attract foreign investments. For instance, at the Government–Private Sector Forum held in Phnom Penh in March 2019, the government laid out new commitments and concrete reforms to reduce the cost of production and logistics (Chheang 2019). Moreover, the investment law is being reviewed to provide more incentives to investors.

The Cambodian government has taken efforts to attract more Chinese investments, primarily through the reduction of costs of production and logistics. Speaking at the dinner party of the Cambodia–China

Business Forum on Cambodia in December 2016, Prime Minister Hun Sen said that the government would continue to improve investment and businesses climate by improving logistics, proving stable and low-cost electricity, skills development for the workforce, and reducing irregular fees (Hun 2016). China is a key trading partner of Cambodia. In 2020, the bilateral trade volume reached US$8.118 billion. Both sides aim to achieve more than US$10 billion by 2023 (MOFAIC 2020). In terms of FDI, China is the top investor. By 2019, the accumulated investment capital from China reached more than US$9 billion. Industry and manufacturing and infrastructure are the two main investment sectors followed by tourism and agriculture. China is the top investor in the hydropower sector, with a total investment of US$2.36 billion in seven projects with a total capacity of 1,328 megawatts (MOFAIC 2020).

Chinese investments in Cambodia have been facilitated by deep mutual political trust, iron-clad friendship, Cambodia's stable macroeconomic conditions, political predictability, low labour cost, and relatively easy access to land and other natural resources. The bilateral agreement on the protection and promotion of investment that came into force in August 1999 provides a legal framework to facilitate Chinese investments in Cambodia. In 2010, both countries signed a landmark Comprehensive Strategic Partnership Agreement to advance their bilateral ties (this was the first strategic partnership agreement that Cambodia had signed with an external partner). The signing of the bilateral free trade agreement (FTA) in October 2020 will further boost trade and investment flow between the two countries. The FTA negotiation was remarkable as it took less than one year to conclude the deal. China offered about 98 per cent of tariff line while Cambodia offered about 90 per cent of tariff line. In the FTA, there is a section on investment cooperation which consists of six articles aiming at facilitating and protecting investment projects between the two countries.

Moreover, the ASEAN–China Free Trade Agreement took effect in 2010, the Belt and Road Initiative (BRI) launched in 2013, and Lancang–Mekong Cooperation (LMC) established in 2016 provide a conducive environment for regional economic cooperation and integration as well as the enhancement of bilateral economic ties between China and Cambodia. These multilateral frameworks facilitate the inflow of Chinese investments to Cambodia (Sok 2019). In April 2019, the

Ministry of Economy and Finance of Cambodia signed a memorandum of understanding (MOU) with the Bank of China on "Cooperation under the Rectangular Strategy and the Belt and Road Initiative" with the aim to promote the implementation of BRI projects, especially those pertaining to infrastructure development, trade facilitation and financial collaboration. The Bank of China agreed to assist the Ministry of Economy and Finance to bring in Chinese investments, host or organize investment promotion activities and provide favourable credit policies to the key projects. Moreover, since early 2019, Cambodia has started using Chinese currency, the renminbi, as a floating currency, making Cambodia one of the early supporters of the internationalization of the renminbi (see as well Mierzejewski, this volume, for the case of Myanmar).

Chinese investments in infrastructure development especially under the BRI framework have gained steam after the signing of the bilateral cooperation on the BRI. In 2016, thirty-one agreements were signed, including a concession agreement for the development of Siem Reap airport and a protocol agreement on a 450-megawatt thermal power generation project in Sihanoukville on a Build-Own-Operate basis. In 2017, nine agreements were signed, including strengthening cooperation in the fields of infrastructure and transport-related capacity building. In 2018, nineteen deals were struck, including an MOU on further developing the Cambodia-China technology transfer centre, a concession agreement on the US$2 billion Phnom Penh–Sihanoukville Expressway, a financing cooperation framework agreement for a new airport in Phnom Penh, a framework agreement for the Techo 1 Communication Satellite programme, and a framework cooperation agreement for the Stueng Hav port and special economic zone project. In 2019, six agreements were inked, including the MOU on the Comprehensive Cooperation under the Belt and Road Initiative and the Rectangular Strategy and the Action Plan for Forging the Cambodia-China Community of Shared Future. It remains to be seen how many of these agreements will materialize into concrete projects, how long the actual implementations will take and to what extent the actualized projects will bring transformative development to Cambodia's economy.

China's financial aid to Cambodia totalled US$5.27 billion in the period from 2001 to 2018, with an additional US$600 million pledged from 2019 to 2021. China is now the main creditor of Cambodia with the amount of more than US$4.5 billion, about 40 per cent of its total foreign debt. However, it is still at low risk of external debt distress (IMF 2017). Prime Minister Hun Sen stated at the 2nd Belt and Road Forum in April 2019 that

> it's not like the view of those who believe BRI will make some countries fall into a debt trap. Cambodia will negotiate and prepare projects in the interests of the nation and its people, and not increase financial burden and public debt. As a sovereign country, we have the right to make whatever choices we want and receive the loans necessary. We will implement these projects for national development based on self-reliance (Chheng 2019a).

The Chinese government also supports the Cambodian government in addressing external pressures. For instance, under mounting diplomatic and economic pressures from the US and the EU, Cambodia has sought assistance from China to mitigate the risks and hedge against the pressures from the West. Wang Huning, a member of the Politburo Standing Committee of the Communist Party of China (CPC) and Secretary of the Party's Secretariat, told Prime Minister Hun Sen in April 2019 that China would help Cambodia with its problems, including those arising from the withdrawal of the quota-free and tariff-free preferential treatment under the Everything-but-Arms (EBA) scheme by the EU (Chheng 2019b). The statement demonstrates China's firm commitment to assist Cambodia in all circumstances. The editorial of *Khmer Times* warns that "the threat to revoke the EBA, which costs Cambodia up to 650 million dollars a year, will force Cambodia to fall completely into China's camp and this might be an irreversible trend" (*Khmer Times*, 9 May 2019).

The role of the local Chinese ethnic community plays a bridging role in connecting Chinese investors with local Cambodian stakeholders, given that some local Chinese tycoons have strong political connections with local political leaders. O'Neill (2014) correctly observes that to avert risks, Chinese firms in Cambodia receive and secure political support from China (in the case of state-owned enterprises), and political connections and protection from the local elites. Chinese investments in Cambodia are varied in terms of ownership type and asset specificity. China's state-owned enterprises have focused on hydropower plant projects—facilitated through grant aid or soft loans from the Chinese government—which largely enjoy investment approval and political protection (some of these projects have been criticized for the lack of transparency and accountability). China's private firms, on the other hand, have concentrated their investments in the garment industry. In the land and resource sector, Chinese firms have strong political connections with local political elites (O'Neill 2014).

The estimated number of Chinese nationals residing in Cambodia was around 700,000 at its peak in 2019, not counting the annual 2 million Chinese tourists who visited the country. There are twenty-one capital and provincial cities that have established sister-city relations with forty-one Chinese cities and provinces. However, the growing presence of the new Chinese in Cambodia caused certain local discontent and cultural tensions with local Cambodians (Puy 2019).

TRANSFORMATIONS CAUSED BY CHINESE INVESTMENTS

Chinese investments have caused remarkable systemic transformations in Cambodia, ranging from economy, society, politics, environment and local governance. There are mixed, diverse views on the impacts of Chinese investments. The ruling elites feel confident and convinced that Chinese investments contribute to the socio-economic development of the country which in turn will strengthen the regime's legitimacy and authority. For the ruling elites, China has played a critical role in developing the Cambodian economy, especially through the development of infrastructure, investment and job creation, and trade relations. China is most responsive to Cambodia's development needs, especially in mega infrastructure development projects. Secretary of State at the Ministry of Economy and Finance said: "Without China, there would be no Cambodia today—one must learn to accept that. Why should we go to China for assistance? We don't want to favour China, but if they give us what we need, shouldn't we take it?" (*Radio Free Asia* 2019). Moreover, the Under-Secretary of State of the Ministry of Economy and Finance, wrote that "the prospect of shifting and relocating some of China's industries and production base to countries along the Belt and Road can only be promising for small economies like Cambodia" (Hem 2019).

Local business communities have mixed views. Generally, local big corporations have more opportunities and advantages to link up with

Chinese companies, especially under the framework of joint ventures. Local small and medium-sized enterprises (SMEs) gain much less, and some are even marginalized due to their loss in competition to Chinese companies. In some cases, the local community has not fairly benefited from the influx of Chinese investment. For instance, in the case of Sihanoukville, improperly managed Chinese investments led to the rise in crime rate, environmental degradation, rising cost of living, land grabbing, and social and cultural tensions (Po and Heng 2019). The local community does not fairly benefit from the influx of Chinese investments. The Chinese are the key beneficiaries (*Deutsche Welle* 2020).

There is a certain degree of public concern that local Cambodians are marginalized, and Cambodia might fall into a debt trap, especially under the mega infrastructure projects under the Belt and Road Initiative (BRI) (Touch 2018). Due to some concerns over debt traps and mismanagement of some investment projects, it is suggested that "mechanisms for transparency and accountability for BRI projects, especially in infrastructure, should be established to prevent elite capture and corruption in these gigantic, loan-based infrastructure projects" (Keo 2019).

There is also an issue of the unequal spatial distribution of benefits and costs between the national and local stakeholders. The national policymakers are largely positive towards Chinese investment projects, while the local stakeholders are facing certain issues resulting from the mismanagement or negative effects caused by the investment projects. The Chinese investment project, Kamchay hydropower dam, in Kampot province is a case in point, illustrating the divergence in perception and interest between the local and national stakeholders. The bamboo collectors, firewood collectors and fruit sellers were affected by the construction of the hydropower plant. This is due to the lack of objective and comprehensive environmental and social impact assessment and the absence of inclusive, transparent and proper mitigation, consultation, and compensation (Siciliano et al. 2015).

The local community and civil society are quite critical of Chinese investments. Some are concerned over the fact that their livelihood has been affected due to the rising cost of living and environmental degradation as some Chinese investment projects do not strictly follow the social and environmental safeguard measures. Some local observers and analysts have raised their concern over the "unchecked development by Chinese investors" which might change Cambodia's local identity and beauty (Sim 2019), cause disruptions to local community development and social cohesion (Heng 2019), labour disputes, and environmental degradation (Chheang 2017).

Social and cultural tensions between the locals with Chinese immigrants have been rising due to the lack of respect by some Chinese towards Khmer culture and values. Misspelling of Khmer language on commercial signboards and other related identity conflicts are some of the causes of the tensions. For instance, some residents in Sihanoukville protested against the presence of Chinese immigrants (Hannh 2018). As a result, anti-China sentiment has been on the rise, fuelled by some opportunist politicians (*Capital Cambodia* 2019). A local analyst argues that "if the situation continues to deteriorate and more social chaos is caused by the Chinese community in Cambodia … it is possible that it will create a negative sentiment towards Chinese nationals in Cambodia…. It's a real risk for Cambodia" (Millar 2018).

LOCAL GOVERNANCE TRANSFORMATION

The influx of Chinese investment to Cambodia has a significant impact on local governance, which combines "resource frontier" with governance. The governance in the context of the resource frontier involves the negotiation and contestation of policy framework on the use and reproduction of natural resources, and the development of socio-economic and ecological change (Thaler, Viana, and Toni 2018). This development forms a "governance frontier" which is defined as the "boundaries of distinct political-economic formations, each with a characteristic set of governance arrangements" (ibid., p. 63).

Some cases are showing that Chinese investments breed corruption and weaken the rule of law and governance (Burgos and Ear 2010). Others (Heng 2016) argue that the "economic gains from China are taking place at the expense of social dislocation and environmental destruction" and the deterioration of good governance. Their arguments are based on some cases involving Chinese investment projects in Cambodia. For instance, some Chinese investors bribe local government officials to get access to local resources and licences. Some even collude with local officers to use cars with government official number plates for their own interests (Po and Heng 2019). These observations are in line with the fact that the local political system is not transparent and the legal system relatively weak.

Corruption has been a key governance issue in the country. In 2020, Cambodia's corruption index was 162 out of 180 by Transparency International. Therefore, the existing Cambodian governance conditions constrain the potential positive impacts of Chinese investments. Some Chinese investors try to adapt to the local political environment and legal system, but some try to manipulate the weak local governance system.

Regulatory Regime

The amount and speed of Chinese investment in Cambodia are remarkable, outpacing the speed and capacity of the local governance and regulation to monitor and manage the investment projects. Due to the lack of regulation and weak law enforcement, Cambodia is vulnerable to "irresponsible" Chinese investors (*Khmer Times*, 4 June 2019). Cambodia's judicial system lacks institutional capacity and faces political constraints (Cox and Ok 2012). As a result, there are associated crimes, social and cultural tensions, environmental issues and other unintended negative impacts on the local people.

Weak law enforcement and corruption are the main root causes of these adverse impacts. In January 2018, for instance, Preah Sihanouk provincial governor Yun Min expressed frustration over growing crime and public disorder in Sihanoukville associated with the mushrooming gambling industry and Chinese influx (Nachemson 2019). The collapse of a building under construction by Chinese developers in June 2019 which lead to the death of twenty-eight people and many others injured was another case in point illustrating the weakness of the local government in enforcing construction laws and regulations. Five Chinese nationals including the owner of the building, one Cambodian, and one Vietnamese were charged with involuntary manslaughter and conspiracy. The incident led to the resignation of the provincial governor and deputy prime minister in charge of disaster management and sparked a public outcry about the quality and nature of Chinese investments in Cambodia (Prak 2019a). Subsequent inspections exposed an alarming scale of substandard construction, leading the Cambodian authorities to order the demolition of at least fourteen buildings (Luo and Un 2020).

To address the public concerns over the quality of Chinese investments in Cambodia, it is proposed that strengthening the capacity of the public institutions and law enforcement agencies, conducting a comprehensive assessment of Chinese investment projects, better management of foreign workers and fair and just distribution of benefits and opportunities arising from the investments are some of the possible measures for Cambodia to better govern Chinese investment projects (Keo 2019). Hence regulatory framework for managing FDIs needs to be developed to improve the quality of foreign investments.

Land Disputes

Land ownership registration and land disputes are complex governance issues. The ambiguity of land ownership creates land disputes in some areas. Some Chinese companies are allegedly involved in land grabbing and disputes. According to the local NGO Coalition of Cambodian Farmer Community (CCFC), some 20,000 families have suffered because of land disputes related to Chinese investment since 2003 (Hul 2018).

The forced eviction and land disputes in Boeung Kak Lake district in Phnom Penh capital city is the case in point. Thousands of residents were affected by the Chinese-financed real estate company called Shukaku. Under the terms of a 99-year lease granted in February 2007 by Phnom Penh Municipality, Shukaku gained the right to turn the lake and a swath of surrounding land into a new residential and business district. Shukaku agreed to pay US$79 million for 328 acres of prime real estate, far less than the market value of such a large piece of land in the centre of the capital (Higgins 2012).

According to Cambodia's Investment Law, ownership of land for the purpose of carrying on promoted investment activities shall be vested only in natural persons holding Cambodian citizenship or in legal entities in which more than 51 per cent of the equity capital is directly owned by natural persons or legal entities holding Cambodian citizenship. However, there are some loopholes in implementation. Some Chinese investors use their Cambodian proxies to invest in land and real estate.

Labour Issue

The mass inflow of Chinese workers to Cambodia has caused some social tensions. Concerning employing Chinese workers, Cambodia's Investment Law stipulates that investors can hire foreign employees with the condition that their qualifications and expertise are not available in Cambodia among the Cambodian populace. In addition, the investors have the obligation to provide adequate and consistent training to Cambodian employees and promote Cambodian staff to senior positions over time.

In accordance with Cambodia's Labour Law from 1997, foreign workers must apply for a work permit and an employment card issued by the Ministry of Labour. The work permit is valid for one year and may be extended. The maximum percentage of foreigners who can be employed in each of the enterprises shall be determined by a *Prakas* of the Ministry of Labour. However, the implementation of the investment law and labour law has some limitations, mainly due to corruption and the lack of transparency. Some labour legal issues are unclear types of employment contracts, limited determination of minimum wage and the absence of a labour court (Nop 2017). Some Chinese investment projects, from the garment industry to construction and casino, do not fully comply with the Cambodian labour law. There are some cases of poor working conditions and labour abuses (Frost, Pandita, and Hewison 2002; Buckley and Eckerlein 2020).

Technology Transfer

Technology and knowledge transfer by Chinese companies is low (Lam 2019). There is a weak link between Chinese investment projects with local small businesses (Ng 2019). Chinese firms have little interaction with local firms and do not contribute much to the capacity and skill development of the local workforce (Kubny and Voss 2010). Chinese companies prefer to hire Chinese workers over local Cambodians because of easier language communication and work ethics (Tann 2019). Chinese investments do not have a strong multiplier effect for both backward and forward linkages with the local firms. According to the survey findings, only 13 per cent of the local firms sold their goods or services to the Chinese firms and 22 per cent of the local firms felt competitive pressure from Chinese firms (Senh and Chan 2016).

Therefore, the spillover effect of Chinese investments on local SMEs is limited. The local investment law and other regulations do not bind foreign investors to transfer or diffuse technology and know-how with the local firms or staff. It rests upon the decision of the firms. In 2014, Cambodia and China signed an agreement to establish the Cambodia-China Technology Transfer Center and in 2018, the MOU on promoting the development of the centre was signed. However, concrete project implementation on the ground is limited.

THE CASE OF SIHANOUKVILLE

Located along the coastline and 220 km from Phnom Penh's capital, Sihanoukville is one of the three economic pillars after Phnom Penh and Siem Reap. The government has the ambition to transform this coastal city into Cambodia's Shenzhen, inspired by the successful development model of the free trade zone of Shenzhen in China. The Urban Planning and Design Institute of Shenzhen has developed a master plan for urban planning and development of the city. The Sihanoukville Autonomous Port, the only deep-sea port in Cambodia, was established in 1998 and the Sihanoukville Special Economic Zone was created in 2009. The Sihanoukville Port can accommodate 700,000 containers in 2020 and up to 1 million in 2023. Currently, 90 per cent of sea transport goes through the port.

Prime Minister Hun Sen said: "Let us work together to make this city, named after the King Father Norodom Sihanouk, become a city that will open for economic growth ... The province of Preah Sihanouk will certainly contribute to national economic growth. It will contribute to our national coffer." (Hun Sen 2019). He added: "The city of Preah Sihanouk is one with multipurpose or covering almost every fields. We have here transportation facilities, deep-sea port, industrial and service sector development. There is a possibility that it could become one of the financial hubs in the region as Hong Kong, Singapore, or Shanghai. We have such ambition" (ibid.). Aside from its industrial and financial potential, Sihanoukville is also considered one of Cambodia's four tourism poles which include Phnom Penh, Siem Reap, the coastal region, and the northeast region. The city's natural beach, biodiversity, natural resorts and accessibility (international airport, international port and railway services) make Sihanoukville an attractive tourist destination.

Chinese investments and economic presence have a tremendous impact on the local economy, society, urban landscape and environment. It is estimated that about 70 per cent of foreign investments in the city are from China. The explosive inflow of Chinese investors and tourists started in mid-2017. About 200,000 Chinese were in the city before the COVID-19 pandemic (Lan 2020). Chinese economic dominance has raised certain local resentment and anxiety as reflected in the following observation:

> By 2019, through large-scale investment in the special economic zone, hotels, resorts, condominiums, casinos, alongside small Chinese-owned retail shops, restaurants and other service sectors, the Chinese have literally taken over the city. Although Chinese investment, trade, and aid contributed to economic growth in Sihanoukville and elsewhere in Cambodia, Cambodian perceptions of the Chinese have been overwhelmingly negative (Luo and Un 2020).

Urban Planning and Development

Historically, there have been several urban development plans in Sihanoukville, including the Vann Molyvann's Plan (1959), the Ariston-ACER (Malaysian company) Plan (1995), the Sihanoukville Development Plan by the Royal Government of Cambodia (RGC) (2002), the Sihanoukville Coastal Development Plan by RGC (2003), the Stueng Hav Development Plan (2003), the Vinci (French company) Plan (2006) and the Draft Master Plan of Sihanoukville (as part of the South Coastal Area Development Plan) supported by the Japan International Cooperation Agency (JICA) as part of the study on a national integrated strategy for coastal development and master plan (2010). In 2019, the Cambodian government commissioned the Urban Planning and Design Institute of Shenzhen to develop the master plan for Sihanoukville to transform this provincial city into Cambodia's Shenzhen. The institute developed the 1991 Shenzhen Master Plan, which helped transform the poor fishing village into an international gateway and a growth centre.

Xiao Sima, president of the Institute and Chief Technology Officer was quoted as saying "We have the experience in developing Shenzhen from ground zero to a sprawling metropolis. In Sihanoukville, we are not starting from ground zero and this gives an edge and also a better understanding of the local elements which dictates development there." He added, "We are under no illusion about the massive challenges we will face in undertaking the master plan. But I am confident that with the support and consultations with the Royal Government of Cambodia, the provincial authorities and other stakeholders, including residents, we will be able to prevail" (Soumy 2019).

The fast-changing urban landscape and rapid real estate development have posed significant challenges for the future development of the city. With no land use plan to guide development, the cityscape has changed dramatically, with new high-rise developments out of place in a traditionally low- to medium-rise urban environment. As such the construction permits are granted on a case-by-case basis, also known as "built first, license later". The granting of permits and control of construction is beyond the authority of individual provincial departments and municipalities (World Bank 2018).

In 2019, the central government allocated US$294 million to build thirty-four roads and streets in the provincial city of Sihanoukville with a total length of 84 km. In early 2021, the Chinese company (Prince Holding Group) started developing an 834 ha "Ream City" in Sihanoukville. The total investment in the project is about US$16 billion. The master plan of the city development has been developed by Surbana Jurong from Singapore (Goh 2021).

Economic Management

The Preah Sihanouk airport is being expanded to 3,200 metres to accommodate larger aircrafts (a French company VINCI is developing the project) (Hun 2019). There are nine special economic zones (SEZs) in Preah Sihanouk province of which five are in full operation. Four of the nine SEZs are built and operated by Chinese firms. It was reported that the Sihanoukville Special Economic Zone operated by Hodo Group attracted about 200 enterprises, mainly from China, providing nearly 30,000 jobs. It is estimated that the zone will attract 300 more enterprises and provide about 80,000 to 100,000 new jobs. The industrial output of the economy of Preah Sihanouk province is over 50 per cent (Lan 2020).

There are numerous news reports on Chinese investments in Sihanoukville illustrating that small local businesses do not benefit from the influx of Chinese investments to the province. The local analyst Heng Pheakdey (2018) argues that:

> even though Chinese investment is bringing wealth to Cambodia, this wealth is mainly kept within Cambodia's Chinese community. Chinese residents and visitors in Cambodia buy from Chinese businesses, eat in Chinese restaurants and stay in Chinese hotels. The trickle-down effect to local businesses is minimal.

News reports quoted local entrepreneurs as saying:

> Hundreds of family-owned businesses have put up the shutters in the past year. Many were evicted because the landlords preferred to lease properties to Chinese businessmen, who can afford to pay up to five times more. To make matters worse, local businesses have lost their traditional customer base: Western tourists who used to flock there for the sun, sand and sea (Ng and Phang 2018).

Many Chinese working in Cambodia are young men with limited education and without overseas travel experiences. Their loud behaviour and lack of respect for local customs and etiquette strongly irritate Cambodians (Luo and Un 2020).

Social Issues

The increased crime rate, human trafficking, sex industry, drug smuggling, kidnapping, cybercrime and money laundering are the key social issues facing the community in Sihanoukville. In January 2018, local governor Yun Min warned that Chinese investments bring organized crime and instability to Sihanoukville, sending a three-page letter to the interior minister. Governor Yun warned that the Chinese influx had "created opportunities for Chinese mafia to come in and commit various crimes and kidnap Chinese investors, causing insecurity in the province". The then Chinese ambassador to Cambodia, Xiong Bo, also acknowledged the rising crime rate amongst Chinese living in Cambodia, including drug and sex trafficking and online or telephone scams (Benjamin 2019).

The governor also raised concerns over rising rents, the inability of local businesses to compete with Chinese companies and the oversaturation of Chinese labourers in the construction sector (Nachemson 2019). In addition, Chea Munyrith, director of project and planning, Civil Society Alliance Forum, said that "these crimes tarnished

Sihanoukville's image and gave a bad reputation for Chinese people in Cambodia. Chinese enterprises bring benefits to Sihanoukville, but some online gambling companies have brought crimes, which won't do any good for the long-term cooperation between the two countries" (Lan 2020).

The enforcement of the ban on online gambling in January 2020 and the pandemic outbreak in March 2020 left the Chinese investments and businesses in this coastal city in limbo. There was a significant decrease in Chinese nationals in Sihanoukville, from around 200,000 people. Only around 15,000 Chinese nationals were remaining in the city in June 2021. Many Chinese workers were stuck there, unable to collect enough money to fly back to China (Khan and Aun 2020). More than 7,000 Cambodian workers lost their jobs due to the ban on online gambling (Prak 2019b). Both Chinese and Cambodian construction workers in Sihanoukville suffered from poor, difficult living conditions as they only got paid a fraction of their daily wage. Thus, their dream to work in Sihanoukville became a nightmare (Franceschini 2020). In addition, more than 8,000 workers lost their jobs due to the COVID-19 induced closures of twenty factories (Sen 2020).

Environmental Management

The construction boom has caused significant stress on the city's infrastructure and waste management system. The current waste management system does not keep up with the drastic urbanization. The extensive construction has also resulted in loose soil and mud, making many roads unwalkable when it rains (Lim 2019). Sihanoukville is vulnerable to floods, affected by the sea-level rise and coastal erosion. Homes in low coastal areas are highly exposed to flood risks, often exacerbated by the poor quality of housing and lack of basic urban infrastructure. Flood problems are also exacerbated by the lack of adequate drainage, sewerage, and solid waste management (World Bank 2018). Local authorities have raised concerns that the pollution would be alarming while the provision of urban environmental infrastructure is underdeveloped (World Bank 2018). The town also faces serious traffic congestion (*Asia Sentinel*, 18 December 2019).

In response to these mounting environmental pressures, the government has allocated a national budget to renovate and build new environmental infrastructure as part of China's efforts to beautify and justify Chinese massive investments in the area. Waterways and canals have been renovated and expanded to prevent floods with a budget of US$2.5 million. Water treatment facilities are being developed with a grant from China of US$170 million. Four water sewage stations are being constructed. In 2019, the government allocated about US$200 million to increase the capacity of water treatment plants. As of 2019, a water treatment plant has the capacity to treat only about 5,700 cubic metres per day while up to 25,000 cubic metres of wastewater are produced every day. The government plans to increase the water treatment capacity to 64,000 cubic metres per day (Sen 2019).

CONCLUSION

China is the top foreign investor in Cambodia, enabled and facilitated by deep political trust and ties between the two governments, a relatively open and liberal investment regime in Cambodia and bilateral and multilateral agreements and mechanisms. The influx of Chinese investments has a significant impact on the resource frontiers in Cambodia by triggering a systemic transformation. Cambodian society, economy, environment and governance have been affected by the inflow of Chinese capital and people. For Chinese investors, Cambodia is their emerging resource frontier and an extension of Chinese production networks.

While Chinese investments have brought about some opportunities for the local people, they also trigger certain local resistance and discontent. Chinese investments have systematically transformed the local economy, society, environment and governance. There is an upsurge of anti-China sentiment across Cambodia because of the mismanagement of the Chinese investments in Sihanoukville. Rising living costs, increasing crime rate and environmental degradation are some of the local concerns. The local authority finds it difficult to regulate and manage the investments, especially those in the gambling industry. The government's decision to ban online gambling gained public applause although the closure of online gambling caused certain short-term economic losses.

One of the viable ways for Cambodia is to convince and legally bind the Chinese investors to improve the quality of their investments. Both China and Cambodia need to work closely together to address the perception gap and the outstanding challenges and issues arising from Chinese investments. Developing a regulatory framework and creating an independent oversight body to manage foreign investments would promote the transparency and quality of foreign investments in Cambodia.

References

Asia Sentinel. 2019. "Sihanoukville Re-engineered: The Way Forward". 18 December 2019. https://www.asiasentinel.com/p/sihanoukville-reengineered (accessed 19 December 2019).

Barbier, Edward. 2011. *Scarcity And Frontiers. How Economies Have Developed through Natural Resource Exploitation*. Cambridge: Cambridge University Press.

Barney, Keith. 2009. "Laos and the Making of a "Relational" Resource Frontier". *Geographical Journal* 175, no. 2: 146–59. http://dx.doi.org/10.1111/j.1475-4959.2009.00323.x (accessed 19 December 2019).

Benjamin. 2019. "Foreign Investors Do Not Only Bring Economic Growth to Cambodia". *Capital Cambodia*, 17 May 2019. https://capitalcambodia.com/foreign-investments-do-not-only-bring-economic-growth-to-cambodia/ (accessed 19 December 2019).

Buckley, Joe, and Christian Eckerlein. 2020. "Cambodian Labour in Chinese-owned Enterprises in Sihanoukville: An Insight into the Living and Working Conditions of Cambodian Labourers in the Construction, Casino and Manufacturing Sectors". *Sozialpolitik.ch* 2: 1–17. http://dx.doi.org/10.18753/2297-8224-163 (accessed 19 December 2019).

Burgos, Sigfrido, and Sophal Ear. 2010. "China's Strategic Interests in Cambodia: Influence and Resources". *Asian Survey* 50, no. 3: 615–39. https://doi.org/10.1525/as.2010.50.3.615 (accessed 19 December 2019).

Capital Cambodia. 2019. "If Not China, Then Who?". 31 May 2019. https://capitalcambodia.com/if-not-china-then-who/ (accessed 9 December 2019).

Chheang, Vannarith. 2017. *The Political Economy of Chinese Investment in Cambodia*. Trends in Southeast Asia, no. 16/2017. Singapore: ISEAS – Yusof Ishak Institute.

⸺. 2019. "Cambodia's New Era of Reforms". *AVI Commentary* 4/2019. Phnom Penh: Asian Vision Institute.

Chheng, Niem. 2019a. "Hun Sen: Cambodia Will Not Fall into Belt and Road Debt Trap". *Phnom Penh Post*, 29 April 2019. https://www.phnompenhpost.com/national-politics/hun-sen-cambodia-will-not-fall-belt-and-road-debt-trap (accessed 19 December 2019).

⸺. 2019b. "Questions Asked over 'Post-EBA' China Help". *Phnom Penh Post*, 30 April 2019. https://www.phnompenhpost.com/national-politics/questions-asked-over-post-eba-china-help (accessed 10 December 2019).

Cons, Jason, and Michael Eilenberg. 2019. *Frontier Assemblages: The Emergent Politics of Resource Frontier in Asia*. Oxford: Wiley.
Cox, Marcus, and Sereu Sopheak Ok. 2012. "Cambodia Case Study, Evaluation of Australian Law and Justice Assistance". Canberra: Australian Agency for International Development. https://www.oecd.org/countries/cambodia/cambodia.pdf (accessed 10 December 2019).
Deutsche Welle (website). 2020. "Cambodia. Chinese Investors in Sihanoukville". 16 March 2020. https://www.dw.com/en/cambodia-chinese-investors-in-sihanoukville/av-52761895 (accessed 5 July 2020).
Franceschini, Ivan. 2020. "As Far Apart as Earth and Sky: A Survey of Chinese and Cambodian Construction Workers in Sihanoukville". *Critical Asian Studies* 52, no. 4: 512–29. https://doi.org/10.1080/14672715.2020.1804961 (accessed 5 July 2020).
Frost, Stephen, Sanjiv Pandita, and Kevin Hewison. 2002. "The Implications for Labour of China's Direct Investment in Cambodia". *Asian Perspective* 26, no. 4: 201–26. http://www.jstor.org/stable/42704391 (accessed 5 July 2020).
Goh, Gayle. 2021. "Surbana Jurong's Masterplan for US$16b 'Ream City' in Cambodia Gets Go-Ahead". *Straits Times,* 10 February 2021. https://www.straitstimes.com/business/companies-markets/surbana-jurongs-masterplan-for-16b-ream-city-in-cambodia-gets-green-light (accessed 20 March 2021).
Hannh, Ellis-Petersen. 2018. "No Cambodia Left: Now Chinese Money Is Changing Sihanoukville". *The Guardian,* 31 July 2018. https://www.theguardian.com/cities/2018/jul/31/no-cambodia-left-chinese-money-changing-sihanoukville (accessed 10 December 2019).
Hem, Vanndy. 2019. "Closing Remarks at the 3rd Policy Dialogue on 'Belt and Road Initiative in Cambodia: Economic Diversification and Debt Management'". *AVI Policy Brief* 3/2019. Phnom Penh: Asian Vision Institute.
Heng, Kimkong. 2019. "Chinese Investment Strains Cambodian Society". *Nikkei Asian Review,* 21 July 2019. https://asia.nikkei.com/Opinion/Chinese-investment-strains-Cambodian-society (accessed 19 December 2019).
Heng, Pheakdey. 2016. "Chinese Investment and Aid in Cambodia's Energy Sector: Impacts and Policy Implications". Unpublished PhD dissertation, Vrije Universiteit Amsterdam.
———. 2018. "Are China's Gifts a Blessing or a Curse for Cambodia?". *East Asia Forum* (blog), 29 August 2018. https://www.eastasiaforum.org/2018/08/29/are-chinas-gifts-a-blessing-or-a-curse-for-cambodia/ (accessed 8 December 2019).
Higgins, Andrew. 2012. "Land Disputes in Cambodia Focus Ire on Chinese Investors". *Washington Post,* 25 September 2012. https://www.washingtonpost.com/world/asia_pacific/land-disputes-in-cambodia-focus-ire-on-chinese-investors/2012/09/24/1e64dce6-fd9c-11e1-98c6-ec0a0a93f8eb_story.html (accessed 8 December 2019).

Hul, Reaksmey. 2018. "Activists Claim Chinese Investment Fuelling Land Disputes in Cambodia". *Voice of America*, 31 October 2018. https://www.voacambodia.com/a/activists-claim-chinese-investment-fueling-land-disputes-in-cambodia/4637185.html (accessed 11 December 2019).

Hun, Sen. 2016. "Keynote Speech at the Dinner Party of Cambodia-China Business Forum on Cambodia: The Kingdom of Opportunities along 'One Belt, One Road'". *Cambodia New Vision* (website), 1 December 2016. http://cnv.org.kh/dinner-party-cambodia-china-business-forum/ (accessed 11 December 2019).

———. 2019. "Launching the Constructions of the USD294 Million 34 Roads/Streets in the Province of Preah Sihanouk [Unofficial Translation]". *Cambodia New Vision* (website), 16 November 2019. http://cnv.org.kh/34-roadsstreets-province-preah-sihanouk/ (accessed 10 December 2019).

International Monetary Fund (IMF). 2017. "Staff Report for the 2017 Article IV Consultation – Debt Sustainability Analysis", 30 August 2017. https://www.imf.org/external/pubs/ft/dsa/pdf/2017/dsacr17325.pdf (accessed 10 December 2019).

Keo, Piseth. 2019. "The Belt and Road Initiative: Risks and Opportunities for Cambodian Sustainable Development". *AVI Policy Brief* 6 (2019). Phnom Penh: Asian Vision Institute.

Khan, Sokummono, and Aun Chhengpor. 2020. "A Pandemic and Gambling Ban Has Left Cambodia's 'New Shenzhen' Unfinished". *Voice of America*, 11 June 2020. https://www.voacambodia.com/a/a-pandemic-and-gambling-ban-has-left-cambodia-new-shenzhen-unfinished/5458750.html (accessed 20 March 2021).

Khmer Times (website). 2019a. "Can Cambodia Balance China with the West?". 9 May 2019. https://www.khmertimeskh.com/50601997/can-cambodia-balance-china-with-the-west/ (accessed 9 December 2019).

———. 2019b. "Cambodia Embraces East and West". 4 June 2019. https://www.khmertimeskh.com/50610630/cambodia-embraces-east-and-west/ (accessed 9 December 2019).

Kubny, Julia, and Hinrich Voss. 2010. "The Impact of Chinese Outward Investment: Evidence from Cambodia and Vietnam". *Discussion Paper*, no. 16/2010. Bonn: German Development Institute.

Lam, Thanh Ha. 2019. "Chinese FDI in Vietnam: Trends, Status and Challenges". *ISEAS Perspective*, no. 2019/34, 24 April 2019. https://www.iseas.edu.sg/articles-commentaries/iseas-perspective/201934-chinese-fdi-in-vietnam-trends-status-and-challenges-by-lam-thanh-ha/ (accessed 13 October 2021).

Lan Hui. 2020. "Sihanoukville Eyes a Bright Future to Become 'Shenzhen of Cambodia'". *Global Times*, 24 February 2020. https://www.globaltimes.cn/content/1180622.shtml (accessed 9 December 2020).

Lim, Damon. 2019. "Urbanization in Southeast Asia: Field Notes from Cambodia". *Data Driven Environlab* (blog), 9 August 2019. http://datadrivenlab.org/fieldwork-2/urbanization-in-southeast-asia-field-notes-from-cambodia/ (accessed 9 December 2019).

Luo, Jing Jing and Kheang Un. 2020. "Cambodia: Hard Landing for China's Soft Power?". *ISEAS Perspective*, no. 2020/111, 6 October 2020.

Millar, Paul. 2018. "Anti-Chinese Sentiments in Cambodia". *Southeast Asia Globe*, 13 November 2018. https://southeastasiaglobe.com/anti-chinese-sentiment-in-cambodia/ (accessed 10 December 2019).

Ministry of Foreign Affairs and International Cooperation (MOFAIC). 2020. "Cambodia-China Cooperation". Internal paper.

O'Neill, Daniel. 2014. "Playing Risk: Chinese Foreign Direct Investment in Cambodia". *Contemporary Southeast Asia* 36, no. 2: 173–205. http://www.jstor.org/stable/43281288 (accessed 10 December 2010).

Nachemson, Andrew. 2019. "Chinese Investment in Cambodia Is Bringing Phnom Penh Closer to Beijing – and Further from the EU". *South China Morning Post*, 1 May 2019. https://www.scmp.com/news/asia/southeast-asia/article/3008451/chinese-investment-cambodia-bringing-phnom-penh-closer (accessed 9 December 2019).

Ng, Desmond. 2019. "China's Chequebook Diplomacy in Cambodia a Double-Edged Sword Creating Resentment". *Channel NewsAsia* (website), 5 March 2019. https://www.channelnewsasia.com/news/cnainsider/china-chequebook-diplomacy-cambodia-investments-resentment-debt-11311662 (accessed 9 December 2019).

_____, and Charles Phang. 2018. "China Brings Casino Boom to Cambodian Town—But Doom to Local Businesses?". *Channel NewsAsia*, 20 October 2018. https://www.channelnewsasia.com/news/cnainsider/china-belt-road-casino-boom-sihanoukville-cambodia-phnom-penh-10846730 (accessed 10 December 2019).

Nop, Kanharith. 2017. "Overview of Labour Legal Issues in Cambodia". *Japan Labor Issues* 1, no. 3: 95–101.

Po, Sovinda, and Heng Kimkong. 2019. "Assessing the Impact of Chinese Investments in Cambodia: The Case of Preah Sihanouk Province". *Issues and Insights* 19, no. 4: 7–14 https://cicp.org.kh/publications/assessing-the-impacts-of-chinese-investments-in-cambodia-the-case-of-preah-sihanoukville-province/ (accessed 9 December 2019).

Prak, Chan Thul. 2019a. "Cambodia Charges Chinese Nationals over Deadly Building Collapse". Reuters, 25 June 2019. https://www.reuters.com/article/us-cambodia-construction-accident-idUSKCN1TQ0CZ (accessed 9 December 2019).

_____. 2019b. "Thousands Lose Jobs, Casinos Shut as Cambodia Bans Online Gambling". Reuters, 31 December 2019. https://www.reuters.com/article/us-cambodia-gambling-idUSKBN1YZ0O3 (accessed 20 March 2021).

Puy, Kea. 2019. "Large Chinese Presence in Cambodian City Clashes with Local Culture". *Kyodo News*, 13 July 2019. https://english.kyodonews.net/news/2019/07/a9ad537f6c19-focus-large-chinese-presence-in-cambodian-city-clashes-with-local-culture.html (accessed 10 December 2019).

Radio Free Asia (website). 2019. "Transparency of Chinese Loans". https://www.rfa.org/english/news/special/chinacambodia/loans.html (accessed 10 January 2020).

Sen, David. 2020. "Preah Sihanouk Sees Factory Suspensions and Massive Job Losses". *Khmer Times*, 10 June 2020. https://www.khmertimeskh.com/732092/preah-sihanouk-sees-factory-suspensions-and-massive-job-losses/ (accessed 20 March 2021).

———. 2019. "$170 Million More Earmarked for Sihanoukville's Sewage Woes". *Khmer Times*, 18 November 2019, https://www.khmertimeskh.com/50660635/170-million-more-earmarked-for-sihanoukvilles-sewage-woes/ (accessed 10 December 2019).

Senh, Senghor, and Sophal Chan. 2016. *Research Paper. Inclusive Development and Chinese Direct Investments in Cambodia*. Phnom Penh: Centre for Policy Studies. http://www.cps.org.kh/wp-content/uploads/inclusive-development-and-chinese-direct-investments-in-cambodia.pdf (accessed 20 March 2021).

Siciliano, Giuseppina, Frauke Urban, Sour Kim, and Pich Dara Lonn. 2015. "Hydropower, Social Priorities and the Rural-Urban Development Divide: The Case of Large Dams in Cambodia". *Energy Policy* 86: 273–85. https://doi.org/10.1016/j.enpol.2015.07.009 (accessed 20 March 2021).

Sim, Vireak. 2019. "Sihanoukville: A Cambodian City Losing its 'Cambodian-ness'". *The Diplomat*, 20 April 2019. https://thediplomat.com/2019/04/sihanoukville-a-cambodian-city-losing-its-cambodian-ness/ (accessed 10 December 2019).

Sok, Kha. 2019. "Cambodia: Transforming China-led and Other Regional Initiatives into a Source of Development". *AVI Commentary* 6. Phnom Penh: Asian Vision Institute. https://www.asianvision.org/archives/publications_tag/mr-sok-kha (accessed 15 October 2021).

Soumy, Phan. 2019. "Chinese Urban Planning Institute to design Sihanoukville's Masterplan". *Real Estate Cambodia* (blog), 18 November 2019. https://www.realestate.com.kh/news/china-based-planning-institute-to-produce-sihanoukville-masterplan/ (accessed 10 December 2019).

Tann, Somethea. 2019. "How Chinese Money Is Changing Cambodia". *Deutsche Welle*, 22 August 2019. https://www.dw.com/en/how-chinese-money-is-changing-cambodia/a-50130240 (accessed 9 December 2020).

Thaler, Gregory, Cecilia Viana, and Fabiano Toni. 2019. "From Frontier Governance to Governance Frontier: The Political Geography of Brazil's Amazon Transition". *World Development* 114: 59–72. https://doi.org/10.1016/j.worlddev.2018.09.022 (accessed 9 December 2019).

Touch, Daren. 2018. "What Does Chinese Investment Mean for Cambodia?". *The Diplomat*, 2 February 2018. https://thediplomat.com/2018/02/what-does-chinese-investment-mean-for-cambodia/ (accessed 9 December 2019).

World Bank Group. 2018. *Cambodia: Achieving the Potential of Urbanisation*. Phnom Penh: Cambodia Country Office. http://documents1.worldbank.org/curated/en/580101540583913800/pdf/127247-REVISED-CambodiaUrbanizationReportEnfinal.pdf (accessed 19 December 2019).

10

THE OPEN ISSUES

Cases between Chinese Investment Companies and Local People in Myanmar

Su Yin Htun

INTRODUCTION

With increasing foreign direct investment (FDI) flow from China, Myanmar's economic growth is depending more and more on Chinese investment. According to FDI data for 1988–2018, China is clearly the number one foreign investor in Myanmar (see as well Mierzejewski, this volume and 2021). Even though the investments coming from China into Myanmar are beneficial in many respects, they entail some major problems. Those are exemplified by the series of strikes that broke out related to three major development projects: The Letpadaungtaung copper mine project, the gas pipeline project, and the Myitsone dam project. As the latter two had been contracted by the former military government before the drafting of the 2008 Constitution, no impact assessments had been conducted and transparency was lacking. As the political reforms that ensued the passage of the 2008 Constitution have initially appeared successful, Myanmar people hoped to move forward in building a democratic nation as guaranteed by the Constitution. They aspire to participate in the decision-making concerning both businesses as well as political affairs. Myanmar, as an International Person, respects the ratified International Conventions and carries out their provisions by integrating them into national laws. Likewise, Myanmar Parliament has moved forward to update the national laws according to international standards of foreign investment, environmental and social impacts, employment, land rights and political reforms.

This paper investigates the three aforementioned Chinese investment cases such as the Letpadaungtaung copper mine project by the Wanbao Company, the gas pipeline project by China's National Petroleum Corporation, and the Myitsone dam project by the Chinese Power Investment Company. The Belt and Road Initiative (BRI) provides a new context for these open issues of environmental, social and human rights. The paper addresses the question of how to reduce the negative local impacts of Chinese investment projects that are allegedly dedicated to Myanmar's sustainable development. Local people had often not been informed about the projects before construction started. Moreover, the projects neglected the human rights impact assessment for local people and indigenous people. It is evident that the "Free, Prior and Informed Consent" method of public participation was not used.

INVESTMENT INFLOWS FROM CHINA TO MYANMAR

In Myanmar's investment history, the government enacted foreign investment law three times—in 1988, 2012 and 2016 following political reforms. Only the recent law of 2016 merged both foreign investment and citizen investment. Foreign investment law[1] and citizen investment law[2] were separately enacted before 2016. Through the investment law, Chinese companies operate foreign investments in different sectors. FDI inflows between Myanmar and China are apparent in resource extracting sectors of common interest since the beginning of foreign investment in 1988. According to the yearly approved amount of foreign investment (by country) as of 31 December 2018, China was the largest investor bringing a total foreign capital of US$20,353.528 million (accumulated 1988–2018).[3]

Myanmar's abundance of natural resources and cheap labour easily attract multinational companies to invest. Chinese investment enterprises are particularly keen to invest in Myanmar, especially with regard to minerals and other natural resources. It is indicative that until 2016, the natural resources sector was the one that China was most interested in investing in. In 2016, Parliament (Pyidaungsu Hluttaw) enacted the Myanmar Investment Law and repealed the Foreign Investment Law 2012. The new Law introduced strict provisions for environmental and social protection, new methods of treatment of investors, as well as more stringent rules concerning exemptions and reliefs. As a result, according to data from 2017 and 2018, while Chinese investments in explorations of natural resources have decreased significantly, they have at the same time increased in the manufacturing and service sectors.

Resource extraction remains a contested issue (see the introduction to this volume by Rowedder and Tappe). The three largest Chinese investment projects in Myanmar—the Letpadaung copper mine, the Sino-Myanmar oil and gas pipelines, and the Myitsone dam—have sparked local opposition and criticism in Myanmar to varying degrees, creating problems and uncertainties for Chinese investors (Zhang 2020; Kiik 2016).

BENEFITS OF CHINESE INVESTMENT

China's "going global" policy emerged in 1999 to take advantage of booming global markets (Mierzejewski 2021 and in this volume). China had played a key role in Myanmar's investment development since the US and other Western countries started economic sanctions in 1988. According to the official statistics of the Myanmar Investment Commission (MIC), from 1988 to 2018 China invested US$20,353,528 in Myanmar's economy.[4] As a result, by December 2018 China ranks first among all countries investing in Myanmar. Chinese investments have become an economic growth engine for Myanmar. They led to GDP growth and contributed positively to job opportunities, tax performance, development of production, export and import, technical know-how, integration into global markets, and capital inflows.

Chinese investors are entitled to tax exemptions and reliefs. Tax exemption is granted for investment activities in those economic zones which are categorized by the MIC as Zone 1 for the least developed region, Zone 2 for the less developed region, and Zone 3 for the developed region. Income tax is exempted for up to seven years in Zone 1, up to five years in Zone 2 and up to three years in Zone 3.[5] In addition, Myanmar investment law offers "Most–Favoured Nation" treatment and fair and equitable treatment to foreign investors. Chinese investment in Myanmar targets China's increasing energy demand through investments in the natural resources sector.

Data provided by the US Energy Administration Information (EAI) document the rapid rise of energy consumption for the major powers in the world. While the United States' consumption remained relatively stable over the course of forty-five years, and India's growth was steady yet slowly, China's consumption rapidly spiked in the early 2000s and continues to outpace the other two nations. Indeed, China overtook the US in terms of consumption in 2009 and continues to rise steadily over the next decades. While China consumed approximately 30 quadrillion Btu in 1990, estimations hold an over sixfold increase by 2035—a total of approximately 190 quadrillion Btu in 2035, equating to almost four times India's total and only little less than half of the United States' total (EAI 2011). To satisfy energy demand, China will have to re-evaluate how it secures energy and then modify its approach to find ways of providing for this monumental increase (Mitchell 2012). Arguably, patterns of extracting Myanmar's natural resources might mitigate the pressures of rising demand for energy in China.

With regard to Chinese investments, both Myanmar and China expect mutual benefits. However, we can identify problems of natural resource extraction in Myanmar as the respective enterprises affect local communities in terms of environmental, social, political and community impacts.

OPEN ISSUES OF THE IDENTIFIED CASES

There are widely well-known cases involving Chinese investment companies that lack a properly implemented regulatory framework to ensure sustainability. This has resulted in far-reaching detrimental consequences.

Letpadaungtaung Mining Project

Geographically, the Letpadaungtaung Copper Mine Project is situated about 7 miles from the Nyaung-Pin-Gyi Port in Sarlingyi Township of Monywa District in the Sagaing Region. On 5 March 2010, a large-scale production agreement on the mining of copper ore on the Letpadaungtaung site was signed between the Union of Myanmar Economic Holding Ltd (UMEHL) and Myanmar Mining Enterprise 1 (ME). The agreement included a licence to undertake mining in an area of 32 square kilometres for a twenty-eight-year period. In April 2010, UMEHL added Norinco Company, a Chinese weapon factory, as a new partner for copper production (with a production sharing type by the joint-venture contract and return of the share ratio of ME 1 from the first deal). In May 2011, the Chinese Embassy in Myanmar confirmed the agreement between Wanbao, a subsidiary of the Chinese Norinco Company, and UMEHL.

Since the project commenced construction, Wanbao increased business activities and acquired much land area. Then, Wanbao acquired additional land of over 7,000 acres which extended into adjoining village land. Although Wanbao compensated about 530,000 kyats[6] per acre to the current landowners of the neighbouring villages for a three-year term, the villagers felt deprived of the use of the lands for that period. This adversely affected the food crop production and local livelihoods more generally. Facing this situation, the residents of areas affected by the copper mine became increasingly dissatisfied with the arrangement and launched protests against the company. As a reaction, the company built new villages so that the villagers from Wat-Hmey, Saetai and Zeedaw villages could relocate.[7]

Due to the strikes by local people in November 2011, the elementary school closed for the safety of children, and the teachers left, notwithstanding that the final exam was near. The primary students could not attend the school of nearby villages as they did not receive the required authorization letter from the township office on time. They failed to reach their graduation exams in that term. In December 2011, the denial of compensation was used by Wanbao as a means to threaten the residents into evacuating their homes. After that, the construction of Wanbao mining went into full operation. There had been many protests eventually, and UMEHL signed many agreements with local people. Nonetheless, the intensity of the villagers' protests had increased with supporters across the country joining the protests. On 18 and 19 October 2012, the villagers created a so-called meditation event "Contemplating Letpadaungtaung". Unfortunately, several participants in that campaign were arrested and detained for the unlawful assembly under the Criminal Law. A few days later, monks and people from other towns joined the protestors and the movement became bigger. The news of the incident soon spread throughout the country. In the early morning of 29 November 2012, a contingent of police forces reached the protest area and used firebombs against the protestors.[8] The participants of the strike suffered injuries from chemical burns.[9]

The government issued a curfew order explaining that the strikes would be perceived dangerous to human life, health or safety, or a disturbance of the public order, or a riot, of an affray from 1 January 2013 to 28 February 2013 by sections 127, 128 and 144 of the Criminal Procedure Code.[10] Through the President's Office Notification No. 95/2012, issued on 3 December, the National League of Democracy Party (NLD) leader Daw Aung San Suu Kyi chaired the investigation committee involving thirty members.[11] Three days later, the investigation committee was reinstituted with sixteen members including the chairperson, Daw Aung San Suu Kyi. Thereafter, the Commission submitted the final report to the government which was published in the Myanmar newspapers and journals on 12 March 2013.[12]

In the years 2013 and 2014, several consultations were made between the villagers and the company. After the consultations, two groups formed up: one accepted the compensation for their lands as well as relocation to the new villages while the other refused to relocate. In the meantime, local people became dissatisfied with the company's efforts aimed at compensating for their loss of livelihood, which turned into a long-term problem. The company, for example, destroyed the growing crops of extended land areas near the Hsetae village with bulldozers on 22 December 2014. Although this action was officially announced, the widespread strikes erupted again and then, the fencing was suspended. To prevent these clashes between the company and local people, the police forces used firearms against the community. Tragically, a woman named Daw Khin Win was killed by the police forces and many suffered injuries (Amnesty International 2015). And yet, in March 2015, the Commission announced that out of forty-two points, thirty-seven had been implemented.[13] On 11 March 2016, Letpadaungtaung Copper Mine officially started business.

Although the clashes between local people and the Wanbao Company have been continuing until the present day, the company has managed to finish the site construction and has begun the copper production under the new contract (Htwe 2016). Based on this, the No. 1 Mining Enterprise, on behalf of the Myanmar government, received 51 per cent stakes, the Myanmar Economic Holding Co., Ltd 19 per cent and the Myanmar Wanbao Mining Copper Limited 30 per cent.[14] The Letpadaungtaung mining project is envisaged to run until the year 2043 starting from the completion of construction in 2015.

Gas Pipeline Project

The Myanmar-China Gas Pipeline Project involved six parties from four countries: the Chinese National Petroleum Corporation (CNPC), the Daewoo Group of South Korea, the Oil and Natural Gas Corporation Ltd (ONGC) from India, the Myanmar Oil and Gas Enterprise (MOGE), the Korea Gas Corporation (KOGAS) and the Gas Authority of India Limited (GAIL). This project comprises two subprojects: the Shwe Natural Gas Production Project and Myanmar-China Oil Transport Project. In December 2005, CNPC signed a deal with the Myanmar government to purchase natural gas over a thirty-year period. The project was approved by China's National Development and Reform Commission in April 2007. In November 2008, China and Myanmar signed investment agreements to set up an oil pipeline worth US$1.5 billion and a natural gas pipeline worth US$1.04 billion. In June 2009, an agreement to build a crude oil pipeline was made. The inauguration ceremony marking the start of construction took place on 31 October 2009 in Maday Island of Rakhine State. On 12 June 2013, the construction of the gas pipeline was completed, and the oil pipeline was completed in August 2014.

The pipelines make up multiple separate projects combining distinct contracts and ownership structures. The main contractual parts are as follows:

   a. Shwe Natural Gas Field that takes Daewoo International Ltd 51 per cent, ONGC Ltd 17 per cent, MOGE 15 per cent, KOGAS 8 per cent and GAIL 9 per cent stakes;

b. Onshore natural gas pipeline which takes the ownerships of CNPC 51 per cent, Daewoo International Ltd 25 per cent, ONGC 8 per cent, MOGE 8 per cent, KOGAS 4 per cent and GAIL 4 per cent stakes; and
c. Onshore crude oil pipeline which consists of CNPC 51 per cent and MOGE 49 per cent stakes.

The 2,520-km pipeline starts at Kyaukpyu on Myanmar's western coast, enters China at Ruili in Yunnan province and ends at Guigang in Guangxi Zhuang Autonomous Region. The project will produce natural gas in Myanmar and transport it to the southwestern provinces of Guangxi, Yunnan and Guizhou in China. Some 793 km of the trunk line are in Myanmar, and there are four offtake points: Kyaukphyu, Yenangyaung, Taungtha, and Mandalay.

Along the pipeline from the Rakhine State of Myanmar to China, widespread abusive land confiscations occurred. On Maday Island, fifty-six villagers lost approximately 60 acres of farmland to make way for the natural gas storage facility. Another twenty villagers in Kyaukpyu faced land confiscations because the villages were located on the pipeline route. Villagers in Magway Division also experienced land grabbing. Although many local people impacted by the pipeline construction have lost land upon which they rely for their livelihood, only some of the villagers received compensation payment, while others have received nothing so far (Earthrights International 2011).

However, responding to the villagers' voices and publicly displayed protests, CNPC carried out the compensation process according to the old Land Law. The land compensation standards included crop compensation: the crop compensation term for permanent land acquisition is equal to the payment of the value of crops for five years, while that for temporary land acquisition is three years. After the new Land Administration Law of Myanmar had been promulgated at the end of 2012, the provisions required that for permanent land acquisition, only three years' fee of crop compensation needed to be paid. After the promulgation of this new law, the company still compensated land owners, who had not finished the land acquisition process at that time, according to the five-year crop compensation standard for permanent land acquisition (Business & Human Rights Resource Centre 2013). Finally, the gas pipelines and crude oil pipelines were completed in 2014 and the business has run ever since.

Myitsone Dam Project

The Myitsone dam project is situated in the Kachin State which is the northernmost part of Myanmar, bordered by China to the north and east, by Shan State to the south, and by Sagaing Division and India to the west. The population of Kachin State is 1,689,441 according to the 2014 Census Report. The inhabitants are Kachin (Jingpaw, Rawang, Lisu, Zaiwa, Longwo, Lachit), Shan, Bamar, Chinese and Indian in four districts and twenty-nine townships. The Myitsone dam is above the confluence of two rivers, the May-Kha and Mali-Kha, in the upper Ayeyarwaddy basin that is listed in the United Nations Environment Programme's World Conservation Monitoring Centre as one of the world's top thirty high-priority river basins for its support of high biodiversity and high vulnerability to future pressures (IFC 2017, p. 5). The Ayeyarwaddy river is 2,170 km long and its basin is 413,674 square km, flowing through the land which accounts for 61 per cent of the country's total area (ibid., p. 8).

The Myitsone dam project is a joint venture business of CPI (Yunnan International Power Investment Company China) (80 per cent), Myanmar Ministry of Electric Power (15 per cent) and Myanmar Asia World Company (5 per cent), established in 2006. CPI is a wholly-owned subsidiary of state-owned China Power Investment Corporation, one of China's five largest power generation groups (Mon and Hammond 2015). Since the investment contract between the CPU and the Ministry of Electric Power was concluded in 2006 in the period of military government before the 2008 Constitution, the contract had not been implemented for over three years before construction could start only in 2009. The local people did not know about the project before its commencement and could not see its advantages. The reservoir construction, which is located very close to the banks of these rivers, began nonetheless.

After the construction of the dam reservoir, the dam would affect around 766 square km of forest areas in the Kachin State and cause immense damage to the navigation system on the river, as well as damage to downstream communities whose livelihoods depend on agriculture and livestock. Local communities believe that they would suffer environmental impacts such as landslides, water flooding, or earthquakes by dam failure due to the extremely high waterfall or installation of hydroelectric power generation. In 2013, opinions by twelve experts were invited to seek the Environmental Impact Assessment (EIA) which is done by the Chinese investment company. Experts found significant flaws in the environmental impact statement (EIS) in the structure of the report, a superficial analysis of the dam's impacts on freshwater biodiversity and inadequate public participation.[15]

Like the Wanbao project, the revolt and objections of local communities were driven by concerns over land relocation, environmental problems and lack of transparency. Since early 2010, local people started strikes and demanded to stop the Myitsone dam project (Kristensen 2016). After that, the Kachin National Organization (KNO) based in the UK organized protests against the Myitsone dam in front of Myanmar embassies in several countries. Armed conflicts between the Kachin Independence Army (KIA) and Myanmar military troops occurred as well, adding another violent dimension to this specific frontier context. As a result, a lot of local people who had been involved in the strikes were arrested. This hydropower project was indeed suspended in 2011 due to public opposition (Myint 2016). However, an investment contract cannot be just terminated because of the contractual terms. If Myanmar cancels that project, Myanmar will be liable to pay US$800 million to China. As of 2020, Myanmar annually pays the bank interests of the business deposits to the CPI. Myanmar should do ad hoc decisions about the Myitsone dam project by taking into account the country's energy needs and its relations with China, while at the same time preserving the precious natural and cultural heritage of its river systems.

Myanmar's Resource Contestation in Regional Context: The Belt and Road Initiative

China's rebalancing was a response to economic imperatives. As demographics have changed, wages have risen, and with productivity growth not keeping pace, unit labour costs have gone up. That has forced China to start reducing its exports of labour-intensive light manufacturing industries such as garments, footwear, toys and furniture. This has created opportunities for CLMV (Cambodia, Laos, Myanmar and Vietnam) economies which need to be seized with proactive policy measures. Approximately 17 per cent of the global daily oil production is transported via the Straits of Malacca. This delivers oil from the

Middle East to the likes of China, Japan and South Korea. Issues that are becoming problematic with this trade route include:
- increasing piracy;
- longer steam times between ports; and
- port and channel congestion, particularly in Singapore.

Significant oil and gas exploration activities in the Bay of Bengal and the Andaman Sea—in the countries of Myanmar and India—aim at Chinese future energy security needs. The "New Silk Road" brings all of these markets closer (Mierzejewski 2021, this volume; Rowedder, this volume). The opening of the Chongqing rail route, the cheapest of five railway routes from China to Europe, opens up a new mode of transport that is twice as fast as shipping and is more effective for moving hi-tech and automotive parts. A new road, rail and air infrastructure provide the central city of Kunming with better access, particularly ocean access via Myanmar. Arguably, Kunming aims to compete with Singapore as a key Southeast Asian transport hub.

RESPONSIBILITIES AND ACCOUNTABILITIES TO SOLVE THE INVESTMENT ISSUES

To solve the investment issues, states have to adopt a legal framework in line with international standards. The Constitution of the Republic of the Union of Myanmar 2008 provides the legal basis for the development of the national economy by permitting economic activities through such business vehicles as cooperatives, joint-ventures, or sole proprietorships (for businesses conducted by private individuals).[16] Myanmar is implementing its investment policy by including the main components such as the adoption of a market-oriented system for the allocation of resources. the encouragement of private investment and entrepreneurial activity, and the opening of the economy for foreign trade and investment. The government adopted more laws and regulations related to investments. If a foreign investor wants to invest in Myanmar, she or he must observe the rules contained in section 40 of the Investment Law according to which the investors will have to apply the requirements imposed on the chosen type of economic activity. In the case of Chinese investment corporations, the main law is the Investment Law 2016 and the related laws are Myanmar Mines Law 1994, Law Amending Myanmar Mines Law 2015, Myanmar Special Economic Zone Law 2014, Myanmar Companies Law, Tax Laws, Myanmar Land Laws, Myanmar Labour Laws, Environmental Conservation Law and Contract Law.

The responsibilities of foreign investors are provided in Chapter 16 of the Investment Law 2016. They must obey the regulations, notifications, procedures of the concerned department, orders and directives.[17] Then, they shall follow the procedures and standards for the impacts on the environment and social and cultural heritage.[18] They have legal liabilities to pay adequate compensation to the victims when they suffer any loss due to the investment activities.[19] They are responsible for carrying out the necessary environmental protection and conservation measures, protecting the project and its environment in accordance with the existing laws, managing the system to dispose of industrial waste from the factories, contributing the funds for corporate social responsibility (CSR) and submitting the reports to the ministries concerned and MIC (see as well Einzenberger 2018; for the case of Laos, see Tappe, this volume).

The identified three cases are all about the exploitation of natural resources which are likely to cause environmental problems. The enterprises need to prepare Initial Environmental Examination (IEE) and Environmental Impact Assessment (EIA) reports. Depending on the outcome of the IEE report, they will be allowed to apply for a Myanmar Investment Commission (MIC) permit to the commission under the Investment Law. Investors also need to carry out Social Impact Assessment (SIA), Environmental Impact Assessment (EIA) and Health Impact Assessment (HIA).[20] The manufacturing of minerals is included in the list of economic activities which required an environmental impact assessment.[21]

Investment companies can lease the land or buildings up to an initial fifty years of land use and extend that for an additional ten plus ten years depending on the amounts invested and on whether the activity will be continued without disruptions after the expiration of the initial term.[22] However, investors shall compensate for any loss caused by the damage of extraction and socio-economic losses to affected people.[23] As the state is the original owner of all lands,[24] it is the government that grants the right to farming in conformity with the rules, regulations and by-laws of this law so that agricultural resources can be developed except for natural resource extraction such as gems, mines, petroleum, etc.[25] To use this right, a person has to apply to the Township Land Records Department Office for getting the Land Use Certificate, passing it through the relevant Ward or Village Tract Farmland Management Body.[26] After the person has paid the prescribed registration fees and has been registered at the Township Land Records Department's Office, he will get the certificate of eligibility for farming.[27] In awarding compensation, the owners of confiscated land have to provide land certificates and they have the right to get the market value price for their lands.[28]

REFLECTION ON INTERNATIONAL LAW

In addition to the national laws and rules, a number of international frameworks address the adverse impacts of large-scale extractivism. Stakeholders of investments have to adhere to international regulations such as the Extractive Industries Transparency Initiative (EITI), International Council on Mining and Metals (ICMM), Sustainable Development Framework, Voluntary Principles on Security and Human Rights (VPSHR), China Chamber of Commerce of Metals Minerals & Chemicals Importers and Exporters (CCCMC), Guidelines for Social Responsibility in Outbound Mining Investments, and OECD Due Diligence Guidance for Responsible Supply Chains of Minerals from Conflict-Affected and High-Risk Areas. The Chinese companies are required to prepare the EIA reports that include the necessary information for decision-making on an executive summary, results from EIA studies, information on data gaps and major sources of uncertainties, technical appendices, visual aids and easy-to-read text. In the Environmental Conservation Rule 2014, foreign investors of large-scale production have to provide an EIA report with the environmental management plan.[29] In preparing the EIA report, they can follow the principles of the International Association for Impact Assessment (IAIA). EIA processes are based on screening, scoping, examination, mitigation and impact management and evaluation. After the completion of the EIA process, they have to write the environmental impact statement (EIS) which clearly states the proposed measures for mitigation, satisfactory assessment of the proposals, information required for decision-making, and establishment of the terms and conditions for its implementation. On the other hand, the concerned department needs to follow up on this process and monitor the development and the effectiveness of mitigation measures (Interorganizational Committee 1994).

As Myanmar and China are member countries of the World Bank Group and International Finance Corporation (IFC), the investors have to apply the 2007 Environmental, Health and Safety (EHS) Guidelines and the 2012 Performance Standards of IFC. The EHS guidelines are applied by their respective policies and standards on wastewater management, hazardous materials management, control of air emission, land contamination, energy conservation and emergency preparedness and response. Multinational corporations shall create the Environmental Management Policy and Plan by following up on the EHS Guidelines. This is because of the nature of exploitation, the use of hazardous materials, and heavy machinery equipment. The Performance standard 1 of IFC, "Assessment and Management of Environmental and Social Risks and Impacts", establishes the Environmental and Social Assessment and Management System (ESMS) incorporated with the policy; identification of risks and impacts; management programmes; organizational capacity and competency; emergency preparedness and response; stakeholder engagement; and monitoring and review (IFC 2012).

Ideally, the process of identification of risks and impacts will consist of an adequate, accurate, and objective evaluation and presentation, prepared by competent professionals. The ESMS will maintain an emergency preparedness and response system so that the enterprises will prepare to prevent and mitigate any harm to people and/or the environment. The clients will establish the procedures to monitor and measure the effectiveness of the management programme, as well as compliance with any related legal and/or contractual obligations and regulatory requirements. Moreover, the enterprises will develop and implement a Stakeholder Engagement Plan that is scaled to the project risks and impacts and development stage and be tailored to the characteristics and interests of the affected communities (IFC 2012).

The enterprises have to follow the regulatory requirements, including technical feasibility and cost-effectiveness of the available options for prevention, control and release of emission, wastewater management, water conservation programme, sanitary water conservation techniques, and internationally accepted hazard assessments such as Hazardous Operations Analysis (HAZOP), Failure Mode and Effects Analysis (FMEA) and Hazard Identification (HAZID), noise monitoring programme, risk management actions involving the risk screening, interim risk management, detailed quantitative risk assessment, permanent risk reduction measures, and plan for community health and safety which means the projects including the life and fire safety systems, health and education facilities, transport project of hazardous materials, disease prevention and emergency preparedness and response plan (IFC 2007).

The UN Guiding Principles on Business and Human Rights are essential principles on business and its impacts. There are three pillars such as protect, respect and remedy which identify the responsibilities of states and business corporations. The former shall be the regulator or policymaker, economic actor, multi-complex actor and adviser in conflict zones (United Nations 2011).

CONCLUSION

With regard to FDI, the provisions relating to the flow of investments by foreign investors in Myanmar are enshrined at the very outset of International and Investment Agreements (IIAs). The approach that has been sought to liberalize conditions for the investors is the "Pre-establishment" or "Combined National Treatment (NT) and Most-favoured Nation Treatment (MFNT)" model (Reinisch 2008, p. 11). In the Bilateral Investment Treaties, NT and MFNT must be granted at any time of the investment activities: establishment, acquisition and expansion, management, use, conduct, operation, sale, and other disposition of the investment (ibid., p. 13). The host country and foreign investors consider the "fair and equitable standard" and "security and protection standard" for investors' legitimate expectations. These two standards are put for transparency, stability and legitimacy for any dispute. The standard of full protection and security is less frequently applied than other standards, hence arbitration practice is not common and the legal literature on Myanmar is rather scarce. This research on three major Chinese infrastructure projects has identified the political conditions and public demonstrations in Myanmar as major uncertainties and problems for Chinese investors. These issues persisted because of the lack of trust among the stakeholders and deficient transparency. These shall be solved with different methods by considering the sustainable development of the environment, human rights, state economy, and investment relations by the Myanmar government including local authorities, and Chinese investors.

To gain sustainable economic growth, both the Myanmar government and Chinese investors should be willing to consider not only their own interests but also those of the local communities in the impacted area. In particular, as the political economy perspective can contribute to the sustainable development of Myanmar's democratic transition, the stakeholders need to use the Free, Prior, Informed Consent (FPIC) method in doing business for public purposes. To build trusted relations between investment companies and local people, and to mitigate problems of trust and accountability, greater transparency is needed. As the State/Region Government are vested with the delegated legislative power by Schedule 2 of the Constitution, the local government shall legislate on the "Energy, Electricity, Mining and Forestry Sector" in the concerned regions. Arguably, the stakeholders of Chinese investors, local government and the Myanmar government should encourage public participation to solve the challenging issues. To assess these developments in the present context of the expanding Chinese BRI as a new dynamic of frontier capitalism in Myanmar, further research will be needed.

Notes

1. The Union of Myanmar Foreign Investment Law was enacted in 1988 and the Republic of the Union of Myanmar Foreign Investment Law was enacted in 2012 and repealed by the Investment Law 2016.
2. The Union of Myanmar Citizen Investment Law was enacted in 1993 and the Republic of the Union of Myanmar Citizen Investment Law was enacted in 2013 and repealed by the Investment Law 2016.
3. Source: Myanmar Investment Commission, https://www.dica.gov.mm/en/data-and-statistics.
4. Ibid.
5. Investment Law, Pyidaungsu Hluttaw Law No. 40/2016, p. 75, 18 October 2016.
6. In 2011, 530,000 kyats were equivalent to US$500 by currency exchange rate.
7. http://www.myanmarwanbao.com.mm/en/our-latest-news.html, press statement, 24 August 2016.

8. Para 63 of Submission of Evidence to Myanmar Government's Letpadaung Investigation Commission, Lawyers' Network and Justice Trust, 28 January 2013.
9. Final report of the Investigation Commission on Letpadaungtaung Copper Mine Project, April 2013. https://www.charltonsmyanmar.com/letpadaung-investigation-commission-issues-final-report/ (accessed 10 October 2021).
10. *The Global New Light of Myanmar* 10, no. 255, 31 December 2012.
11. http://www.president-office.gov.mm/en, 2 December 2012.
12. Myanmar Ahlin Newspaper 52, no. 163, 12 March, 2013.
13. Final report of the Investigation Commission on Letpadaungtaung Copper Mine Project, April 2013. https://www.charltonsmyanmar.com/letpadaung-investigation-commission-issues-final-report/ (accessed 10 October 2021). *Myanmar Ahlin* (newspaper) 52, no. 163, 12 March 2013. Presidential Notification No. 92/2012.
14. EITI Report of Myanmar Economic Holding Ltd, 25 June 2018.
15. https://archive.internationalrivers.org/campaigns/irrawaddy-myitsone-dam-0 (accessed 10 October 2021).
16. Section 36 of the Constitution of the Republic of the Union of Myanmar, 2008.
17. Section 65(c) of the Investment Law 2016, Pyidaungsu Hluttaw Law No. 40/2016, 18 October 2016. http://www.myanmar-embassy-tokyo.net/eco2017/Investment/Myanmar-Investment-Law-2016-English.pdf (accessed 13 October 2021).
18. Ibid., section 65(g).
19. Ibid., section 65(o).
20. Ibid., section 71.
21. MIC Notification No. 50/2014, 14 August 2014.
22. Ibid., section 50.
23. Investment Law 2016, Pyidaungsu Hluttaw law No.40/2016, 18 October 2016, section 65.
24. Constitution of the Republic of the Union of Myanmar, 2008, section 37.
25. Myanmar Land Law, Pyidaungsu Hluttaw law No.11/2012, 30 March 2012, section 3. https://www.burmalibrary.org/sites/burmalibrary.org/files/obl/docs15/2012-Farmland_Act-Habitat-en-red-t%26p.pdf (accessed 13 October 2021).
26. Ibid., section 4.
27. Ibid., section 6.
28. Myanmar Land Acquisition Act, 1894, section 23.
29. Rule 2(p) of the Environmental Conservation Rule 2014, Notification No. 50/2014 by the Ministry of Environmental Conservation and Forestry, 5 June 2014.

References

Amnesty International. 2015. Urgent Action, UA: 98/15 Index: ASA 16/1563/2015 Myanmar. https://media.business-humanrights.org/media/documents/files/documents/ASA1615632015ENGLISH.pdf (accessed 10 October 2021).

Business & Human Rights Resource Centre. 2013. "Chinese National Petroleum Corporation (CNPC) Response to Reports on Alleged Human Rights Impacts of Shwe Gas & Myanmar-China Oil Transport Projects". https://www.business-humanrights.org/en/latest-news/chinese-national-petroleum-corporation-cnpc-response-to-reports-on-alleged-human-rights-impacts-of-shwe-gas-myanmar-china-oil-transport-projects/ (accessed 10 October 2021).

EAI. 2011. "China and India Account for Half of Global Energy Growth through 2035". https://www.eia.gov/todayinenergy/detail.php?id=3130 (accessed 5 January 2022).

Earthrights International (blog). 2011. "The Burma-China Pipelines; Human Rights Violations, Applicable Law and Revenue Secrecy". 29 March 2011. https://earthrights.org/publication/the-burma-china-pipelines/ (accessed 10 October 2021).

Einzenberger, Rainer. 2018. "Frontier Capitalism and Politics of Dispossession in Myanmar: The Case of the Mwetaung (Gullu Mual) Nickel Mine in Chin State". *Austrian Journal of South-East Asian Studies* 11, no. 1: 13–34.

Htwe, Chan Mya. 2016. "Wanbao Prepares to Restart Letpadaung". *Myanmar Times*, 23 February 2016. http://www.mmtimes.com/index.php/business/19128-wanbao-prepares-to-re-start-letpadaung.html (accessed 10 October 2021).

International Finance Corporation (IFC). 2007. *Environmental, Health, and Safety (EHS) Guidelines: General EHS Guidelines*. https://www.ifc.org/wps/wcm/connect/29f5137d-6e17-4660-b1f9-02bf561935e5/Final%2B%2BGeneral%2BEHS%2BGuidelines.pdf?MOD=AJPERES&CVID=jOWim3p (accessed 10 October 2021).

———. 2012. *Guidance Note 1: Assessment and Management of Environmental and Social Risks and Impacts*. https://www.ifc.org/wps/wcm/connect/6df1de8f-2a00-4d11-a07c-c09b038f947b/GN1_English_06142021_FINAL.pdf?MOD=AJPERES&CVID=nF3z-gq (accessed 10 October 2021).

———. 2017. *Baseline Assessment Report. Fisheries, Aquatic Ecology and River Health. Strategic Environmental Assessment of the Hydropower Sector in Myanmar*. Washington: International Finance Corporation. https://www.ifc.org/wps/wcm/connect/56a6cad6-cd92-4288-8a29-7d348e89c074/Chapter+5_SEA_Baseline+Assessment_+Fisheries+and+Aquatic+-+21+Sep.pdf?MOD=AJPERES&CVID=maaMcCO (accessed 10 October 2021).

Interorganizational Committee on Guidelines and Principles. 1994. "Guidelines and Principles for Social Impact Assessment". *Impact Assessment* 12, no. 2: 107–152. DOI: 10.1080/07349165.1994.9725857 (accessed 10 October 2021).

Kiik, Laur. 2016. "Nationalism and Anti-Ethno-Politics: Why 'Chinese Development' Failed at Myanmar's Myitsone Dam". *Eurasian Geography and Economics* 57, no. 3: 374–402.

Kristensen, Joern. 2016. "Fourth Option of the Myitsone Dam". *Frontier Myanmar*, 30 June 2016. https://www.frontiermyanmar.net/en/there-fourth-option-the-myitsone-dam

Mierzejewski, Dominik. 2021. *China's Provinces and the Belt and Road Initiative*. London: Routledge.

Mitchell, Travis. 2012. *Chinese Foreign Direct Investment in Myanmar: Remarkable Trends and Multilayered Motivations*. Unpublished thesis, Lund University. https://lup.lub.lu.se/luur/download?func=downloadFile&recordOId=2756649&fileOId=2756655 (accessed 10 October 2021).

Mon, Ye, and Clare Hammond. 2015. "CPI Pushes for Restart of Myitsone Dam". *Myanmar Times*, 5 June 2015. https://www.mmtimes.com/business/14887-cpi-pushes-for-restart-of-myitsone-dam.html (accessed 10 October 2021).

Myint, Sithu Aung. 2016. "The Myitsone Dam: China's Three Options". *Frontier Myanmar*, 26 June 2016. https://www.frontiermyanmar.net/en/the-myitsone-dam-chinas-three-options/ (accessed 10 October 2021).

Reinisch, August. 2008. *Standards of Investment Protection*. Oxford: Oxford University Press.

Shwe Gas Movement. 2006. "Supply and Command: Natural Gas in Western Burma Set to Entrench Military Rule". https://burmacampaign.org.uk/media/shwe_gas.pdf (accessed 10 October 2021).

United Nations. 2011. "Guiding Principles on Business and Human Rights". https://www.ohchr.org/documents/publications/guidingprinciplesbusinesshr_en.pdf (accessed 10 October 2021).

Zhang, Ruosui. 2020. "To Suspend or Not to Suspend: A Cost-Benefit Analysis of Three Chinese Mega-Projects in Myanmar". *Pacific Review*. https://doi.org/10.1080/09512748.2020.1776757 (accessed 10 October 2021).

11

INTERNATIONALIZATION OF RMB AND TIN ORE TRADE IN CHINA-MYANMAR FRONTIER GOVERNANCE
Views from Yunnan Province

Dominik Mierzejewski

INTRODUCTION

Ever since China and Myanmar have shared a border, Yunnan as the melting point of different cultures and civilizations plays a critical role in China's policy towards South and Southeast Asia. In this regard being named the "bridgehead" (*qiaotoubao* 桥头堡) and later "radiation centre" (*fushe zhongxin* 辐射中心) or "pivot" in Chinese foreign policy, Yunnan has enjoyed an essential place for China's actions in the region (Summers 2019; Lu 2013). The "bridgehead" is understood mainly as a military term that refers to a strategic chokepoint on the field of battle. It mainly relates to a sturdy structure that defends and controls a bridge or ferry crossing. In economic terms, however, it acts as a port and facilitates the ease of transportation while it constitutes an international centre of trade, integrating shipping, finance and information. Going further as being located at the edge of the Chinese civilization, "bridgeheads", namely Heilongjiang and Yunnan provinces, and Xinjiang Autonomous Region, cater to resource frontiers as they are responsible for managing frontier governance with a particular focus on cross-border trade and providing stability for China's energy security and mineral resources. Moreover, the term "bridgehead" entails the role of the centre for logistical and supply chains, serving the specific purpose of controlling the flow of resources along international trade routes (Steinberg and Fan 2012, pp. 213–20). Moreover, as part of the frontier regions, "bridgeheads" are responsible for managing the non-traditional transnational security threats and identifying their origins, conceptions and effects, like irregular migration, human trafficking, drug trafficking or climate changes (Caballero-Anthony 2016). Apart from playing an important role in national policy, the essential characteristics of a bridgehead are its powers to control, develop, and influence the regions in the neighbourhood (Jinxin 2019). To have a better understanding of Yunnan's role in China's interactions with Myanmar, the paper looks into the issues of cross-border governance and discusses the role of Yunnan in China's investment policies and the internationalization of the Chinese currency RMB, with a particular focus on the micro level across the border. The first part introduces basic Western and Chinese understandings of cross-border governance. Then, by analysing the documents and academic discourse, the paper identifies the willingness and challenges in Yunnan's actions in Myanmar and discusses a further understanding of frontier governance in Sino-Myanmar relations. The final part presents cross-border projects and their realities with particular emphasis on infrastructure projects sponsored from the provincial and city level as well as the dynamic in the tin ore cross-border trade. In the context of China-Myanmar frontier cooperation, similar questions arise: Are the incentives given by the country in the asymmetrical relations sufficient and is it possible to shape collective actions across the border? To what extent might China's investment, productivity cooperation and trade be useful in providing stability in the very turbulent areas? And finally, what is the significance of frontier trade agreements for the Chinese currency, and to what extent does the frontier capitalism supported by Chinese currency supremacy shape the current frontier dynamics between China and Myanmar?

CROSS-BORDER GOVERNANCE THEORIES: A BRIEF INTRODUCTION

Within Western scholarship, the concept of cross-border governance has been mainly discussed through the lenses of the Euroregion as the vehicle for delivering European integration. Governance, then, is the capacity of public and private actors to (a) build an organizational consensus and define common objectives and tasks; (b) agree on the contribution of each partner to attain the purposes previously defined; and (c) decide on a shared vision for the future of their territory (Global Development Research Centre n.d.). The second concept of the border is mainly based on geographical conditions, cultural differences, and political and economic disparities, which all appear as the natural obstacle to cooperation. To limit the negative impact of the challenges listed above, cross-border governance systems are defined as a set of differently organized institutions of cross-border cooperation between various actors mainly at the subnational level to overcome difficulties due to a shared national border. That means that cross-border governance systems are seen as the simultaneous existence of different transnational organizations as well as their various functional relationships (Fricke 2015).

Chinese narratives often position border areas as backward to coastal areas. Xing Guangcheng from Wuhan University points out that in the border areas "everything" is weaker: innovations, living standards, education, medical care, and social contradiction are more profound than in the rest of China, and the people in the border places are "less civilized" than of those living in China. Going further he identifies the biggest challenges to the stability across the border: terrorism, separatism and ideological struggles (Xing 2018, pp. 5–17). Enrico Gualini (2003) writes that cross-border governance is an institutional construct resulting from complex processes of coevolution that consist of three dimensions: political-economic (is related to the operation of strategic selectivity of aims), institutional (involves institutional aspects of collaboration) and symbolic-cognitive (deals with the creation of transborder communities and invention of a cross-border identity). In the research of Gualini the critical points touch on the incentives for cross-border sustainable cooperation: Are the incentives for cross-border cooperation sufficient for participating parties to promote innovative forms of collective action and for realizing an adequate concurrence of resources? Are the incentives for cross-border operations enough for building new coalitions and governance regimes? Under the Belt and Road Initiative (BRI), China can offer two-track incentives: tax and infrastructure incentives. In both cases, as usually promised by the policymakers from Beijing, the relations with China might stimulate economic growth and limit unemployment. But the practical side of China's frontier cooperation has been planned and managed by the provincial and lower-level governments. In this context, the central government takes the position of an agenda-setter and arbiter. In the context of Sino-Myanmar cross-border governance, the local Chinese apparatus faces the dilemma of cooperation with numerous non-state actors, e.g., military groups, local policymakers or minorities that hope to gain as much as possible from the Chinese side (Kato 2013, p. 293). Apart from economically driven incentives, China, with its non-interference principles, offers political incentives and politically unconditional economic cooperation—as the majority of Chinese scholars admit. Sometimes, however, it is far from reality, but in the case of the Rohingya crisis, China indeed does not interfere in domestic affairs and only supported the government in Myanmar. Joachim Blatter suggests two models of governance: Territorial governance characterized by "vertical interaction lines and information flow within national units where the border is crossed at the top of the hierarchy", and functional governance that consists of "direct contacts between different level actors across a border" (Blatter et al. 2008, p. 468). Territorial governance is understood as the process of territorial organization of the multiplicity of relations that characterize interactions among actors and different, but non-conflictual, interests. Functional interdependencies have acted as the most important driving forces for the acceleration of cross-border cooperation during the last decades, mainly, but not only in Europe. Functional orientation is mainly based on horizontal relations, project-based management, integration of social and private actors and fuzzy borders (Rosenau 1995, pp. 13–43). Both orientations are visible in Chinese practices. The territorial orientation is reflected in the hierarchical organization: The upper level should approve a decision taken at the lower level, there are many actors across the borders: military, business, social groups and the local government have many tasks to complete. Functional orientation is less critical in China's practices, but still visible when the frontier regions are asked to seek breakthroughs in the two aspects of "property system" and "process of marketization" and deepen the process of reforms in their regions (Xing 2018, pp. 5–17).

YUNNAN: PROVINCE RESPONSIBLE FOR FRONTIER GOVERNANCE

Yunnan province has been named "bridgehead" by Hu Jintao (2006) and "radiation centre" or "pivot" by Xi Jinping (2015). On the one hand, the Yunnan government has enjoyed this superior position, but on the other, it "needs to satisfy the central government expectations that sometimes are not realistic and usually very high" (see Mierzejewski 2021 for a more detailed discussion). While responsible for the infrastructure projects in upper Myanmar and constituting a platform for a reconciliation process between competing groups from Kachin and Shan states, Kunming has been at the same time put into a challenging position by the central government. Moreover, Yunnan province is less developed than other regions in China and has no leverages for opening up China on its own, as asked by the central government. In reverse, the local authorities prefer cooperation with more stable regional partners like Shanghai or Guangdong.[1] This, however, does not translate into the passiveness of the provincial-level government that is willing to "run" for more money transfers from Beijing. Interestingly, the driving force behind the corridor of Bangladesh-China-India-Myanmar Economic Corridor (BCIM-EC) was the Yunnan provincial government. The first conference on regional collaboration was held in Kunming in August 1999 after Jiang Zemin declared the "Open Up the West" campaign. Since then, the concept was further developed by both local and central governments; in 2012, the four concerned countries established the BCIM Business Council, and in 2013, the BCIM-EC agreement was signed. Myanmar, however, is less important from the viewpoint of Beijing's overall foreign policy, while Yunnan is a matter of domestic development and stability. In this regard, when the economic issues are discussed, Kunming plays a decisive role. Since 2015 the Yunnan provincial government has set up a leading group for the construction of a pivot for South Asia and Southeast Asia. The body is managed by the governor, the deputy governors as the deputy leaders, and forty-five provincial-level departments (Li 2016, pp. 150–51).

Critical for Yunnan's position in the BRI is the effectiveness of external actions taken by the provincial government. In its designated function as a "bridgehead", Yunnan needs to accomplish five tasks, in particular concerning the interactions with Myanmar: (1) internationalization of RMB and stable cross-border trade, (2) negotiating, lobbying, finding funds and implementing infrastructure projects, (3) limiting anti-Chinese sentiments and providing the basis for elite cultivation in the target areas, (4) being a hub for companies from more advanced regions in China like Shanghai or Guangdong, and (5) providing the political platform for ceasefire talks in Kunming and managing humanitarian crises.

It is needless to say that it is the settlement in Chinese currency that is critical for the success of the foreign trade "go global" policy. In this regard, Chinese central institutions like the Bank of China, Agriculture Bank of China, and the Industrial and Commercial Bank of China are involved. Regarding the internationalization of RMB, critical jobs were placed in the hands of local banks and financial institutions (Yunnan Government 2016a). In fact, local banks and the Kunming branch of the People's Bank of China (PBOC) actively tried to navigate the trade policy towards the RMB settlement so that in 2007, 95 per cent of border trade was settled in the Chinese currency. From the Chinese perspective, the internationalization of RMB improves cross-border transactions: "the cross-border flows of the renminbi brought about by real economic activities such as cross-border trade and travel could provide an effective settlement method in bilateral transactions; and it could also enlarge bilateral trade and economic cooperation and promote the economic development of frontier regions inhabited by minority nationalities" (Gao and Yu 2009, p. 8). From the perspective of the neighbouring countries, however, the situation looks the opposite. The domination of RMB facilitates deals but at the same time infiltrates the markets of partner countries and challenges their sovereign right to have their own currency. In the case of Vietnam, the rule of the Chinese currency is perceived as a critical issue that might have a significant impact on China-Vietnam relations.[2] RMB has formed in the border areas of Laos, Myanmar and Vietnam adjacent to China, where its circulation area generally covers 70–180 km inward, and its farthest circulation range extends to 300 km. In Myanmar's Shan State RMB even replaced the official currency, the kyat (MMK), and became the currency of primary circulation (Steinberg and Fan 2012, p. 245).

Yunnan's second "bridgehead" task field includes perusing the big infrastructure projects in Upper Myanmar. Starting with the economic activities, it is worth mentioning that usually, Chinese local governments need to fulfil their obligations placed in the very detailed plans and projects. One among many is the plan declared by the local level of the National Development and Reform Commission (NDRC) that by 2020, obligated the provincial government to achieve US$50 billion in foreign trade.

This objective could only be achieved by the active participation of Yunnan's government in Myanmar infrastructure projects. One example of China's inland navigation project is based on its activities in the Irrawaddy River. The Governor of Yunnan province first raised the prospect of using the river artery for mass transportation from China to the Indian Ocean in 1989. The negotiations between the Chinese and Myanmar governments to construct the water route began in 1996. The two governments reportedly reached a transportation agreement in principle and agreed to a "Build, Operate, Transfer" (BOT) financing model. Yunnan's Dehong Prefecture, bordering Myanmar, was responsible for coordinating the project. Again in June 2018, the Yunnan Provincial Development and Reform Commission (YPDRC) proposed to the central government that works on the Irrawaddy River passage project should be resumed. In this case, Dehong Prefecture is responsible for coordinating with Myanmar enterprises to obtain approval from the Myanmar government to upgrade the road between Zhangfeng and Bhamo to connect to the Irrawaddy River. In other words, the lobbying in Myanmar is in the hand of Dehong's prefecture administration (Transnational Institute 2019). In 2014, the YPDRC took the lead and attracted the state-owned enterprise (SOE) China International Trust and Investment Corporation (CITIC) to invest in the China–Myanmar Irrawaddy River–Land Water Intermodal Transport

Corridor. This powerful ally in Beijing allows the local government to play a bigger role in China's global economic outreach with the project of the "China–Myanmar Economic Corridor and Ruili–Kyaukpyu Channel Plan" (Tun and Mclaughlin 2015).

The third important part of Yunnan's participation in cross-border relations with Myanmar lies in governing and navigating the activities of Chinese living in Myanmar. This, however, is far from easy. Lower Myanmar is inhabited by Southern Chinese Hakka and Hokkien while mainly Yunnan's Chinese reside in upper Myanmar. Apart from this, the Yunnan provincial government needs to limit the anti-Chinese sentiments. According to surveys conducted in Myanmar, published by Yunnan Academy of Social Science (2016), the picture of China according to public opinion was negative. First, Burmese prefer to conduct business with Americans (approximately 87 per cent in cities, 83 per cent in the countryside), while 43 per cent in cities and 40 per cent in the countryside prefer doing business with China. Moreover, the majority of society in Myanmar placed relations with the United States higher than those with China. The importance of relations with China did not exceed 15 per cent, while relations with the United States registered close to 60 per cent (Mierzejewski 2021, p. 94).

The fourth main task of Yunnan province is building a platform for Chinese companies from the developed areas to facilitate their "go global" position. In this regard, the critical place for cooperation was designated in the Central New District of Yunnan in Kunming with the policy named "Kunming Service and Peripheral Manufacturing" model. This domestic integration is based on two significant facts: First, the construction of the Chongqing-Kunming and Kunming-Shenzhen high-speed railways and second, the "mutual assistance" plan between Kunming and Shanghai. The municipal government, due to a similar structure of economic (mainly agrarian) structures with bordering countries, has preferred to cooperate with domestic partners from more developed areas in the coastal areas of Shanghai or Guangdong. The biggest challenge faced by the Yunnan government and lower administrative levels is the ethnic insurgency in Myanmar. Local cooperation with ethnic armed organizations challenged Myanmar's central government to achieve the state-led resources management system. Some local communities from upper Myanmar have attempted to tax the trade often bypassing government treasuries (Woods 2019, p. 2).

Moreover, through cross-border trade, the Chinese local authorities aim to provide the venue for peace talks. For example, in 2012 Ruili hosted the third round of peace talks between Myanmar and Kachin State since a seventeen-year truce with the Kachin Independence Organization (KIO) fell apart in June 2011. In February 2019 representatives from Northern Alliance–Burma (NA-B) and the government's National Reconciliation and Peace Center (NRPC) met in Kunming to examine the possibility of how to conduct the peace process based on the Nationwide Ceasefire Agreement (NCA) (Yhome 2019).

In recent events, when the global pandemic of COVID-19 and military *coup d'état* influenced cross-border activities, the role of the local government in Yunnan shifted from outward-oriented to inward-oriented with the critical focus on governing the pandemic within China's borders. This inward-oriented policy shift has been visible in limiting the cross-border trade by rising freight costs and possible strict inspections at the border points or even closing the border points between China and Myanmar (Dan and Ma 2021). Regarding the stability in upper Myanmar, Cissy Zhou (2021) predicts that "Myanmar's military is expected to have a tougher stance in ethnicity issues, and the military conflict in northern Myanmar is likely to become more intense, which would further disrupt the passages alongside the border". The situation brought more responsibilities to the Yunnan provincial government in Kunming; to keep its position within the Chinese system, it needs to take more responsibilities in peace process management.

INTERNATIONALIZATION OF RMB AND TIN ORES: FRONTIER CAPITALISM IN PRACTICE

During the period of Deng Xiaoping's reforms, the central government allowed the provincial level to experiment while delivering stability and economic growth. By decentralizing and relocating development priority to southwestern Yunnan and its border region, the Chinese government has scaled down administrative decision-making to allow these underdeveloped areas to catch up. In this regard, the border cities act as the primary site and vehicle for cross-border mobilities between the two countries. Besides, the border city is the direct actor for implementing any national and provincial policies intended to make different border cities more prosperous and cooperative across borders. China-Myanmar border trade includes five types: formal and official business, informal border trade, illegal border trade, transit trade and barter trade. More importantly, the border city is the actual producer of economic growth and also serves to distribute the benefits of new development and greater mobility. In 1992, the Beijing government also granted Yunnan specific preferential policies to bolster its border trade. One of the plans designated Ruili, Wanding and Hekou as state-level border towns. The central government also approved, within these three towns, the creation of an economic cooperation district in collaboration with Myanmar, Laos, and Vietnam, respectively. In this case, the Yunnan provincial government have been given authority to manage five centrally approved state-level border towns with minimal central intervention. Apart from the central planning, the local communities took the initiative to facilitate frontier trade and RMB circulation. In 2015, for example, Dehong Prefecture described the China-Myanmar Corridor as a priority in their planning, and the promotion of the passage is referred to in Luanchuan County's 2019 plan. Yunnan helped Myanmar build the Bhamo-Xinkang land-water intermodal hub port. In the first phase of the project, four docks were built with a quayside of 1,200 metres, including one 1,000-ton container terminal, two 1,000-ton bulk terminals, and one passenger terminal. New passenger buildings, large reporting buildings, warehouses, storage yards, parking lots and other ancillary facilities were also planned. Further construction works were designed, such as dredging of the waterway from Bhamo to Mandalay downstream and Bhamo to Myitkyina upstream, and setting of navigation marks along the Irrawaddy River. However, to secure the relatively efficient use of the river port in Bhamo, the local governments strive for funds to build or repair the highway from Luanchuan county to Bhamo (Rippa 2020, pp. 95–96). Chinese sources estimate the total costs borne by the Chinese side at MMK85.8 billion (for 92 km of the road) and the project plans to complete the road construction in June 2020 and open to traffic at the end of June 2021 (163.com 2019). The above-discussed plans are facing limited financial resources of the local government so Chinese authorities find themselves cooperating with semi-legal groups in upper Myanmar, thus leading to frontier capitalism co-produced by both state- and non-state actors (see the introduction to this volume by Rowedder and Tappe). The

China-Myanmar highway to Myitkyina, jointly led and financed by the Yunnan provincial government, Baoshan city and Tengchong city, is a case in point. As acknowledged by the Yunnan province leadership, the problems arise from the other side: Myanmar's borders have poor traffic and a lack of funds. The localities need to deal with the situation that competing forces in northern Myanmar discourage border trade by imposing extra duties and tools (Kudo 2013, p. 292).

The second pillar of border prefectures' actions is based on the internationalization of the Chinese currency RMB. It is needless to say that the government in Kunming plays the "internationalization of RMB" card to receive more benefits from Beijing. Thus, in January 2004, Yunnan was granted the special export taxes repayment programme which stipulates that taxes on the export of goods of small border trade in Yunnan settled in RMB could be refunded 70 per cent and 40 per cent, respectively. The centrally granted policies allow local authorities to limit illegal business practices across the border. The traders preferred to use black market banks to settle the accounts instead of China's and Myanmar's official financial institutions (Yunnan Government 2016b). Moreover, the provincial-level government has transferred annual special subsidies of RMB100 million from 2013 to 2020 and arranged exclusive money transfers for particular projects such as infrastructure construction, economic and trade development along the border, border stability, drug control and HIV/AIDS control and inland navigation projects. Moreover, the local government encourages financial and tax incentives to support equity investment funds and venture capital funds to settle in pilot zones and encourage the use of non-financial corporate bond financing instruments in the interbank bond market, broaden financing channels and reduce financing. With all these measures local governments support the establishment of development funds in the pilot areas and the experimental zone to speed up the construction of import and export processing zones, international logistics and warehousing zones, and actively undertake industrial transfer. The three industrial parks of Ruili, Mangshi and Longchuan are unified under the management and support of provincial parks with particular provincial finances. The experimental zone in Ruili speeds up the construction of import and export processing zones, international logistics and warehousing zones, and actively undertakes industrial transfer. Finally, the project addresses the issues of encouraging qualified enterprises to conduct pilot trials for direct power purchases by large customers and support the development of regional electricity price reforms (China FDI 2019). Taking the individual plan of the Dehong prefectural government and Yunnan provincial NDRC as an example, the majority of projects are related to the digital economy and social management. The detailed list of the projects reveals that the biggest part is given to tourism, agriculture, machinery industry, digital economy (38 per cent), social management (*shehui guanli*), medical care, social insurance, local government engineering (*shizheng gongcheng*) (27 per cent), followed by the environmental protection (17 per cent), road, airports, railroads (15 per cent), and cultural exchange (3 per cent). The common project sponsored by Yunnan companies and Myanmar counterparts is in the energy sector based on the BOT model financed through central or local government subsidies (40 per cent), local funds (25 per cent) and other sources (35 per cent). Once the BOT is mainly sponsored by government subsidies and local funds, the domination of the Chinese currency is not in dispute (Xinhua 2018). Apart from drawing attention to road construction and internationalization of the RMB, the critical issue is given to cross-border trade. Due to the unstable political situation in upper Myanmar, the critical point is placed on the sustainability of trade between China and Myanmar. The data collected from Kunming Custom Office, Ministry of Commerce and SilkRoad News webpage indicates that the business is turbulent and not stable. In 2015 the trade dynamic dropped down by 29.7 per cent, followed by an increase of more than 50 per cent in 2016 before it dropped down again by more than 20 per cent (see Figure 11.1).

Regarding the structure of cross-border trade, the priority is given to natural resources, mainly tin ores, iron ores, or rare earth materials. The major producing areas in upper Myanmar include the Man Mawtin district, Namkham and Muse, all in the northern Shan States (Gardiner et al. 2015). The close relations between Ruili and Muse facilitate border trade and provide access to resources in the eastern part of Myanmar. Analysis of the structure of cross-border trade in 2019 indicates that Chinese companies are mainly interested in Myanmar's natural resources. Tin ores take the big portion of China's imports through cross-border trade (49 per cent), followed by non-agglomerate iron ores (12 per cent) and rare earth oxides (11 per cent) (Custom Statistic Office 2019). Taking the import of tin ores from Myanmar as an example, there

FIGURE 11.1
The Dynamic of Cross-Border Trade of Yunnan Province, 2014–18

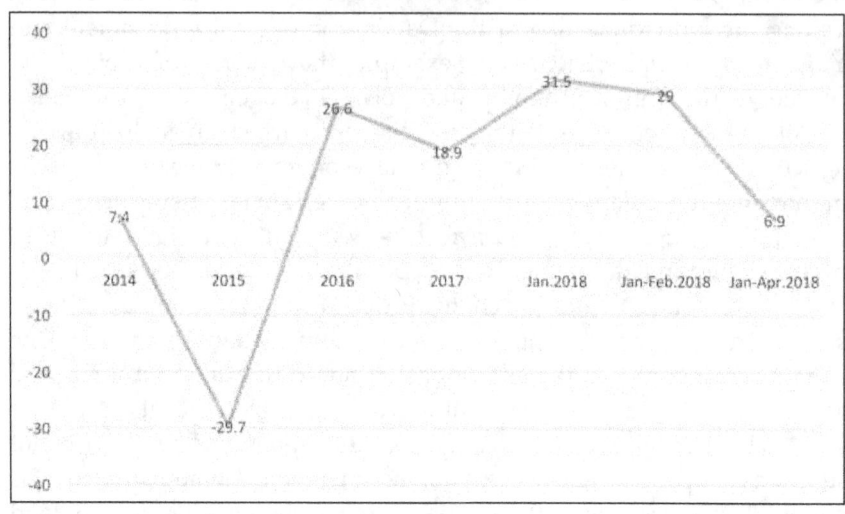

Source: Author's Internet query based on the webpage of Kunming Custom Office http://www.customs.gov.cn/, Ministry of Commerce of the People's Republic of China http://www.mofcom.gov.cn and SilkRoad News http://silkroad.news.cn (accessed 12 November 2020).

are three primary reasons for China's interest in Myanmar's mineral resources. First, with large resources of tin ores within its borders, China is imposing strict environmental protection laws that limit extraction; second, the cost of labour in China is higher than in Myanmar; third, companies have enjoyed the pleasant political climate at the central level between China and Myanmar (News SMM 2019).

As of the end of 2017, 448 tin mines have been identified in China, with 4.5 million tons of reserves. The base resource reserves amounted to 1.04 million tons. They are mainly concentrated in Yunnan (29 per cent), Hunan (17 per cent), Guangxi (16 per cent), Guangdong (13 per cent), and Inner Mongolia (13 per cent), and they account for 88 per cent of Chinese reserves of tin mines. In 2017, China's geological exploration investment continued its downward trend in recent years and continued to decline with 2012 as the inflexion point. The Chinese government invested less in non-oil and gas geological exploration (RMB19.8 billion), a year-on-year decrease of 19.8 per cent. In the first half of 2018, non-oil and gas exploration was RMB7.5 billion, a decrease of 7.2 per cent. This limitation encouraged local companies to "go global", and invest in the closest destination with huge natural resources—Myanmar. The newly introduced policies by the government in Beijing make China dependent on cooperation with Myanmar. In 2005, the largest supplier of tin ore to China was Bolivia, followed by Myanmar, the Netherlands and Germany. After thirteen years in 2018, Myanmar occupied first place with a 98 per cent share in China's market (see Table 11.1; News SMM 2019).

Being dependent on Myanmar as a natural resources supplier, Chinese local governments need to deal with instability across the border. The lack of stability is important for stable import of tin ore from Wa state; part of Shan state however with the strong connections to China known as Self-administered Division for the Wa ethnic people. In the long term, the ad hoc transaction might end the supply chains and tin ore shortages in China's and global markets. In this regard, the approach of Chinese businesses differs from that of local governments: "We don't specifically pay attention to where they source their materials from." (Lee and Schectman 2016). While from the perspective of the local Chinese administration responsible for

TABLE 11.1
China's Tin Ore Significant Suppliers by Country (2005, 2018)

Country	2005	Country	2018
Bolivia	75%	Myanmar	98%
Myanmar	13%	Australia	1%
The Nederlands	2%	Others	1%
Germany	3%		
Indonesia	2%		
Vietnam	1%		
Nigeria	1%		
Laos	1%		

Source: Zong guan quanqiu xi kuang fenbu, kaifa, gongji xianzhuang xiuqiu zengjia ziyuan youxian xi jia changqi shangzhang? [Looking at the global tin ore distribution, development, supply status, increasing demand, limited resources, and the long-term rise of the tin price?], accessed 12 May 2021, https://news.smm.cn/news/100883489.

the development, the local economy still has "chronic diseases" such as traditional, less advanced pillar industries that are mainly based on trade (jade and fruits), rather low levels of foreign investment, and the slow pace of institutional transformation. Moreover, the gap between revenue and expenditure has been widening and provincial-level government, not to mention the central level, neglects the city of Ruili; due to the turbulent situation and the recent pandemic, people panic and do not want to cooperate with Myanmar's businesses. The development is targeted by the chaos created by smuggling, drug trafficking, overseas gambling, village bandits and "village hegemons", and illegal land purchasing so that "comprehensive social governance has a long way to go" (Ruili Government 2018). Managing security on the border remains a challenge, however, mainly due to weak governance and capacity on the Myanmar side—as declared by the Chinese. Civilian officials in border counties in Yunnan highlighted that while the border remains open and relatively secure, there is little they can do to accelerate economic development or deepen their local-level relations (Mining.com 2019).

CONCLUSION

As a "bridgehead", "radiation centre" or "pivot", Yunnan province with the multidimensional obligations under the national policy serves as the transmitter of resources from Myanmar to more developed provinces in China. On the contrary, Kunming needs to lobby Beijing for more preferential policies and better treatment. While the central government's bilateral relations are subject to political ties and Beijing's strategic interests in the country, local connections have fewer political considerations and are more immediate and practical. It can be seen in the particular context of tin ores import and the growing dependency on the stability on the border with Myanmar. In this regard, three factors provide stability in the border areas: Central political relations, political relations between China and militant groups in northern Myanmar and cross-border economic interdependence. For the first, after Xi Jinping visited Myanmar (January 2020), political relations are seen as cordial and close, with the potential for further economic and strategic engagement. The second and the third, however, play critical roles. To manage the relatively stable environment for frontier capitalism, the

Chinese government at the various levels faces the "incentives gap". Talking to only one side of the conflict in upper Myanmar, or trying to approach only the central government, fails to fulfil its promise of stability. The nexus between the three aforementioned factors produce the frontier capitalism that is governed by state actors from the Chinese side and competing non-state actors from the upper Myanmar side. It leads to the never-ending process when once the Chinese government promises more incentives for a particular group, e.g., in Wa state, Beijing immediately faces the backlash from the other competing groups like the Kachin Independent Army. Because Myanmar ranks worst among the fragile states in Southeast Asia, China can utilize the situation to the fullest, by creating economic interdependence through RMB settlement and thereby expanding its zone of influence. On the other hand, the constant uncertainty of managing different competing groups by the Chinese local and central governments creates shortfalls in China-Myanmar cross-border governance. Against this backdrop, security across the border is critical for the further development of China's BRI, Bangladesh-China-India-Myanmar Economic Corridor Strategy, and China-Myanmar Economic Corridor.

Notes

1. Interview, Local Government, Kunming, Yunnan Province, March 2019.
2. Interview, Diplomatic Academy, Hanoi, Vietnam, February 2018.

References

163.com (blog). 2019. "858 Yì, 92 gonglǐ, mian Zhong zhe tiao kuaguo lu zhengzhi donggong jiang gaixie Mian Zhong wuliu lishi" [85.8 billion, 92 kilometres, Myanmar-China cross-border road officially started and will rewrite Myanmar-China logistics history]. 4 December 2019. https://www.163.com/dy/article/EVI2GVQA0517R1QV.html (accessed 15 November 2020).

Blatter, Joachim, Matthias Kreutzer, Michaela Rentl, and Jan Thiele. 2008. "The Foreign Relations of European Regions: Competencies and Strategies". *West European Politics* 31, no. 3: 464–90. https://doi.org/10.1080/01402380801939743 (accessed 16 November 2020).

Caballero-Anthony, Mely, ed. 2016. *An Introduction to Non-Traditional Security Studies: A Transnational Approach*. London: Sage Publications.

Chen, Xiangming, and Curtis Stone. 2017. "Rethinking Border Cities: In-between Spaces, Unequal Actors and Stretched Mobilities across the China-Southeast Asia Borderland". In *The Sage Handbook of the 21st Century*, edited by Suzanne Hall and Ricky Burdett, pp. 478–501. London: Sage.

China FDI. 2019. "Ruili—Essential Investment Condition". http://www.fdi.gov.cn/1200000020_5_51_0_7.html (accessed 13 November 2020).

Custom Statistic Office. 2019. "Haiguan tongji shuju zaixian chaxun pingtai" [Online query platform for customs statistics]. http://43.248.49.97/ (accessed 12 March 2021).

Dan, Zhang, and Ma Jingjing. 2021. "New COVID-19 Lockdown Worsens Trade in China's Border City with Myanmar". *Global Times*, 5 July 2021. https://www.globaltimes.cn/page/202107/1227884.shtml (accessed July 19 2021).

Fricke, Carla. 2015. "Spatial Governance across Borders Revisited: Organizational Forms and Spatial Planning in Metropolitan Cross-border Regions". *European Planning Studies* 23, no. 5: 849–70.

Gao, Haihong, and Yu Yongding. 2009. "The Internationalization of RMB". In *Asia and China in the Global Economy*, edited by Yin-Wong Cheung and Guonan Ma, pp. 191–217. Singapore: World Scientific. https://doi.org/10.1142/9789814335270_0007 (accessed 20 January 2021).

Gardiner, Nicholas, John P. Sykes, Allan Trench, and Laurence J. Robb. 2015. "Tin Mining in Myanmar: Production and Potential". *Resources Policy* 46: 219–33. https://doi.org/10.1016/j.resourpol.2015.10.002 (accessed 20 January 2020).

Global Development Research Centre (blog). n.d. "Understanding of the Concept of Governance". http://www.gdrc.org/u-gov/governance-understand.html (accessed 14 November 2020).

Gualini, Enrico. 2003. "Cross-Border Governance: Inventing Regions in a Transnational Multi-level Polity". *Disp – The Planning Review* 39, no. 152: 43–52. https://doi.org/10.1080/02513625.2003.10556833 (accessed 18 November 2020).

Htun, Than, Than Htay, and Khin Zaw. 2017. "Tin–tungsten deposits of Myanmar". In *Myanmar: Geology, Resources, and Tectonics*, edited by A.J. Barber, Khin Zaw, and M.J. Crow, pp. 625–47. London: The Geological Society. https://mem.lyellcollection.org/content/48/1/625/tab-figures-data (accessed 14 November 2020).

Jinxin, Liu. 2013. "China's Bridgehead Strategy and Yunnan Province". *East By Southeast* (blog), 13 November 2013. http://www.eastbysoutheast.com/chinas-bridgehead-strategy-yunnan-province/ (accessed 18 November 2019).

Kato, Toshihiro. 2013. "Myanmar's Border Trade with China: Roads, Gates, and Peace". In *Border Economies in the Greater Mekong Subregion*, edited by Masami Ishida, pp 279–95. New York: Palgrave Macmillan.

Kudo, Toshihiro. 2013. "Myanmar's Border Trade with China: Roads, Gates, and Peace". In *Border Economies in the Greater Mekong Subregion*, edited by Masami Ishida, pp. 279–95. London: Palgrave Macmillan. https://doi.org/10.1057/9781137302915_11 (accessed 18 November 2020).

Lee, Yimou, and Joel Schectman. 2016. "How a Rebel Myanmar tin Mine May Upend a Global Supply Chain". Reuters, 25 November 2016. https://www.reuters.com/article/uk-myanmar-tin-insight-idUKKBN13N1XY (accessed 29 January 2021).

Li, Meiting. 2016. "Xin xingshi xia Kunming Shenhua Nanya dongnanya guoji you cheng fazhan yanjiu" [A study of Kunming's further development of its relationships with its sister cities in South Asia and Southeast Asia in the new situation]. *Yunnan Minzu Daxue Xuebao (Shehui xue)* 33, no. 3: 149–56.

Lwin, Nan. 2019. "China Quietly Pushing Myanmar to Back Its Development Plan for Irrawaddy River". *The Irrawaddy*, 30 December 2019. https://www.irrawaddy.com/opinion/analysis/china-quietly-pushing-myanmar-back-development-plan-irrawaddy-river.html (accessed 13 March 2020).

Lu, Guangsheng. 2013. "China (Yunnan)-GMS Economic Cooperation: New Developments and New Problems". In *Greater Mekong Subregion: From Geographical to Socio-Economic Integration*, edited by Omkar L. Shrestha and Aekapol Chongvilaivan, pp. 103–18. Singapore: Institute of Southeast Asian Studies.

Mierzejewski, Dominik, ed. 2021. *China's Provinces and the Belt and Road Initiative*. London and New York: Routledge.

Mining.com (blog). 2019. "Rare Earth Trade between China, Myanmar Facing Challenges". 24 December 2019. https://www.mining.com/rare-earths-trade-between-china-myanmar-facing-challenges/ (accessed 16 November 2020).

News SMM. "Zong guan quanqiu xi kuang fenbu, kaifa, gongji xianzhuang xiuqiu zengjia ziyuan youxian xi jia changqi shangzhang?" [Looking at the global tin ore distribution, development, and supply status, increasing demand, limited resources, and the long-term rise of tin price?]. https://news.smm.cn/news/100883489 (accessed 14 November 2020).

Rippa, Alessandro, ed. 2020. *Borderland Infrastructures. Trade, Development, and Control in Western China*. Amsterdam: Amsterdam University Press.

Rosenau, James. 1995. "Governance in the Twenty-First Century". *Global Governance* 1, no. 1: pp. 13–43.

Ruili Government 2018. "Ruili 2018 nian zhengfu gongzuo baogao" [Ruili Government Work Report 2018]. January 2018. http://www.ahmhxc.com/gongzuobaogao/11418.html (accessed 13 October 2021).

Steinberg, David I., and Hongwei Fan, eds. 2012. *Modern China-Myanmar Relations: Dilemmas of Mutual Dependence*. Copenhagen: NIAS Press. https://

norden.diva-portal.org/smash/get/diva2:844047/FULLTEXT01.pdf (accessed 16 November 2020).

Summers, Tim. 2019. "The Belt and Road Initiative in Southwest China: Responses from Yunnan Province". *Pacific Review* 34, no. 2: 206–29. https://doi.org/10.1080/09512748.2019.1653956 (accessed 17 November 2020).

Transnational Institute (Myanmar Policy Briefing). 2019. "Selling the Silk Road Spirit: China's Belt and Road Initiative in Myanmar". 22 November 2019. https://www.tni.org/files/publication-downloads/bri_myanmar_web_18-11-19.pdf (accessed 13 November 2020).

Tun, Aung Hla, and Timothy Mclaughlin. 2015. "China's CITIC Wins Projects to Develop Myanmar Economic Zone". Reuters, 31 December 2015. https://www.reuters.com/article/myanmar-citic-project-idUSL3N14K1D720151231 (accessed 5 November 2020).

Woods, Kevin M. 2019. "In Myanmar, Conflicts Over Land and Natural Resources Block the Peace Process". *East-West Wire*, 19 January 2020. https://www.eastwestcenter.org/system/tdf/private/ewwire022woods.pdf?file=1&type=node&id=36975 (accessed 5 November 2020).

Xing, Guangcheng. 2018. "Xin shidai Zhongguo bianjiang zhili de xin silu" [The New Ideas for the Governance of Chinese Borderlands in the New Era]. *Bianjie yu Haiyang yanjiu (Journal of Boundary and Ocean Studies)* 3, no 2: 5–17.

Xinhua. 2018. "Dian Mian gongmou fazhan zhilu" [The road for joint development between Yunnan and Myanmar]. 6 April 2018. http://m.xinhuanet.com/yn/2018-04/06/c_137091323.htm (accessed 12 November 2020).

Yao, Qinhua. 2018. "Zhong Mian jiaotong hulian hutong xianzhuang yu qianjing fenxi–yi Yunnan jichu sheshi jianshe wei shijiao" [Analysis on the Current Situation and Prospect of Sino–Myanmar Traffic Connectivity: from the Perspective of Infrastructure Construction in Yunnan]. *Shehui Kexue* (2017), no 5: 25–37. https://doi.org/10.13644/j.cnki.cn31-1112.2017.05.003 (accessed 13 October 2021).

Yhome, K. 2019. "Understanding China's Response to Ethnic Conflicts in Myanmar". *ORF Occasional Paper*, no. 188. https://www.orfonline.org/research/understanding-chinas-response-to-ethnic-conflicts-in-myanmar-49759/ (accessed 30 December 2019).

Yunnan Government. 2016a. "Yunnan sheng renmin zhengfu guanyu jianshe mianxiang Nanya yu Dongnanya jinrong fuwu zhongxin de shishi yijian" [The opinion of the Yunnan provincial government on building the financial centre for South and Southeast Asia]. http://www.yn.gov.cn/zwgk/zcwj/zxwj/201910/t20191031_183814.html (accessed 14 November 2020).

———. 2016b. "Yunnan sheng renmin zhengfu guanyu zhichi yanbian zhongdian diqu kaifa kaifang ruogan zhengce cuoshi de shishi yijian" [The Opinion of the People's Government of Yunnan Province on Supporting the Development and Opening of Key Border Areas]. http://www.yn.gov.cn/zwgk/zcwj/yzf/201910/t20191031_183828.html (accessed 15 November 2020).

Zhou, Cissy. 2021. "Myanmar Coup: China Border Trade Could Be Disrupted if Military Conflict Intensifies, Analysts Say". *China Macro Economy*, 3 February 2021. https://www.scmp.com/economy/china-economy/article/3120361/china-myanmar-border-trade-could-be-disrupted-if-military (accessed 18 July 2021).

index

A
Action Plan for Forging the Cambodia-China Community of Shared Future, 201
afforestation, 62
Agriculture Bank of China, 245
animism, 39, 191
anti-China sentiment, 205, 214, 245, 247
Ariston-ACER Plan, 210
artisanal and small-scale mining (ASM), 175, 177–89, 191
  see also industrial large-scale mining (LSM)
ASEAN, 80, 178
ASEAN–China Free Trade Agreement (ACFTA), 79–80, 200
Asian Development Bank (ADB), 3, 5, 80, 146–47, 168, 178
Aung San Suu Kyi, 226
Ayeyarwaddy River, 229
  see also Irrawaddy River

B
bamboo shoots, collection of 70–72
Ban Huay Meng village, development of, 84–90, 92–96
Bangladesh-China-India-Myanmar Economic Corridor (BCIM-EC), 244, 255
Bank of China, 201, 245
Banmai resettlement, 149–52, 154–64, 166–67
BCIM Business Council, 244
"Beijing's Shadow", 2
Belt and Road Initiative (BRI), 2, 6, 7, 9, 15–16, 19–20, 80, 147, 167, 178, 200–4, 222, 230–31, 236, 243, 245, 255
black market, 250
Boon Suang Rua (longboat racing), 33
border areas, perception of, 242
  see also cross-border governance
"Boten Beautiful Land Specific Zone", 15
Boten Special Economic Zone, 15
Buddhist Lent, 33
"Build, Operate, Transfer" (BOT), 246, 251
"built first, license later", 211
Buntharik–Yot Mon Wildlife Sanctuary, 55

C

Cambodia, 3, 6, 18, 40–41, 50, 139, 185, 198, 212, 215, 230
  Chinese investments in, 199–205, 214
  Chinese nationals in, 202, 213
  environmental management, 213–14
  labour legal issues, 208
  local governance, transformation of, 205–9
  regulatory regime in, 206–7
  urban planning and development, 210–11
  see also Sihanoukville
Cambodia–China Business Forum, 199–200
"Cambodia–China Community of Shared Future", 18
Cambodia–China Technology Transfer Center, 209
capitalism, 18, 50, 173–74, 179, 185, 189, 236, 242
  see also frontier capitalism
cash crop, 2–3, 13–14, 51, 53, 65, 82, 113–14, 135, 137
cash economy, 67, 121
cassava, 51–52, 61, 63–66
charcoal production, 177, 180
Charoen Pokphand Foods (CP), 115–16, 119, 123
Chea Munyrith, 212
China
  anti-China sentiment, 205, 214, 245, 247
  dams in, 31, 35–37
  fruit imports, 79–80
  fruit trade, 92–95
  "go global" policy, 178, 223, 226, 245, 247, 253
  investments in Cambodia, 199–205, 214
  investments in Myanmar, 221–24
  nationals, in Cambodia, 202, 213
China Chamber of Commerce of Metals Minerals & Chemicals Importers and Exporters (CCCMC), 233
China–Indochina Peninsula Economic Corridor, 80
China International Trust and Investment Corporation (CITIC), 246
China–Laos Railway, 20, 80
China–Myanmar Corridor, 249, 255
China–Myanmar frontier cooperation, 241
China–Myanmar Irrawaddy River–Land Water Intermodal Transport Corridor, 246–47
China Power Investment Corporation (CPI), 229–30
"China's Backyard", 2
Chinese Academy of Tropical Agricultural Sciences (CATA), 99
Chinese mafia, 212
Chinese National Petroleum Corporation (CNPC), 227–28
Chinese Power Investment Company, 222
Chinese RMB, internationalization of, 14, 201, 241, 245, 248–54
citizen investment law, 222, 236
civil society, 29–31, 37–39, 41, 43–44, 204
Civil Society Alliance Forum, 212
civilization, expansion of, 4
climate change, 31, 241
CLMV (Cambodia, Laos, Myanmar and Vietnam), 230
Coalition of Cambodian Farmer Community (CCFC), 207
coastal erosion, 213
"collaborative borders", 12, 100

colonialism, 7, 180, 185
Combined National Treatment (NT), 235
commoditization, 2, 5–9, 17, 190
Communist Party of China (CPC), 202
communist regime, 177, 186, 190
community forest, 13, 56, 59–60, 62–66, 68–71, 73–74, 139
community-led approach, resource management and, 36–39, 43–44, 50, 73, 130
Comprehensive Cooperation under the Belt and Road Initiative, 201
Comprehensive Strategic Partnership Agreement, 200
contamination, 66, 70, 73, 91, 234
"Contemplating Letpadaungtaung", 226
contract farming, 7, 110–11, 118, 120–26, 135–36
Contract Law, 232
contract system, 121
contract worker, 189
"coolies", 185, 189
"Cooperation under the Rectangular Strategy and the Belt and Road Initiative", 201
corporate social responsibility (CSR), 232
corruption, 18, 55, 58, 160, 165, 167, 204–6, 208
corvée labour, 179
"Council Study", 41
coup d'état, 248
COVID-19 pandemic, 19–20, 80, 152, 190, 210, 213, 248
CP Vietnam, 115, 125
crime rate, 204, 206, 212–14
Criminal Law, 226
cross-border governance, 241, 255
theories, 242–44

see also border areas
cross-border trade, 12, 14, 20, 83–84, 91, 95–100, 111, 117–21, 125, 241, 245, 248–52
opening up to, 87–90
customary rights, 6, 8, 13, 69, 132, 134–38, 181–82
cybercrime, 212

D
Daewoo Group, 227–28
Damrong Phidet, 59
dams in China, impacts of, 31, 35–37
debt trap, 19, 95, 186, 202, 204
deforestation, 37, 55–56, 66, 177, 183
see also forest destruction
degraded forest, 55, 57, 73, 126, 131
Deng Xiaoping, 248
Department of Forestry (DoF), 133–34
Department of Land (DoL), 133–34
Department of Water Resource, 39
"development contributions", 124
Doi Moi reforms, 115, 117–18, 124
Dong Saramoen Forest, 56, 75
Draft Master Plan of Sihanoukville, 210
"Dragon's Shadow", 2
drought, 29, 31, 42, 39–44, 161
drug trade, 20
drug trafficking, 212, 241, 254

E
ecological impact, and rubber cultivation, 55–56, 65–68
ecosystem, 9, 29, 35–36, 39, 49, 56
El Niño, 31
electric grid connection, in rural settlement, 153–58
Électricité du Laos (EDL), 148
employment contract, 162, 186–87, 208

Energy Administration Information (EAI), 224
energy consumption, by country, 224
Environmental and Social Assessment and Management System (ESMS), 234
Environmental Conservation Rule, 233
environmental degradation, 15, 37, 65, 73, 110, 177, 179–80, 189, 204–5, 214
environmental governance, 42
Environmental, Health and Safety (EHS) Guidelines, 234
Environmental Impact Assessment (EIA), 230, 232–33
environmental impact statement (EIS), 230, 233
environmental management, 38, 213–14, 233–35
Environmental Management Policy and Plan, 234
Everything-but-Arms (EBA) scheme, 202
"experimentarian ethic", 83
Extractive Industries Transparency Initiative (EITI), 233
extractivism, 7–8, 17–18, 189, 233
"Eyes on the Earth", 31

F

Failure Mode and Effects Analysis (FMEA), 235
"family forest" project, 60–61, 70–71
fishery decline, 36
Five-Year Plan of Action on Lancang–Mekong Cooperation, 41
flood, 36, 42, 66, 168, 185, 191, 213–14, 229
foreign direct investment (FDI), 146–47, 166, 177–78, 199–200, 207, 221–22, 235

foreign investment law, 222–23, 236
forest destruction, 56, 112, 117
  see also deforestation
Forest Industry Organization, 62
forest ordination, 30, 39
Forest Protection Unit, 59, 65, 69
forest rehabilitation, 134
forest reserve, 57–58
Free, Prior, Informed Consent (FPIC), 236
free trade agreement (FTA), 200
free trade zone, 209
French Indochina, and mining, 175–77, 179
"frontier assemblage", 2, 4, 9, 83, 99, 109, 112, 175, 199
frontier capitalism, 6–9, 13–14, 19, 82, 174–76, 186, 189–90, 236, 242, 248–55
  see also capitalism
"frontier commoditization", 190
"frontier cultures", 11
"frontier from below", 83–84
frontier imaginaries, 16–18
frontier micropolitics, 11
frontier mobilities, 11–14
"frontier myth", 10
frontier space, 131–32, 137, 145
frontier temporalities, 14–16
frontier territorialities, 9–11
"Frontier Thesis", 148
"frontier time", 15
frontierization, 4–5, 17–20, 82, 132, 145–46, 173–75, 178, 190
  agents of, 117–21
fruit cultivation, 13, 99
"fruit frontier", 83–87, 99, 117
  transnational, 90–91
fruit quality, 94–96
fruit trade, 88, 92–94, 100–1

G

gambling, 188, 206, 213–14, 254
Gas Authority of India Limited (GAIL), 227–28
"gate-cities", 7
geopolitics, 32
ghosts, worship of, 34
Global South, 148
globalization, 180
Go Out policy, 178, 223, 226, 245, 247, 253
"governance frontier", 205
Government–Private Sector Forum, 199
Greater Mekong Subregion (GMS), 80, 147, 168
"Green Mekong" strategy, 42
Guidelines for Social Responsibility in Outbound Mining Investments, 233

H

Hazard Identification (HAZID), 235
Hazardous Operations Analysis (HAZOP), 235
health diplomacy, 20
Health Impact Assessment (HIA), 232
"Health Silk Road", 20
Heilongjiang province, 241
herbicide, 65–67, 70
Hodo Group, 211
Hu Jintao, 244
Huai Se, river, 66
human trafficking, 212, 241
Hun Sen, 200, 202
hydropower, 3, 6, 8–9, 18, 28–29, 43, 109, 145–50, 157–59, 163, 165–68, 202, 204, 229–30

I

imperialism, 7

Industrial and Commercial Bank of China, 245
industrial large-scale mining (LSM), 175, 179–80, 182–83
  see also artisanal and small-scale mining (ASM)
informal contract, 125
infrastructure, conceptualization of, 15
Ing People's Council (IPC), 29–30, 44
  formation and activities of, 37–39
Ing River, 36–38
Initial Environmental Examination (IEE), 232
Innovative Farmers Association, 57
Integrated Water Resource Management (IWRM), 41
International and Investment Agreements (IIAs), 235
International Association for Impact Assessment (IAIA), 233
International Conventions, 222
International Council on Mining and Metals (ICMM), 233
International Finance Corporation (IFC), 234
investment contract, 229–30
Investment Law, 207–9, 231–32
Irrawaddy River, 246, 249
  see also Ayeyarwaddy River

J

Japan International Cooperation Agency (JICA), 210
Jiang Zemin, 244
Jinghong Dam, 31

K

Kachin Independence Army (KIA), 230, 255
Kachin Independence Organization (KIO), 248

Kachin National Organization (KNO), 230
Kachin State, population of, 229
Kamchay hydropower dam, 204
kamnan (village headman), 85–88, 92, 101
Kanchanaburi Province, 58
kenaf, 51, 61
Khao Yai National Park, 59
Khin Win, 226
Khmer Times, 202
kidnapping, 212
knowledge politics, 30
Kongka Goddess, 33
Korea Gas Corporation (KOGAS), 227–28
Kunming–Bangkok Highway, 80–81
Kunming Custom Office, 251
"Kunming Service and Peripheral Manufacturing" model, 247

L
Labour Law, 208
labour legal issues, in Cambodia, 208
Lai Rua Fai festival, 32–33
Lancang–Mekong Cooperation (LMC), 29–31, 39–44, 200
Lancang–Mekong Environmental Cooperation Center (LMECC), 42
Lancang–Mekong Water Resources Cooperation Center (LMWRC), 42
Lancang River, 31
Land Administration Law of Myanmar, 228
land concession, 109, 137, 139
land degradation, 183
land dispute, 207
land grab, 12, 50, 204, 228
land rights, 135, 137–38, 179, 222
land titling, 139

Land Use Certificate, 233
Lao National Day, 20
Laos, 3, 8–13, 15–16, 18, 20, 33–34, 37, 40–41, 49–50, 85, 87–91, 99–102, 106, 108, 109–16, 122, 124, 129–30, 132, 134, 137, 139, 145, 163, 165–68, 172–74, 190–91, 246, 249, 253
  cross-border traders, 95–98
  feed sector, and, 117–21
  fruit trade, 92–94
  hydropower development in, 146–59
  mining legislation, 181–83
  mining practices in, 175–79, 183–89
  "new frontier", as, 5–7, 173
  regional connectivity, and, 80–84
  "last frontier", 147, 166
Law on Minerals, 8, 181–83
"lazy Lao", 90
Letpadaungtaung Copper Mine Project, 221–23, 225–27
Loy Krathong festival, 32–33

M
Mae Ya Nang (guardian of boats), 35
maize cultivation, 7, 12, 51, 61, 82, 106–10, 118–21, 125–26, 135
  animal feed complex, and, 114–17
maize frontier, 7, 12, 17, 121–24
  origins of, 110–14
Malaysia, 7, 210
"mangosteen incident", 94–97
market economy, 51, 67–68, 74, 139
Mekong Agreement, 40
Mekong River, 16, 18, 28–30, 37, 39–44, 80, 84–85, 88, 191
  communities along the, 32–35
  drought and low flows, 31–32
  flow conditions, 35–36
Mekong River Commission (MRC), 29–31, 39–44

migrant labour, 2, 10–11, 50–51, 61, 176, 185–89, 191
military coup, 20
miner-peasant, 180, 186
minimum wage, 187, 208
mining concession, 182, 190
mining legislation, 181–83
mining practices, in Laos, 175–79, 183–89
Ministry of Agriculture and Cooperatives, 57
Ministry of Agriculture and Forestry (MAF), 133
Ministry of Commerce, 251
Ministry of Economy and Finance, 201, 203
Ministry of Electric Power, 229
Ministry of Energy and Mines, 177, 181
Ministry of Labour, 208
Ministry of Mines and Electric (MEM), 148
Ministry of National Defense (MND), 133
Ministry of Natural Resources and Environment (MoNRE), 133–34
Mohan port, 80
money laundering, 212
Most-Favoured Nation Treatment (MFNT), 224, 235
mushrooms, collection of 70–72
Myanmar Oil and Gas Enterprise (MOGE), 227–28
Myanmar, 3, 6, 8, 12, 14, 20, 41, 101, 190, 201, 240–55
   2008 Constitution, 222, 229, 231
   China investments in, 221–24
   citizen investment law, 222, 236
   environmental management, 233–35
   foreign investment law, 222–23, 236
   GDP, 223
   military coup, 20
   Parliament (Pyidaungsu Hluttaw), 223
Myanmar Asia World Company, 229
Myanmar–China Gas Pipeline Project, 223, 227–28
Myanmar–China Oil Transport Project, 227
Myanmar Companies Law, 232
Myanmar Investment Commission (MIC), 223–24, 232
Myanmar Investment Law, 223
Myanmar Labour Law, 232
Myanmar Land Law, 232
Myanmar Mines Law, 232
Myanmar Mining Enterprise 1 (ME), 225
Myanmar Special Economic Zone Law, 232
Myitsone dam project, 221–23, 229–30

N

naiban (village head), 106–8
Nakhon Phanom Province, 56
Nakhon Ratchasima Province, 55
Nam Nua 1 (NNua1) Hydropower Project, 146–47, 149–50, 157–62, 165–68
National Development and Reform Commission (NDRC), 227, 246, 251
National Land Management Authority (NLMA), 133
National League of Democracy Party (NLD), 226
national master plan on land allocation (NMPLA), 130, 132–34
new territorial frontier, as, 132–34
National Natural Rubber Policy Committee, 57

National Park, Wildlife, and Plant Conservation Department, 58–59, 61
National Petroleum Corporation, 222
National Reconciliation and Peace Center (NRPC), 248
National Socioeconomic Development Plans (NSEDP), 111
Nationwide Ceasefire Agreement (NCA), 248
natural forest, 56–57, 61–62
natural resources, 6–7, 9, 17–18, 50
Nature Care, 60
New Economic Mechanism, 146
"New Economic Zone", 10
"New Silk Road", 231
NGOs (non-governmental organizations), 16, 19, 37–38, 56, 59–60, 62–63, 65, 73–74, 108, 207
Norinco Company, 225
Norodom Sihanouk, 209
Northern Alliance–Burma (NA-B), 248
North-South Economic Corridor, 80

O
OECD Due Diligence Guidance for Responsible Supply Chains of Minerals from Conflict-Affected and High-Risk Areas, 233
Office of Agricultural Economics, 57
Office of Forest Department, 39
Office of Rubber Replanting Aid Fund (ORRAF), 56–57
"1 million *rai* project", 54
Oil and Natural Gas Corporation Ltd (ONGC), 227–28
"Open Up the West" campaign, 244
opium, 108, 110, 112–14, 121, 124–26, 179
Opium Replacement Policy, 114
"oriental Klondike", 7

P
paddy cultivation, 13, 49, 57, 60–61, 67–68, 74, 106
see also rice crop
Party Resolution on Land, 132
People's Bank of China (PBOC), 245
"persistent frontiers", 16
Pha Taem National Park, 59, 61
Phnom Penh–Sihanoukville Expressway, 201
Phu Kham Forest, 56
Pingxiang Port, 80
pla buek (giant catfish), 34
pollution, 37, 65, 179–80, 182–83, 213
poverty, 106, 110, 112–13, 116, 122, 145, 149, 165–66, 187
Prince Holding Group, 211
private forest, 63, 68–70, 72–74
Progressive Farmers Association, 57, 63
proletarianization, 163, 186, 189
"Prolong Forest and River" ceremony, 30, 39–40
protected forest, 55, 58, 139
protectionism, 99
Provincial/District Agricultural Office, 57

Q
Qing history, 16, 19, 85

R
Rak Chiang Khong, 37
Raquez, Alfred, 183
"Ream City", 211
Rectangular Strategy, 201
reforestation, 53, 131
regulatory regime, in Cambodia, 206–7
renminbi, *see* Chinese RMB
rent-seeking, 138

resettlement community, 9, 144, 146, 149–54, 157–67
resource extraction, 1–2, 10, 18, 65, 74, 82, 179–80, 190, 223–24, 233
"resource frontier", 4, 50, 148, 163, 173–74, 179, 198, 205, 214, 241
resource politics, 29
resourcification, 5
rice crop, 7, 61, 68, 86, 106–8, 115–17, 120–23, 135–36, 139, 144, 154, 156–58, 161, 168, 183–85
see also paddy cultivation
Rohingya, 243
Royal Forest Department (RFD), 58, 62, 73, 75
Royal Government of Cambodia (RGC), 210–11
rubber cultivation, 3, 10–13, 17, 49–50, 58–62, 82, 114, 121, 132, 135–38, 161–63, 185
 adaptation to, 68–74
 ecological impact, and, 55–56, 65–68
 expansion of, 63–65
 government policies, and, 56–57
 income from, 67
 local administration, and, 59–61
 northeast Thailand, in, 51–55
Rubber Research Institute, 56–57

S
sea-level rise, 213
Second Indochina War, 177
"secret war", 177
Self-administered Division for the Wa ethnic people, 253
sex education, 152
sex industry, 212
Shenzhen Master Plan, 210
Shukaku, real estate company, 207
Shwe Natural Gas Production Project, 227

Sihanoukville, 4, 199, 201, 204–6, 209–14
 see also Cambodia
Sihanoukville Autonomous Port, 209
Sihanoukville Coastal Development Plan, 210
Sihanoukville Development Plan, 210
Sihanoukville Special Economic Zone, 209, 211
SilkRoad News, 251
Singapore, 7, 209, 211, 231
Sino-Lao Chilan Rubber Development Company, 135–36, 138
Sino-Myanmar oil and gas pipelines, see Myanmar-China Gas Pipeline Project
small and medium-sized enterprise (SME), 204, 209
"So Po Ko 4–1" deeds, 55–56, 65, 74–75
"So Tho Ko" title, 65, 75
social contract, 4, 132, 138
Social Impact Assessment (SIA), 232
socialism, 173, 180, 190
Société des Études et Éxplorations Minières de l'Indochine, 176, 184
"soft extraterritoriality", 82
souksala (health centre), 151–52, 164
South Coastal Area Development Plan, 210
Special Economic Zone (SEZ), 10, 80, 82, 145, 201, 211
"spirit doctors", 151
Stakeholder Engagement Plan, 234
State of the Basin report, 41
state-owned enterprise (SOE), 202, 246
state territorialization, 133, 135
Straits of Malacca, 230
strike, 225–26, 230
Stueng Hav Development Plan, 210
subsistence ethics, 139

substandard construction, 206–7
Sukhum Wong-ek, 57
Surbana Jurong, 211
Sustainable Development Framework, Voluntary Principles on Security and Human Rights (VPSHR), 233

T
"Tai Lue Cultural Centre", 86
Tai Lue, origin of, 101
"Tai Lue-style", 86
"Tai Lue Weaving Centres", 86
Tambon Administrative Organizations (TAOs), 60
tax exemption, 8, 224
technology transfer, 201, 208–9
Techo 1 Communication Satellite programme, 201
terrorism, 242
Thai Baan research, 38, 39, 44
Thai-Lao Friendship Bridge, 36, 80
"Thai method", 91, 102
Thailand, 3, 7, 10–13, 17, 28–31, 34, 36, 39–44, 49–50, 79–81, 83–84, 99–102, 109, 111, 115, 117, 144, 150–51, 154, 162, 164, 167–68, 177–78, 186–87, 190–91
    cross-border trade, 87–90
    ecological degradation in, 55–61, 65–68
    fruit trade in, 92–94
    national fruit frontier, 85–87
    rubber boom in, 51–61, 63–65
Thap Lan National Park, 55
The Agro-Biodiversity Initiative (TABI), 135–37, 139
Tibetan Plateau, 31
tin mining, 172, 175, 178, 181, 191
    labour relations in, 183–89
tin ore, 251–54
tourism, 34, 199–200, 209, 251

Township Land Records Department Office, 233
trade union, 186
transboundary water governance, 31, 40–43
Transparency International, 206
Trotsky, Leon, 190
Turner, Frederick Jackson, 4, 148
"Turning Land into Capital", 8, 82, 99, 109, 131, 135, 137, 139

U
Ubon Ratchathani Province, 49, 51, 55, 57, 59
    average income in, 52
UN Guiding Principles on Business and Human Rights, 235
UNDP, 60
Union of Myanmar Economic Holding Ltd (UMEHL), 225
United Nations Environment Programme's World Conservation Monitoring Centre, 229
UNODC, 113
"unruly frontier", 149
Urban Planning and Design Institute of Shenzhen, 209–10
urban planning and development, in Cambodia, 210–11
US Energy Administration Information (EAI), 224

V
Vann Molyvann's Plan, 210
Vientiane-Boten railway, 147
Vietnam, 7, 10, 12, 17, 40–41, 80, 82, 101, 108–13, 122–25, 154, 176–79, 183, 185–91, 206, 230, 246, 249, 253
    feed sector, 117–21

maize and animal feed complex, in, 114–17
village head (*naiban*), 106–8
Village Tract Farmland Management Body, 233
VINCI Plan, 210–11
"visa runs", 187

W
Wa ethnic people, 253, 255
wage labour, 61, 136, 162–63, 167, 185
Wanbao Company, 222, 225, 230
Wang Huning, 202
"War on Drugs", 112
Washington Consensus, 146
waste management system, 213, 234
water spirits, 191
water treatment, 214, 234
"water worlds", 29
"wild west" frontier, 148
World Bank, 146–47, 177–79, 234
Wuhan University, 242

X
Xiao Sima, 210
Xi Jinping, 244, 254
Xing Guangcheng, 242
Xinjiang Autonomous Region, 241
Xiong Bo, 212

Y
Yun Min, 206, 212
Yunnan Academy of Social Science, 247
Yunnan, as "bridgehead", 240–41, 244–46, 254
Yunnan International Power Investment Company China, 229
Yunnan Provincial Development and Reform Commission (YPDRC), 246
Yuxi–Mohan railway, 147

www.ingramcontent.com/pod-product-compliance
Lightning Source LLC
Chambersburg PA
CBHW072129290426
44111CB00012B/1843